Spring 200
ISSN: 0276-0045 ISBN: ...

KV-578-512

THE REVIEW OF CONTEMPORARY FICTION

Editor
JOHN O'BRIEN
Illinois State University

Senior Editor
ROBERT L. MCLAUGHLIN
Illinois State University

Associate Editors
IRVING MALIN, DAVID FOSTER WALLACE

Book Review Editor
TIM FEENEY

Production & Design
TODD MICHAEL BUSHMAN

Editorial Assistants
SARA CALDWELL, SARAH MCHONE-CHASE, LAINE MORREAU

Cover Illustration
TODD MICHAEL BUSHMAN

The Review of Contemporary Fiction is published three times a year (January, June, September) by The Review of Contemporary Fiction, Inc., a nonprofit organization located at ISU Campus Box 4241, Normal, IL 61790-4241. ISSN 0276-0045. Subscription prices are as follows:

Single volume (three issues):
    Individuals: $17.00; foreign, add $3.50;
    Institutions: $26.00; foreign, add $3.50.

DISTRIBUTION. Bookstores should send orders to:

Dalkey Archive Press, ISU Campus Box 4241, Normal, IL 61790-4241. Phone 309-874-2274; fax 309-874-2284.

This issue is partially supported by a grant from the Illinois Arts Council, a state agency.

Indexed in *American Humanities Index, International Bibliography of Periodical Literature, International Bibliography of Book Reviews, MLA Bibliography,* and *Book Review Index.* Abstracted in *Abstracts of English Studies.*

The Review of Contemporary Fiction is also available in 16mm microfilm, 35mm microfilm, and 105mm microfiche from University Microfilms International, 300 North Zeeb Road, Ann Arbor, MI 48106-1346.

www.centerforbookculture.org
www.dalkeyarchive.com

THE REVIEW OF CONTEMPORARY FICTION

BACK ISSUES AVAILABLE

Back issues are still available for the following numbers of the
Review of Contemporary Fiction ($8 each unless otherwise noted):

NOVELIST AS CRITIC: Essays by Garrett, Barth, Sorrentino, Wallace, Ollier, Brooke-
 Rose, Creeley, Mathews, Kelly, Abbott, West, McCourt, McGonigle, and McCarthy

NEW FINNISH FICTION: Fiction by Eskelinen, Jäntti, Kontio, Krohn, Paltto, Sairanen,
 Selo, Siekkinen, Sund, Valkeapää

NEW ITALIAN FICTION: Interviews and fiction by Malerba, Tabucchi, Zanotto,
 Ferrucci, Busi, Corti, Rasy, Cherchi, Balduino, Ceresa, Capriolo, Carrera, Valesio,
 and Gramigna

GROVE PRESS NUMBER: Contributions by Allen, Beckett, Corso, Ferlinghetti, Jordan,
 McClure, Rechy, Rosset, Selby, Sorrentino, and others

NEW DANISH FICTION: Fiction by Brøgger, Høeg, Andersen, Grøndahl, Holst, Jensen,
 Thorup, Michael, Sibast, Ryum, Lynggaard, Grønfeldt, Willumsen, and Holm

THE FUTURE OF FICTION: Essays by Birkerts, Caponegro, Franzen, Galloway, Maso,
 Morrow, Vollmann, White, and others

Individuals receive a 10% discount on orders of one issue and a 20% discount on
orders of two or more issues. To place an order, use the form on the last page of this
issue.

Call for Casebook Editors and Contributors

www.dalkeyarchive.com

Dalkey Archive Press/The Review of Contemporary Fiction is seeking editors and contributors for its new web-based casebook series: Studies in Modern and Contemporary Fiction. Each casebook will focus on one novel. It will include an overview essay on the book (its place in the author's oeuvre; its critical reception; the scholarly conversations about it) and four other essays looking at specific dimensions of the book. (Recommended length of essays: 20-25 double-spaced pages.) Also included will be a selected bibliography of critical works on the book. The anticipated audience includes professors teaching the book and graduate and undergraduate students studying it.

All casebooks will be refereed. Successful casebooks will be published on the Dalkey Archive Press website.

The duties of the casebook editor will be to write the overview essay and develop the critical bibliography, to coordinate the other essays, especially avoiding overlapping among them, and to coordinate with the series editor.

The following are the books for which we are seeking casebook editors and contributors:

Felipe Alfau
 Locos
 Chromos
Andrei Bitov
 Pushkin House
Louis-Ferdinand Céline
 Trilogy (*North, Castle to Castle, Rigadoon*)
Peter Dimock
 A Short Rhetoric for Leaving the Family
Coleman Dowell
 Island People
Rikki Ducornet
 The Jade Cabinet
William Eastlake
 Lyric of the Circle Heart
William H. Gass
 Willie Masters' Lonesome Wife
Aldous Huxley
 Point Counter Point
Tadeusz Konwicki
 A Minor Apocalypse
José Lezama Lima
 Paradiso
Osman Lins
 The Queen of the Prisons of Greece

D. Keith Mano
 Take Five
Wallace Markfield
 Teitlebaum's Window
Harry Mathews
 Cigarettes
Nicholas Mosley
 Impossible Object
 Accident
Flann O'Brien
 The Poor Mouth
Fernando del Paso
 Palinuro of Mexico
Raymond Queneau
 Pierrot Mon Ami
Jacques Roubaud
 The Great Fire of London
Gilbert Sorrentino
 Mulligan Stew
Piotr Szewc
 Annihilation
Curtis White
 Memories of My Father Watching TV

Applicants should send a CV and a brief writing sample.

Send applications to:

Robert L. McLaughlin
Dalkey Archive Press, Illinois State University, Campus Box 4241, Normal, IL 61790-4241

Inquiries: rmclaugh@ilstu.edu

Contents

RCF Call for Contributors

The Review of Contemporary Fiction is seeking contributors to write overview essays on the following writers:

Michel Butor, Julieta Campos, Jerome Charyn, Emily Coleman, Stanley Crawford, Carol De Chellis Hill, Jennifer Johnston, Gert Jonke, Violette Le Duc, Wallace Markfield, David Markson, Olive Moore, Julián Ríos, Joanna Scott, Esther Tusquets.

The essays must:

- be 50 double-spaced pages;
- cover the subject's biography;
- summarize the critical reception of the subject's works;
- discuss the course of the subject's career, including each major work;
- provide interpretive strategies for new readers to apply to the subject's work;
- provide a bibliographic checklist of each of the subject's works (initial and latest printings) and the most;
- be written for a general, intelligent reader, who does not know the subject's work;
- avoid jargon, theoretical digressions, and excessive endnotes;
- be intelligent, interesting, and readable;
- be documented in MLA style.

Authors will be paid $250.00 when the essay is published. All essays will be subject to editorial review, and the editors reserve the right to request revisions and to reject unacceptable essays.

Applicants should send a CV and a brief writing sample. In your cover letter, be sure to address your qualifications

Send applications to:

Robert L. McLaughlin
Dalkey Archive Press, Illinois State University, Campus Box 4241, Normal, IL 61790-4241

Inquiries: rmclaugh@ilstu.edu

B. S. Johnson

Philip Tew

Prologue

Writing from 1959, at the age of twenty-six, until his suicide in 1973, B. S. Johnson completed seven experimentally and ideologically intriguing novels.[1] They prefigure by over twenty years the recent phase of critically explicit and reflexive novels of British writers such as Martin Amis and Salman Rushdie and arguably in terms of technique are significantly more radical. Yet despite his formal prescience, Johnson's work is almost never taught and is rarely included in work on Anglophone literature. By contrast, during his short lifetime he threatened to emerge as a significant literary *and* critical figure. Certainly, his oeuvre for such a short career is surprisingly substantial and varied, as will be seen in the ensuing exposition and analysis of his novels. Additionally, I will outline below the major themes found in his life and work, drawing from Johnson's own critical introduction to his narratives found in his collection of essays, *Aren't You Rather Young to Be Writing Your Memoirs?* (1973), and from his other scattered explicit and implicit theoretical fragments, often found even within the novels themselves.

In 1964 Johnson published jointly with Julia Trevelyan Oman an enigmatic book, *Street Children,* consisting of Oman's photographs adjacent to a series of epigrammatic and yet ironic textual narratives by Johnson. This provides an intriguing entry into his world. He writes, "The photographs and text attempt a penetration of the enclosed world of the child, revealing the solemnity of young children who are puzzling out why people do things, why people are, trying to place the new within their own experience, failing, and thus enlarging their experience. . . . The characters of these working-class and immigrant children are seen in relation to the conditions which helped to create them" (n.pag.). Johnson's writing insists that humans are subject to this kind of conditioning, a combination of attitudes, treatment, and surroundings. The book's synthesis of images of postwar Britain shot in grainy black and white together with Johnson's stark narrative of childlike thoughts and comments, offer a glimpse of an environment Johnson found both familiar and representative of his own experience. For one waiflike child of around three Johnson writes, "They don't have to tell me about this human condition: I'm in it. They don't have to tell me what life's about, because I know already, and it's about hardness. Hardness and being on my own, quite on my own. You understand that much right from the beginning, from the first time the pavement comes up and hits you, from the first time you look round for someone you expected to be there and they aren't. Oh, I know you can get close to people, but that's not the same. In the end you're just on your own" (n.pag.). The book centers upon a stark urban setting with few cars on the streets; the buildings and pavements are patched, scratched, and chalked upon; the children playing possess the quality of urchins, swallowed by the immensity of a monochrome Victorian past; and yet amid this uncertainty persists a sense of community. Opposite a group of boys hanging from outside window ledges of the Church of the Nazarene, Clapham Junction, Johnson writes, "The good thing about being a London kid is that there are always other kids around you all the time, living in the same flats or next door or even in the same house, who will be your mates, and there's always something to do if you've got mates . . ." (n.pag.). *Trawl* confirms this kind of street life as Johnson's own, describing how it offered him both his working-class identity and yet a sense of social subjection. Johnson rejects what he saw as an unrepresentative elite class, with both social and intellectual power. This stance won him many readers in his lifetime and recognition from fellow writers, but few plaudits in academic or critical circles.

His very public attack on what he regarded as Britain's privileged and complacent class structures had been initiated in *Travelling People*. In one of the "Interruptions" that are interspersed among a range of other different presentational styles of chapters, the narrator is clear in his dismissal of a certain British character type: "Dunne is about six feet four, heavily built, thirtyish, with straight black hair generally flopping in a trite public school manner over his right eye; loudmouthed in the extreme, rather slow-witted . . . and controller of a business fortune involving the lives of nearly twenty thousand workpeople" (159-60). In *The Unfortunates* Johnson dismisses "crass businessmen, [and] their ideas of the artistic" ("Cast parapet" 3). He is ambivalent about the intellectual traditions of the middle class. Of literary study Johnson recalls telling his academic friend that "the only use of criticism was if it helped people to write better books" ("The opera singer" 1),[2] and Johnson objects even to this friend's academic pedantry ("That was the first time" 4). Together such attacks appear to have limited his appeal among middle-class British intellectuals and critics. He writes to his friend and future novelist Zulfikar Ghose of his antipathy toward "the ponces who feast off the dead body of literature, the carrion who feed on the dead corpses of good men, writers, pay us fuckall and go out to lunch every day of the working week etc, you know the syndrome" (27). This is evident in his analysis of conditions at football grounds in *The Unfortunates*. He notes "an enormous amount of money in football . . . the directors, the owners, who just siphoned off all the money . . . they still don't have to spend money on buildings, they see, the swine, still have these corrugated iron sheds, and charge extra for that, let the men on the terraces, their chief supporters, the sixpences of the masses, stand out in all weathers, and they do, the stupid bastards!" ("Time!" 5). Even years after Johnson's death, one self-proclaimed friend and supporter, Giles Gordon, dismisses him summarily with a loaded put-down: "Bryan Johnson was a working-class lad who had the singular fortune to marry a beautiful middle-class girl, Virginia Kimpton, who had knees that I lusted after. He was extremely aggressive, and quarrelled readily, unnecessarily with those who wished him well as much as with those who couldn't have given a hoot. His working-class chip could hardly have been more blatant" (150-51). Johnson's anger is frequently personalized in similar fashion by critics, thus trivializing his protests; nevertheless his argumentative analyses do far more than articulate simply the personal resentment and the implied inadequacy of which he stands accused. In *Christie Malry's Own Double Entry* the narrator desists from detailing the apparent facts of Christie's life, facing the ontological fear that "All is chaos and unexplainable." Yet he toys immediately with a very specific contextual generalization and opines, "Lots of people never had a chance, are ground down, and other clichés. Far from kicking against the pricks, they love their condition and vote conservative" (82). Some "facts" remain relevant to Johnson despite any notion of an existential maelstrom. Notice the use of the vernacular (and arguably biblical) term *pricks* for the establishment, and that, despite his apparent overall existential despair, a very specific sociopolitical context resurfaces in his narratorial jibe aimed potentially at his readership. This typifies Johnson. As Andrew Hassam concludes, Johnson undertakes "an Orwellian engagement with political reality" (4).

Exposition: Johnson via His Work

Johnson used his own life as an essential source for his fiction and the grounds of his ideology; its coordinates and his awareness of the exploited subtexts of culture's narrative supply both the backdrop and substance of his narratives. Midcareer an interviewer describes

Johnson's insistence that "All writing is autobiographical, because he believes that one should tell the truth and that the only true knowledge is oneself" (Depledge 13). All his primary experience is determined by a class-consciousness and sense of dislocation of the self when matched against the conventional narrative codes and practices of history. Johnson's dislocation was literal as well as existential. He was born in 1933, soon after the Great Depression, of the respectable London working class. As Ghose explains in a 1999 tape-recorded interview with me, "I met his parents and they were very modest people; they were overwhelmed by the fact that they had this brilliant son who was being noticed so widely by the press, by winning prizes and so on. And so every time I went there, his mother would make tea and sit there, and she would just stare at us, you know, at her wonderful son. His father was a very quiet person at the best of times and I don't even know what he did. I think it was some kind of a working-class position." In fact this blue-collar tradition is central to his sense of identity, and Johnson regards his as an underprivileged beginning. One can retrieve a sense of much of his life from the novels.

At four, Johnson attended Flora Gardens Primary School in Hammersmith. His education was disrupted both by two periods of evacuation and the German bombing of London. In 1939 he traveled with his mother to live on a farm in Chobham, Surrey, arranged privately by his family. In *Trawl* he marks out the class dynamics of this existence, specifying such significant minutiae as the choice of newspapers, aspects he sees as part of a scheme of social placement. One senses a seminal time:

Sarah was the daughter of two other refugees from London who were on the farm as guests of Jack, or the old couple, whichever. They did not like my mother and the two children she looked after, Timmie and me, and I see now that this was something to do with class. We were working-class, my mother and I, and the boy Timmie, as the son of a publican, was scarcely better. The newspaper these people, Sarah's parents, read, which had a column in it called "London Day by Day," I now know to have been the *Daily Telegraph*. Their dislike of us, their bare toleration of us, was certainly shared by Jack: my mother was in fact or virtually a servant. Let me think through that again, clearly: not a servant paid by him, not a servant to him unpaid, but just of the servant class, to him. At least, that is what my memory and my instinct insist to be the truth: to him my mother was to be treated as a servant. (51)

During the "phony war," Johnson and his mother returned to London. Later in 1941 during the Blitz, Johnson was sent officially to High Wycombe. Both episodes form the basis of numerous segments in *Trawl*, of which Johnson said in an interview with Alan

Burns published in 1981, "I explored my sense of isolation, my failure to make lasting relationships. I wanted to define this isolation and thereby understand it and ease it, in the classic way" (85). In High Wycombe, as the war moved to its close in Europe, after his local London school had returned to the capital, Johnson suffered an increasing sense of isolation, which may have had a profound effect on his future and his self-regard. While absent from his family, he sat and failed the crucial eleven-plus examination which at this time decided what level of secondary education a state pupil would receive, part of Britain's selective education (in place until the 1970s). As a consequence Johnson "failed" and he went to the most basic kind of school, a secondary modern, in High Wycombe, where he was impressed by at least one teacher named Proffitt who features in *Trawl*. On return, Johnson was sent to Barnes County Modern Secondary School where most of the pupils appeared to Johnson to accept the inevitable fate of dead-end jobs. The more personal feelings of the post-High Wycombe period are reflected and memorialized in his early story "Clean Living Is the Real Safeguard." He describes returning from evacuation in High Wycombe at Mrs. Bailey's, using the genuine name for his character. Johnson plunges the reader into his emotional trauma: "My mother was coming to see the Head because I had slashed my wrist during a History lesson, and she looked very smart" (*Corpses* 19). Johnson has been stopped from seeing a middle-class girlfriend, Jo, by her parents. For Johnson this is not simply an issue of difference in religion and class, but an epiphany. The moment crystallizes his realization of his subjection, his lack of autonomy.

"If I was very ill, desperately ill," she said to me that last day, "they'd *have* to let me see you wouldn't they?"
Her house had a drive, whereas ours did not even have a front garden. She walked away from me, shuffling her feet in dead leaves, small and lovely and unmadeup, her hair wild.
"I'll send for you if I have pneumonia," Jo had turned and called. I watched her out of sight. For the first time I knew there were forces stronger than me and over which I had not the slightest control. Surely this was not how it would always be? (20-21)

Despite this crisis at school, Johnson passed an examination to transfer to Kingston Day Commercial School, and, he details in the Burns interview, here "they taught me shorthand, typing, and bookkeeping. Useful" (90). He qualifies in his final graduation examination for "Matric Exemption," theoretically enabling university entrance. However, at this time no one from his school or many from his background had ever attended university, of which he was very conscious. Rejected for military duties during national service on medical grounds due to sinus difficulties, in the following five years Johnson worked in various accountancy posts of the kind described in *Trawl* and *Christie Malry's Own Double-Entry.* "Clean Living Is the Real Safeguard" records the parameters of his life. It centers around one girlfriend's father, Chicker Mills, who keeps racing greyhounds, a quintessentially lower-class activity. Chicker races a female runt of a litter of four after disasters with all three brothers: "I went and put ten bob on *Chicker's Sweetheart* with the least villainous bookie I could see. At this time I was seventeen and earning three pounds for five and a half days a week at the National Provincial Bank in Hammersmith: ten shillings therefore represented the best part of a day's pay to me" (25). The bank clerk narrator, much like Johnson and Christie Malry, earns very little. Even in his youthful naïveté, Johnson records a dislike that transcends the immediacy of the individual relationships concerned, exploring his objections to the middle-class aspirations of his girlfriend and her family, their obsession with conventional success that he despises: "I liked her father, in a grudging sort of way, for he was really resentful of his daughter loving me and took every chance of humiliating me, of showing up my immaturity. He told Betty that she'd have dozens like me before she settled down; he was wrong in that, she had only one after me, she married the first one with money after me, who never had money in my life" (*Corpses* 26). This antipathy recurs in "Everyone Knows Someone Who's Dead."

In his evenings during his final clerical post, with an oil company on Kingsway, Johnson studied Latin privately for a preliminary examination. He undertook a year of Intermediate BA studying English, Latin, and history at Birkbeck College, University of London, to qualify for degree entry. At twenty-three he enrolled for a B.A. in English at King's College from 1956-1959, another constituent college of London University. Johnson had a significant love affair alluded to frequently in *Albert Angelo,* in "Everybody Knows Somebody Who's Dead" with the comment "My moll had cast me off in favour of a sterile epileptic of variable temperament" (*Memoirs?* 131), and in *The Unfortunates* with the characterization of Wendy. At Birkbeck he was befriended by two of his tutors, Barbara Hardy and Geoffrey Tillotson, well-regarded scholars of their period. He ran the college's literary society and such events as a visit to and discussion of the first London production of Beckett's *Waiting for Godot.* He graduated with a Lower Second Class Honours degree. Even at university level Johnson felt a continuing neglect at the hands of the education system. In rejecting Alan Burns's suggestion that he could learn from other contemporaneous English novelists,

Johnson responds in their interview, "No. I did that at university, studying The English Novel and reading hundreds of them. I've done that bit and come to a position where I am right. If they can't see it then the strength of my case is such that that they haven't properly understood" (93). Throughout his student experience, he seems to have been relatively unaffected by the surge of youth culture in the late 1950s that continued in the 1960s. "Perhaps It's These Hormones" attempts to evoke the youth cultural voice of the record industry insider and remains Johnson's most unconvincing published piece. His teaching deepens his sense of separation from both the young and his own class. In "On Supply" he reflects, "They think you're not human if you're a teacher, like as if you were a copper, only without the power. In the same class as coppers, that is, to be avoided if you're not looking for bother" (*Corpses* 76).

On graduation, Johnson aspired to write professionally, attending courses in the area of film. He can be seen trying to suggest some appropriate credentials to which his unsuccessful appeals for work or commissions from the BBC testify. In a typewritten letter dated 11 November 1959 from his parents' residence in Barnes, Johnson presents himself to a Miss Pughe, giving us a glimpse of this transitional period of his life:

> As I am completely unknown to you, perhaps you might be interested in some autobiographical details. I am twenty-six years old, and I graduated from King's College, London, this summer. At King's I edited five termly issues of the College magazine, *Lucifer,* raising its literary standard higher than ever before, and attracting the favourable attention of John Lehmann and the *New Statesman*. I also edited *Thames,* an anthology of London University poetry, in 1958, and this year I was the London editor of *Universities' Poetry Two,* which was published last month and has been favourably reviewed (to date) in the *New Statesman* and the *Times Educational Supplement.*
>
> Whilst at King's I also wrote, produced, and acted in plays and revues; my production of Jean Genet's *The Maids* (the first non-professional one in England) won an alpha rating at the 1958 British Drama League Festival. Also in 1958 I produced and acted in a production of *Much Ado About Nothing* which toured Germany and Denmark during this summer vacation.
>
> At present I spend most of my time writing (I am working on a novel) and support myself by private coaching. I am extremely interested in writing for radio and television, and I am attending the course on writing for television at the National Film Theatre. (BBC Caversham Archive n.pag.)

Ghose met Johnson during these times of struggle, aspiration, and insecurity. Recording his memories of their first encounter late in the summer of 1959, Ghose recalls their first encounter after graduation:

The first thing I saw of him when I opened the door was his eyes. Not their color, which in the shadow of the threshold appeared a greyish blue, but their look that struck me as sad and *afraid*. Perhaps it was merely the apprehension of meeting someone for the first time with whom previously he had only corresponded; perhaps it was fear of a door opening to beckon him to enter an unknown world. From that moment we were friends for fourteen years, and I never saw that look in his eyes again. . . . My second impression was that he was rather large. In height, perhaps no more than two or three inches taller than my own five feet eight, but there was a bulk about him; a lot of blond hair, the cheeks fleshy and convex, the lips full, a well-proportioned head on a potentially corpulent body. (23)

There followed five years as a supply teacher in innumerable schools in both west and north London, the career anticipated reluctantly in *Travelling People* and outlined in graphic detail in *Albert Angelo*. In 1961 Johnson moved away from his parents in Barnes to a flat in Islington (Ghose 23), a shift confirmed by his correspondence to the BBC recorded in files at Caversham. Johnson worked unpaid on a variety of his own projects including his first novel, while attempting to gain institutional support. In a second letter to Miss Pughe on 15 December 1959 he complains: "It would help me if you could tell me some reasons why this [script proposal] was considered unsuitable. As I realise you must be very busy, a brief indication will be quite sufficient. For instance, was my treatment not good enough? Or was the subject-matter of the novel unsuitable? Or was the whole thing not good compared with other material you have available? Since I spent some time on this adaptation, I would be very grateful if you could indicate where I was at fault so that I might try to avoid wasting time in the future" (BBC Caversham Archive n.pag.).

Johnson's next short letter to Miss Pughe is from 34, Claremont Square, London, N1. on 9 April 1961; the address alone indicates a stage in Johnson's developing independence. Significant is its closeness to the center of artistic avant-garde London in Soho, Camden, and the still cheap and bohemian Angel, Islington. Here he lived within a stone's throw of other struggling writers such as Joe Orton. Through networking, Johnson became a friend and confidant of older novelist Rayner Heppenstall, who identifies *Travelling People*'s indebtedness to *Tristram Shandy* and records Virginia Johnson's good French, polished by time spent previously in Paris. Significantly, he specifies Johnson's attendance at a lecture in English by Nathalie Sarraute (to whom Johnson refers at the begin-

ning of his introduction to the Hungarian edition of *The Unfortunates)* on the Charing Cross Road in 1960 (Goodman 67-68, 120).
Heppenstall explains both his own meeting with and influence
upon Robbe-Grillet as well as the latter's joint visit with Sarraute
to England in February 1961 (Goodman 198-99, 209-10). Heppenstall
is accompanied to these lectures and readings by Johnson, the latter driving a group of people there in his old Bedford van. Such experiences and people suggest themselves as conduits or contact
points, establishing the influence of postwar French thought and
the nouveau roman in particular upon Johnson. In "From Realism
to Reality" Robbe-Grillet concludes, "The discovery of reality can
only continue its advance if people are willing to abandon outworn
forms" (*Snapshots* 154), a sentiment echoed by Johnson's writing in
its practice. Fellow novelist Eva Figes confirms this influence when
she recalls an informal grouping of writers including herself, Ann
Quin, Alan Burns, and Johnson rejecting "mainstream 'realist' fiction at a time when, in England, it seemed the only acceptable sort.
We were concerned with language, with breaking up conventional
narrative, with 'making it new' in our different ways. We all used
fragmentation as a starting point, and then took off in different directions. Bryan concentrated on a kind of literal honesty, on the author as central character, and on the format of the book itself. . . . It
is a measure of English conservatism and insularity when one remembers that this was the prevailing atmosphere in the literary establishment at a time when, abroad, writers like Beckett, Robbe-
Grillet, Grass, and Borges were doing their best work" (70-71). For
Johnson this meant revising the novel form and thus readers' expectations. This became something of a crusade, alienating those
committed to more traditional views. B. S. Johnson responds to a
hostile Bernard Bergonzi in an unpublished BBC radio interview
broadcast on 26 March 1968: "I'm not interested in the slightest in
writing fiction. Where the difficulty comes in . . . where [there ex-
ists] the misunderstanding over terms is that 'novel' and 'fiction'
are not synonymous. Certainly I write autobiography, and I write it
in the form of a novel. What I don't write is fiction" (12). Johnson's
stance reflects Robbe-Grillet's assertion in *Towards a New Novel:*
"Man is no more, from his own point of view, than the only witness"
(82). As Johnson elaborates to Bergonzi, "Yes, I prefer to call inven-
tion lies—I distrust the imagination—I don't think that anyone can
invent anything in the sense that they make something out of nothing. At best what they are doing is combining two things" (10).
Johnson both uses and concurrently subverts narrative's implicit
voice of authority; the purpose is not primarily ludic, but to counter
the traditional social conservatism that the narrative voice came to

represent. In so doing, Johnson also variously resists, critiques, and challenges the sorts of exploitation he saw as inherent in the society that relies upon such elevated and constraining voices. In a rather glib fashion (ignoring the sophistication of modern theory and class politics) many commentators have accounted for Johnson's approach as a "Platonic" position, prioritizing classicism and failing to fully theorize Plato's suspicion of poets. There is a more contemporary context of comparison. Robbe-Grillet insists on the phenomenological nature of the nouveau roman's narrative description of things: "The objects of our novels never have any presence outside human perceptions, whether real or imaginary; they are objects which are comparable to those of our everyday life, objects like those upon which our attention is constantly fixed" (*Snapshots* 138). The perceptual insistence of the world evoked by Johnson draws upon a very similar critically inclined worldview.

On a personal level, Johnson saw his earlier life as being disfigured by romantic and emotional loss. In *Albert Angelo* he hints at the reality for him of such experiences in "Disintegration" by specifying the apparently genuine name of a girlfriend, Jenny, as the source for characterizing Albert's ex-lover, Muriel. This offers an authenticity and accuracy of the emotional referent of Albert by insisting that his loss and anguish represent Johnson's own. In *Trawl* he anguishes over various traumas, but in doing so also explores his defects in such relationships. Of Joan, an unmarried mother he has dated, he admits:

········ It is now easy to see and to understand that I was too selfish: that is, I did not know at the time about enlightened self-interest, that everyone gives in order to receive, that all actions are invariably for selfish motives however much self-delusion there may be about them: and that the enlightenment is all. I took from Joan, and gave little in return. And I did not see at the time—how I could not see it is now difficult to understand—that obviously what she was looking for was security, economic and emotional security, and that I offered her nothing that she wanted, being to her only someone who came from an address he was unwilling to have known, took her for a few drinks, and then screwed her, sometimes when she did not particularly want to be screwed. ·· That is clear. (21)

According to Ghose, "Touched by deep personal tragedy, Bryan carried an enormous quantity of sadness within him. Life had betrayed him, and he was constantly on the guard against fresh betrayals, suspicious of anyone who could not love him wholly. Some time before I met him, he had suffered the worst betrayal of his life: a woman with whom he was deeply in love left him for another man" (24). Later, as he succeeded as a writer, he married and had two children, yet long-term, the happiness and contentment that he desired eluded him. This haunts the fringes and themes of his novels and is not their substance. He reveals an intensity of emotion and judgment, hinting at periods of unhappiness and depression. He was forthright and needy. Ghose recalls a jealous lover: "Once at a dinner party, a male guest greeted Virginia on entering the flat by kissing her on the cheek. Bryan, who was just then coming to the hall and had seen only the end of the perfectly innocent greeting, glared angrily at the man and said in a harsh, accusing voice, 'Did you *kiss* my wife?' The man made a joke of it, but Bryan's evening was ruined. He could never disguise his feelings; if he felt rotten, his face showed it" (25).

In 1973 the underlying conflict within the marriage hinted at in the last novel became an inseparable gulf. There were a number of factors. The initial rejection of his last novel depressed him, and as Gordon Bowker writes, "He then told me that he was unable to get a commission for further novels and talked gloomily of having to return to supply-teaching" (51). He was becoming difficult, confrontational, and threatening. As the breakup of his marriage seemed imminent, he appears to have combined a changed set of obsessions with an irretrievable despondency. Bowker comments, "I heard later, in his last months, Bryan had fallen in with an occultist, who seemed to exercise a strange power over him. He might jump up in the middle of a family meal and leave the house saying that he 'knew' this man wanted him. His behaviour had become increasingly bizarre, and he had even started talking to Virginia about their committing suicide together. It was at this point she had taken the children and fled" (52). There are hints in the fiction that this revived an earlier preoccupation. As Johnson saw matters, he had been abandoned and betrayed again. He was inconsolable. He took his own life alone on 13 November 1973.

Development: Critical and Methodological Contexts

In the literary context Johnson is a thinking, exploratory writer. In one of his first interviews, "Anti or Ultra?," Johnson defines the process of writing as requiring more than the contraction of narrative to verisimilitude and an act of record, and more than any naive realism. He knows narrative must include "the conflict between illusion and reality" (25) and that "my basic problem was that of all novelists: how to embody truth in a vehicle of fiction. Truth, that is, as a personally observed and experienced reality, and not of course autobiographical literalness" (25). Such a notion of complex truth both problematizes and characterizes Johnson's work. He understands writing's potential paradox, which he turns into critical or theoretical one-liners. In "These Count as Fictions" he says of his method of narrative, "I occupy my mind with statements the truth of which interests me, such as *Form follows function,* or it might be on another occasion *Everything is merely or exactly the absence of its opposite.* Or sometimes I will tell myself *You can't have it all ways: at least at once*" (*Memoirs?* 116). The dialectical undertones are open for anyone to read, but the little Johnson criticism that exists mostly refuses to do so.

Johnson looks back to his earlier years for the bulk of his narrative raw material: to childhood, school, adolescence and clerical work, early sexual experiences, student days, and, of course, young adulthood when he was forced into teaching by financial needs. Only *The Unfortunates* and *See the Old Lady Decently* are focused in any concentrated fashion on other significant periods. In the latter he offers several oblique and tantalizing glimpses of his domestic world. Johnson's novels incorporate a number of recurrent themes common to both his fiction and his life: failed or failing relationships with women, an ambivalent, often hostile attitude toward work and authority, and a need to derive truth from such instinctive doubts.

Certainly his work is neither slight nor lacking in critical and/or textual density; as I explain in my article "Chaos and Truth: B. S. Johnson's Theoretical and Literary Narratives," "The reflexive and biographical elements of his work are self-evident, yet there are subcutaneous theoretical aspects to his work that extend this view of narrative. Yet, despite evidence of this scattered throughout his writings, interpreting his significance and evaluating the more profound qualities of his work appear to have eluded the majority of academics and critics. In the decisive struggle of exegetical commentary, until recently Johnson has been almost erased from the literary-cultural field" (38). Johnson's aspirations to theorize his role as writer are self-evident. In *Albert Angelo* Johnson explores the task of writing while accepting this project's innate difficulties:

—And also to echo the complexity of life, reproduce some of the complexity of selves which I contain within me, contradictory and gross as they are: childish, some will call it, peeing in the rainfall gauge, yes, but sometimes I am childish, very, so are we all, it's part of the complexity I'm trying to reproduce, exorcise.

—Faced with the enormous detail, vitality, size, of this complexity, of life, there is a great temptation for a writer to impose his own pattern, an arbitrary pattern which must falsify, cannot do anything other than falsify; or he invents, which is pure lying. Looking back and imposing a pattern to come to terms with the past must be avoided. Lies, lies, lies. (170)

Most critics of Johnson squirm at his central concept of truth, parodying his stance by simplifying it almost out of existence. Such analysis falls into the trap described by Jürgen Habermas in *The Philosophical Discourse of Modernity: Twelve Lectures,* where he explains a reduction of vision caused when "critics commit the error of still starting from the expectation that reality could ever take on a rational shape" (74). His rejection of such basal rationality helps explain why Johnson has failed to attain any "critical mass," and why he is most often dismissed as either derivative or prosaically mundane. He is neither. Poignantly, this reaction is most common in his homeland, exactly where his own critique was directed and where its relevance could still be argued to hold true. In contrast, Morton P. Levitt declares in "The Novels of B. S. Johnson: Against the War against Joyce," "We are struck in each of Johnson's novels not by his veneration of Joyce and the Modernists but, following their example, by his imaginative use of technique and his ability to move us" (575). However, in concluding his observations, Levitt both narrows a notion of truth to literal correspondence, by which he questions Johnson's project, and yet apparently redeems him as Joycean and representing "the one serious novelist of his generation who has been fearless of 'experiment' and of being linked with the Modernists" (585). This is double-edged praise. Johnson, obsessed with truth, simply continues the modernist project. Thus Johnson is denied his own attempt to contextualize the novel, his ambition to supersede "literariness" and its convenient epistemic boundaries (away from "real" life contexts).

Johnson's critical neglect will be reversed only as both his novels and published commentary upon them appear in the marketplace of literary discourse and academic study. Clearly neither Johnson's position nor that of those responsible for literary canonization and textual availability has ever been neutral. Inevitably within the literary-aesthetic and critical fields one can apply as a reservation to any canonical evaluations Pierre Bourdieu's concept, outlined in *The Rules of Art,* of "social agents" and his analysis that "The field is a network of objective relations (of domination or subordination, of complementarity or antagonism, etc.) between positions . . ." (231). Winners in criticism involves neglect of many potentially significant writers and the criteria for these choices are never pure. Judith Mackrell comments, "For much of his writing career, B. S. Johnson regarded himself as one of the very small and embattled minority of writers who were showing any signs of resisting the conservatism of the British literary establishment" (42). What remains notable in this respect is that Johnson's neglect often includes a lack of recognition by middle-class, apparently avant-garde, intellectuals. The question remains why. Addressing the issue of both the textual and nontextual identity of this almost forgotten voice may at least partially explain his neglect. Throughout his work, Johnson expresses multiple aspects of his own identity, paradoxically as both a quintessentially British and yet a counter-cultural novelist. He knew of this contradiction as a characteristic of his society's definition of what constitutes acceptability and saw that narrowing chiefly in terms of the culture's class prejudices. Johnson is notable because he represents a rare combination in British literary narratives. He typifies possibly one of the most representative of voices from the nation's culture, one rarely heard in fiction until very recently, that of an author expressing his own indigenous working-class, everyday experience.

His texts are never straightforward, often appearing contradictory. This is intentional. Johnson questions, almost in frustration, the assumptions of bourgeois narrative and critics: "But why should novelists be expected to avoid paradox any more than philosophers?" (*Memoirs?* 18). Clearly, he approached the task as if it mattered. This is the stuff of life and analysis. The texts offer an interpretative model woven into the simple "facts" of the plots. There are a number of crucial modes or patterns to his narratives. First, the plots are neither elaborate nor tightly focused as expositions of events. Second, his radicalism and socialistically inclined class-consciousness contend with traditionalism; they do so by raising critically the issues of gender relations, notions of honesty, and the possibility of an aesthetic consciousness. Third, he is committed to experimentalism and challenge both as a literary method and reality and as an agent of the ongoing change that is life. "Whether or not it can be demonstrated that all is chaos, certainly all is change: the very process of life itself is growth and decay at an enormous variety of rates. Change is a condition of life. Rather than deplore this or hunt the chimaerae of stability or reversal, one should perhaps embrace change as all there is. Or might be. For change is never for the better or for the worse; change simply *is*" (*Memoirs?* 17). Together all these elements create a remarkable mix: realistic ambitions, experimental structures and styles, moral honesty, radical class awareness, a notion of an almost ethical "truth" or authenticity, a sense of history in a material rather than narrative sense, and a romantic urge in terms of friendship and bonding. This extends beyond his solipsistic concerns, right from the first tentative novel.

(Resisting) Disintegration: The Novels

Travelling People won for Johnson the 1963 Gregory Award for best first novel of the year, with T. S. Eliot and Henry Reid among the judges. Its protagonist, mature student Henry Henry, remains a barely disguised portrait of Johnson. The plot charts an episode based upon the author's, a postdegree summer when, like Johnson, Henry works in a country club in Wales. On Henry's travels to Dublin (not featured in the narrative present, but alluded to in letters to his friend, Robert), he meets the manager of a country club, Trevor Tuckerson. On his return, jobless Henry takes up the offer and spends the summer in among the intrigues of the staff, dividing into two camps. He falls in love with Kim, a student involved with the owner, aging Maurie Bunde (named as pun). The denouement involves Maurie's death, Henry's consummation of his passion with Kim, and their joint sacking by Trevor, influenced by his appalling girlfriend, Mira.

The opening "Prelude" places the narrator in Shandean fashion in Tristram's chair, a telling literal *and* symbolic positioning of the narrator/author figure:

Seated comfortably in a wood and wickerwork chair of eighteenth-century Chinese manufacture, I began seriously to meditate upon the form of my allegedly full-time literary sublimations. Rapidly, I recalled the conclusions reached in previous meditations on the same subject: my rejection of stage-drama as having too many limitations, of verse as being unacceptable at the present time on the scale I wished to attempt, and of radio and television as requiring too many entrepreneurs between the writer and the audience; and my resultant choice of the novel as the form possessing fewest limitations, and closest contact with the greatest audience. (11)[3]

The Sternean reference and influence can be seen in the graying and black pages indicating the losing consciousness and death of Maurie Bunde. As Mackrell says, "the underlying intention is always deadly serious" (45), but she concludes, "The last device is obviously a deliberate lifting from Sterne and reminds us of the latter's wonderfully playful exploitation of the technological potential of the printed page, but it lacks inevitably, the originality and indeed the wit of Sterne's remorseless exposure of the novel's limitations, and like the rather clumsy sound words, succeeds only as a gesture rather than a radical subversion of our expectations . . ." (47). For David John Davies, "the use of innovation is still uncertain and confused . . . at times like the exuberance of a late student's enthusiasms" (73). To respond, firstly, Johnson's allusiveness is not random; it is always directed toward innovators or those concerned with the critical and technical difficulties of relating to reality in a constantly changing culture. Secondly, the chair is far more significant than has been commented upon critically to this point, since it derives from Laurence Sterne's "The Author's Preface" (202ff) where Tristram reflects upon his hatred of "*set dissertations*" (208), and the chair itself is compared to "wit and judgement" where the parts are seen "*to answer one another*" (209) as part of Tristram's recommendation of "*dialectic induction*" (206). Hence Johnson's preface outlines by its Shandean allusions the methodological and ideological approach to his fiction adopted by Johnson that would lead to him developing his own experimental forms. In the text the Shandean critique continues. While hitchhiking, Henry introduces himself to Trevor Tuckerson, later his boss at the Stromboli Club. Johnson reflects of Henry, "He paused at this perpetual social hurdle to see if he had to explain his parents' Shandean fixation with economy in nomenclature" (21). In the novel's world of commodification, dead dogs in transit to be boiled down for glue, and unemployed uncertainty, the Stromboli Club initially offers a symbol of paradise, but its realities negate its Edenic possibilities and, as Kanaganayakam notes, the "image of Paradise dissolves" (92).[4]

Later Johnson rejected *Travelling People,* refusing its republication, but it remains striking, with its mélange of various styles and effects, its collage of methods and structures, and the multiple cultural references drawing from both the literary past and present. This includes gestures toward Joyce, explored by Mackrell (45), for she cites Joyce as motivation for Henry's visit to Dublin. The novel introduces many of the elements that would come to characterize Johnson's writing. He includes comic one-liners: "Henry judged that Crewe station was obsolete about fifty years before the railway was invented" (48). There are reflections which are observationally and morally instructive: "The people most to feared after a row or a crisis are those who behave, often after a very short interval, as though nothing had happened" (122). The text is self-reflexive (or referential), declaring its textual status, as when Henry travels on a train to Wales with a soldier and both are awakened: "The incident which awoke them is rather complex in the describing, so it would perhaps be as well if you paid very careful attention to the next paragraph" (49).

Johnson makes evident the boisterous and ultimately quarrelsome nature of the privileged class (not mentioned by Gordon in his commentary on Johnson's class resentment) in Henry's letter to Robert (62-63). The text offers no attempt at impartiality: "The blueblood sport here is pushing people into the pool, fully clothed:

once one person is in, of course, the whole party goes in. This is the main function of the pool: swimming appropriately clad is almost a misuse of it. How wonderful it must be to have so much money that one can afford to disregard clothes so! They hold races across the pool on lilos, lying down, still clothed, and paddling with their hands" (63). Johnson's instinct concerning the presumptions of English class society was both acute and active. Despite his dismissive class placement, Gordon concedes that Johnson "was the archetypal professional writer in the most discriminating way" (157), but "was like a raging bull, a whale out of water, ultimately floundering fatally in the slightly cynical, very superior, oh so sophisticated literary world of London" (158). In contrast Bowker recollects Johnson's account of an "editor, a product of one of our grander universities, [who] began politely to explain to him why his book had been rejected. 'I leaned over the desk and grabbed the little bugger by the throat and hauled him across the desk,' Johnson told me, 'and I said, "What the fuck does a little cunt like you know about literature?"' He laughed with delight at the memory—it was the Cockney Bard versus the Oxbridge Philistines" (50).

The events of *Albert Angelo* (1964) are even more complex, concerning the social, emotional, and workplace traumas of a London supply teacher who moves to Islington after a failed love affair. Johnson contextualizes his own supply work in north London schools as both exterior and interior setting, but, in doing so, adapts the classroom and schoolyard ephemera and setting from Michel Butor *Degrés* (1960).[5] Some themes or contexts are prefigured in a story in *Statement against Corpses,* "Statement," where the unnamed protagonist articulates a sense of himself as in crisis, between youth and adulthood. It is written from the viewpoint of a character being interviewed by the police after a road accident, with only his side transcribed. He attempts to explain his nocturnal meanderings with a friend in similar circumstances, between classes and dislocated. Significantly, almost exactly the same context and situation is reiterated and developed for several sections of *Albert Angelo.*

—I'm trying to tell you. I know you don't believe I went to college. But I'm a London boy, mate, I'm talking like this to you because you *din't* go to university. See? I can put the right accent on for the right people. Makes you so's you can talk to everybody but be accepted by nobody. That's also why it was good for me and Terry to go down west tonight, like the old times, only there was two of us now and we went in the Minor Terry runs, and the girls ain't on the streets any more. . . . (*Corpses* 41)

Like both Johnson himself, and the eponymous protagonist of *Albert Angelo,* the short story's narrator works as a disillusioned teacher in a Secondary Modern school, the lower part of the two-tier system under the selection system in Britain that lasted into the 1970s. Each of these teachers (particularly Johnson himself) seems ill at ease with his role. Despite Albert's apparent qualifications as an architect (a complex issue in terms of this detail's later significance in the text), he too works as a supply teacher. Johnson's move from his parents' in Barnes to Islington is a real-life experience explored by Ghose (23) and echoed in Albert's own move and the initial decision-making by Albert about the pattern of his life, such as mundane details as when he plans to meet his parents. He fills his life with a synthesis of existential inquiry and Beckettian angst, the latter being politicized by the former. Coming after a failed relationship, about which Albert mopes and the narrative reflects, the plot explores an ensuing transitional phase, a *rites of passage* and a recovery of bachelor life. Albert trawls through the city with another young friend, Terry (these scenes are also a development of the story "Statement"); significantly both are suffering intensely from a period of postrelationship angst that creates a kind of male camaraderie and bonding. Superficially, although these might appear to be angry young (white) men figures, more occurs in Johnson's characterization. These men establish the potentially threatening alterity of women, but in their nocturnal meandering they face the diasporic realities of another form of alterity, the colonial (or postcolonial) presence in the underprivileged quarters of London of Cypriots, West Indians, and Africans, among others. The very technical complexity of the novel's form renders more than a naturalistic account or a notion of liberal intervention. Its viewpoint is various. Its interrogative structure suggests a broader intersection with these everyday realities of urban existence. London is narrowed to the mundane consciousness of various intersubjectivities rather than any grand narrative.

The novel advances Johnson's sophistication and experimentation. The narrative offers many variations and perspectives. A number of semiliterate essays from Albert's pupils, invited to offer their opinion of the hated temporary teacher, break down his viewpoint, offering a glimpse of his violence and anger in response to their unruliness. One pupil outlines an ongoing feud with another where: "I was sent to mr. Harrison and he made us be friends and from that day on we were friends. Next day we had a friendly fight and I busted is nose. FIN" (63); and in "The Killer Master" another pupil records: "Suddenly the boy behind me says something to the boy next to him. The Master in a deadly rage got hold of the boy by his hair, and dragged him to the front of the class where he brutally hit him the boy fell to the floor moaning then the master kicked him, the class by then were shouting their heads off. With that he walked out of the class and that was the last we ever saw of him" (65-66).[6]

Johnson includes holes cut in his text, parallel columns of print representing simultaneous thought and action in the classroom, cartographic battlefield symbols to indicate the conflict between two teachers in a class debate (138-39), and the found object of a spiritualist and medium's card from Chapel Market (120-21), a real street adjacent to Johnson's actual home in Myddleton Square, posing similar questions to the Victorian novel of health, romance, inheritance, and fate. Johnson plays with the central assumption of the found object. The proleptic holes cut into two pages appear to offer a reading of the future, as a textual segment that can be anticipated. On its first encounter after a sectional division, one reads "struggled to take back his knife, and inflicted on him a mortal wound above his right eye (the blade penetrating to a depth of two inches) from which he died instantly" (from 149, reading in advance 153). This is shocking on first encounter. After turning the page, one reads "Terry" as the apparent subject of the sentence, pointing to an appalling outcome of the street confrontation in which he and Albert are involved (151). On turning the page one discovers that this is "Frizer" in his barroom brawl leading to the death of "Christopher Marlowe, Poet, February 1564 to May 1593" (153). This device offers a sense of bifurcation, paradox, and plural possibilities of reading, but also a historical perspective. The parallel columns represent a synchronicity of action, speech, and internalized narrative thought from various viewpoints. Most famously—often the sole feature for which the author is both remembered and dismissed— Johnson emerges into the text, breaking the frame of the literary device, fragmenting the separation of narrative and real-life identifications with "an almighty aposiopesis" (167). The explosive phrase, "OH, FUCK ALL THIS LYING!" (163) is followed by a ranting confession of authorial intention. On first reading this is still shocking. Through this strategy of disrupting readerly expectations and normative structures, Johnson can create the conditions for a critical awareness. As Bhabha says, "The image is only ever an *appurtenance* to authority and identity; it must never be read mimetically as the appearance of reality. The access to the image of identity is only ever possible in the *negation* of any sense of originality or plentitude . . ." (51). Johnson appears to negate both in his text as if to dissociate it from the authority and fixed identity, the movement away from both of which is arguably the central dilemma for Albert.

Subsequently, Johnson admits openly that the architectural profession was an "objective correlative" for poetry (and Albert a device for representing himself) and the need for the poet to work outside of his commitment to art while admitting "this device you cannot have failed to see creaking, ill-fitting at many places, many places, for architects *manqués* can earn livings very nearly connected with their art, and no poet has ever lived by his poetry, and architecture has a functional aspect quite lacking in poetry, and simply, architecture is just not poetry" (168). If such characterization is imperfect and the whole paradigm of creating other identities is prone to error, nevertheless things may be said obliquely and Johnson does observe closely social contexts and the ideological bases of human interaction. This is his other "objective correlative." His textual dismissal of failed parallels is not significant in terms of ineptitude, unless artists are committed to art for its own sake, because what is significant for Johnson are wider realities such as people being forced by labor and capital requirements to conform. Artistic struggle does not potentiate itself in narrow plot features, but within the text's political reality. Johnson's failings are a device to draw attention elsewhere. Once he has abandoned the characterized mediation of Albert's identity, Johnson uses the revelation as an opportunity to hector his reader in irritation as if engaging in a one-sided ideological harangue with the intellectually resistant:

—So it's nothing to you that I am rabbeting on about being a poet and having to earn a living in other ways: but what about your own sector of the human condition then? Eh? Eh? Eh eh eh!

—It is about frustration.

—The poetry comes from the suffering. (169)

Although the apotheosis as an extreme aesthetic act is well noted by critics, the novel's broader contexts and range of elaborations of ideological motifs pass unnoticed in the main. The break in the fiction is taken as an act of critical apoplexy or frustration, and the nuancing of world conditions that has led to this rupture has been effaced or made marginal. The condition of being within social contexts is both structurally and thematically foregrounded so that Johnson's novels balance the personal reflection with a sociological account of urban living.

Arguably, *Albert Angelo* remains Johnson's most experimental work. He writes after his aposiopesis, "——— A page is an area on which I may place any signs I consider to communicate most nearly what I have to convey: therefore I employ, within the pocket of my publisher and the patience of my printer, typographical techniques beyond the arbitrary and constricting limits of the conventional novel. To dismiss such techniques as gimmicks, or to refuse to take them seriously, is crassly to miss the point" (176). Glyn White concludes this is "the novel of his which we can least afford to forget since it contains a full complement of striking experiments, offers its own bludgeoning response to conventional criticism and can be seen to prefigure many of Johnson's later developments" (143). Yet, there are further subtleties often elided by commentators. Far less commented upon than the almost infamous apotheosis is the plural, conflictual, and transitive society in which Johnson locates his characters of various origins and cultures. From recounting his own working-class west London origins in a quasi-Beckettian pastiche, failed architect Albert conveys impressionistically the trauma of imposing in his role as a supply teacher an authority in which he cannot believe. Perhaps significantly for contemporary critical sensibilities, in terms of a sustainable grounds for his recovery, of all white British writers, Johnson, as I detail below, seems acutely attuned to recognizing and critiquing the power and hegemony of the imperial/colonial narrative and its collapse in the postwar world, rather than its narrativization. He offers no trace of nostalgia for the lost bourgeois stability of imperialism that to some degree permeates even supposedly radical novelists touching upon similar contexts or even cultural motifs, often marking the coordinates of a novelistic bourgeois self-identification both familiar and repulsive to Johnson. Albert confronts the conflicts of a classic inner-city London school setting, with absconding adolescents between cultures. In describing the problems to a friend, he opines his fate and negates the romantic portrayal of ethnic presence, doubting the veracity of *To Sir, with Love:*

"I told you the sods pinched my pen a couple of weeks ago? I was reading this novel recently about a teacher in the east end who won over the kids by love and kindness, morality and honesty, against tremendous odds — talk about sentiment and wish-fulfilment! I can just see my lot coming to me at the end of term with a present — or even my pen back — addressed to sir, with their love! These things just don't mean anything to these kids in this school: that's what so frightening, and I've not been frightened in a school before. Not frightened by their violence, though that's bad enough, but just by these unknown forces of character." (130)

He rejects Braithwaite's notion of the imposition of cultured values. Braithwaite's own narrative says, "On my way home that evening I walked to the bus with Miss Blanchard, and told her about what I had done. She was dubious about the wisdom of imposing unfamiliar social codes on the children, yet, as I had already

committed myself, she hoped it would work" (58). His protagonist
gets his girl. Albert is toyed with and rejected by Miss Crossthwaithe
(alluding to and a pun on Braithwaite, surely). In a class debate
about the children's speech, Johnson records, "The offence to Miss
Crossthwaithe's lovely ears, Mr. Albert suggested, came about because these children were not speaking as she spoke herself, these
children were not imposing the same pattern on their worlds as she
imposed on hers; for who approves, Mr. Albert quoted Petronius
without attribution, of conduct unlike his own?" (138).

Underlying Johnson's critique of the world is both his recognition
and avowal of a cycle of violence and oppression, and his indication
of bourgeois complicity in maintaining this pattern, a framework
from which they profit. This applies to the apparently polite, but
actually sarcastic and indifferent headmaster who oversees this
degeneration. Johnson in his engagement with the reality of playground violence and immigrant cultural self-identification attempts something of "the enormous detail, vitality, size, of this complexity, of life" (170). Johnson records the transitions from colonial
to postcolonial realities in their culturally explicit and marginalized
contexts. His *postcoloniality* is complex, a social and ideological
space that can convey both a critical awareness of those imperial/
colonial structures and their problematic continuation in social relations and identity formation.

Early in his classroom duties, Albert faces practical difficulties in
the classroom. His first obstacle is to integrate into his classes four
Greek Cypriot children who have no English language skills or
knowledge. His response is to "Give them games to play with in the
formal lessons, books to look at, and personal coaching, ha, and try
to give as many lessons as possible that do not involve reading or
writing without depriving the other children. Like painting" (33).
Albert calls the register in real time, his words and actions dis-
played in double columns, with thought-responses italicized along-
side the curt, realistic exchanges; this allows Johnson to mark this
process of naming and response, the cultural location and prefer-
ence within which the teacher is implicated. In a textual, physically
represented sense Johnson conveys a dialectical interplay that
Freire summarizes when he says, "The word is more than just an in-
strument which makes dialogue possible; accordingly, we must seek
its constitutive elements. Within the word we find two dimensions,
reflection and action, in such radical interaction that if one is sacrificed—even in part—the other immediately suffers" (75). Johnson
radicalizes the interaction of these dimensions graphically on the
page in *Albert Angelo* in the mundane and habitual act of taking the
class register. Ideological permeation and interplay is thus implied

subtly and obliquely:

"Eray Mustapha"
"Yes, sir."
"Eray? Which one's Eray? Can you understand any more English, Eray?"
"Yes, sir."

Accent like any other North Londoner's. must have been born here.

"Good. John Nash."

John Nash and Regent Street and the Quadrant and All Souls' and the Prince Regent and the Haymarket Theatre and bits of Buckingham Palace, you think, John Nash.

"Yes, sir."
"Andreas Neo . . . Neophytos."
"Yes, sir." (36)

Albert's commentary set beside the verbalization provides by its interrelationship several crucial responses: the acknowledgment of language as the prime factor in subjugation, the cultural density of environment, and the concept of history, and in his final hesitation and uncertainty, he divides the literal approval, the marking of presence of the pupil, and so his ability to redeem his presence. Johnson, by this juxtaposition of the spatial sense of the page and his architectural motif, demonstrates the inscription of power upon a culture, the appropriation of naming by royal and privileged discourses, the hegemony of the familiar, the barriers to interpenetration that culture and authority create. The architectural reminders of the imperial expansion and its profits are overlaid onto his consciousness and his value system. The primary conflict is between himself as an albeit-unwilling agent of those cultural forces and the children themselves. Disruptions of authority and subjugations are central characteristics of the novel against which Albert charts the potential for collective, plural dimensions. Responding to the headmaster's correction of table manners, Albert reflects, again rejecting Braithwaite's model, "these children and their manners are the product of their environment, and therefore suit that environment. You are not sure enough of your own standards to take the responsibility of imposing them on these children for whom they would probably be quite inappropriate" (40).

Albert's contradictions delineate the ground of his growing

awareness, the limitations he feels as to transforming his responses and the limitations of transcending them that come up against his own prejudice and incomprehension: "You set the rest of your class to read, and have the Cypriots out as a group. Eray Mustapha, whom you had hoped to use as an interpreter, you find speaks Turkish and can no more communicate with the Greeks than you can" (44). In one boys' school with a predominance of Afro-Carribean pupils, Albert comments that they are "Blacker than you would think possible, starred by teeth white as the weathered western face of Portland stone, eyes brown as brazil nuts." He teaches in a classroom with "A lean budgerigar in a rusting cage making untimely interruptions" (45). By the very paucity and clichéd nature of Albert's metaphoric comparisons, Johnson highlights the protagonist's unfamiliarity with such figures and the very *Western* range of coordinates that create both his aesthetic and everyday understanding. The boys are objectified, appropriated to natural elements of a prerational presence, a move that serves as a reductive ratio of understanding for their blackness, their otherness, a familiarizing process that has an implicit trope of Western, Eurocentric placement. The budgerigar reminds one comically of the piracy involved in the colonial process, both as an imported product of that process that domesticizes the exotic, and as an ersatz, scaled-down version of the filmic convention of a parrot and pirate. It also evokes Braithwaite's first view of his teaching room, which appears to him like a "menagerie" (12). Also, in Albert's classroom literally the bird's comments both mock and subvert his assumption of authority. In the unruliness of the situation, the apparently liberal Albert reverts to a violence that depresses him, but he reflects, "You feel guilty, but suppress the feeling" (46). The emotional and intersubjective response is subordinated, nevertheless, "Even when you try to entertain you evoke little response from the boys. Yet you like them. You hate yourself" (46).

Albert moves on yet again and has to confront the limitations of his liberal concern and perception. Albert's third school in a week is off Holloway Road, in a run-down north London where "The five-and six-storey schools in this part stand above the three-storey streets like chaotic castellations" (47), and the allusion to power structures is evident. His own powerlessness contrasts his part in "trying to help to teach to take places in a society you do not believe in, in which their values already prevail rather than yours. Most will be wives and husbands, some will be whores and ponces: it's all the same; any who think will be unhappy . . ." (47). Conventional roles, patterned hegemonic behavior and the limitation of its subversion are key to Johnson's and Albert's notion and thematizing of power structures. The school, and its educative process, like the image of the castle Johnson uses, symbolizes itself as a paradigm of modernity and the colonial urge. After the weekend break he talks of religion, the human condition and "How can you think that God is good when you learn in History lessons about terrible wars which have killed thousands of people, and made thousands more, and even millions more, suffer?" (55).

After this initiation into the inner-city school system, the narrative follows Albert on his nocturnal, chthonic meanderings that chart the new subterranean city as if ironically to negate the Victorian philanthropic charting of the underclasses. From all-night cafés in Cable Street that evoke the stand against fascism and where "There must be cafés for ten or a dozen nationalities—Maltese, West Indians, Somalis, West Africans, Turkish and Greek Cypriots, and so on . . ." (51). In contrast to Albert's feelings of commonality, the children describe their lives in terms of racial prejudice and violence in ill-written essays incorporated in the narrative but which culminate in the violence of the teacher figure. Ironically in an atmosphere of growing conflict, where a band of boys from different cultures who call themselves corps drill militaristically, Albert reenacts this descent into control and victimizing others by adopting violence himself, adding to an ongoing spiral of subjection and objectification. The control of the past and history is essential in this process of domination since, as Albert ruminates, "The past of a man's life could always be controlled in this way, be seen to have a fixed order because it was passed, had passed: almost always, that is, for when it could not be controlled then madness was not far away. When something was passed, it was fixed, one could come to terms with it; always the process of imposing the pattern, of holding back the chaos" (133).

In reacting to the migrants he encounters, Albert's irritations are social ones, but the school context confirms that in Albert there is an undercurrent of a need for authority and order despite his liberalism. Of his pupils' unruliness he concludes, "You have to establish your own set of rules, let alone your own obedience of those rules, your own discipline. Which takes all the time, and an incredible amount of nervous energy. It's like I'm working at the frontier of civilisation all the time" (132), and it is clear this is a social process that absorbs and entails all cultures and identities although the rhetoric of blame is evident, a factor explored far more comprehensively in his last novel.

Trawl attempts a version of autobiography, relating the facts of a voyage Johnson undertook on a fishing boat in the Barents Sea with the intention of writing such a book. For Hassam, Johnson writes "diary fiction" that characterizes the author where he is loosening "the autobiographical pact within the novel, or rather its potential, [which] is framed by a fictional pact with the reader" (35). Aboard the trawler the protagonist reviews his life's hurt, betrayal, and failure. His seasickness and confinement to his cabin create the conditions for self-analysis. There is a dominant theme that informs this accumulation of personal, often obsessive minutiae. For me, it becomes clear the character's coordinates are those of Johnson himself. The business of the sea journey intrudes at first peripherally as noises into his cabin: "*CRAANGK!* the towing block goes against my head, it seems, even inside my head, sometimes, it seems . . . the pills I have do nothing for me, do not work, for me . . . " (8). Moving from the perceptually constricted interrogative definition of the Cartesian ego, with which he begins tentatively, Johnson moves to long passages of self-interrogation about the past in a quasi-stream-of-consciousness style, with lacunae representing sleep, doubt, and so forth marked by variable lengths of midline points. As Hassam notes, Johnson's narrator is equivocal about either facts themselves or their meanings (111). The past acquires narrative complexity and the reflection of others. Gradually, contemporary external perspectives reemerge as the narrator recovers and ventures from his psychic cocoon. There, Johnson discovers within the patterns of otherness, a continuation of the sense of almost irredeemable isolation and severance that ties together his reflections and thus the text: "On the whaleback men are busy: when I try to find a place amongst them, I am for the first time cursed for my idleness, the first expressed resentment of my pleasuretripping. Just when I want to be, think of myself as being, one of them, up and around, there is no place for me, no place, I am replaced in my isolation yet again. At least my bunk is my own, I'll go back there, who only an hour ago rose, from my new non-isolation" (179). Johnson's own language and that of the sailors, even in their jocularity, reconfirm his exclusion. The patterns of past minutiae reassert themselves in the apparently insignificant detail of the present. In this self-obsessed circularity and pathological drama of a return to fragmenting identity, the reader is reminded of Louis-Ferdinand Céline and more broadly the nouveau roman as intertextual precursors. As present, past, and reflection intermingle around the pervasive seasickness induced by the voyage, a general unease relates all of these intersecting narrative times at least tangentially to Johnson's frustrations at and responses to the human condition. Intertextually, Johnson develops the motif and substance of the isolated voyager from both Michel Butor's *La modification* (1957) and Alain Robbe-Grillet's *The Voyeur* (1959).

There are central themes and motifs to the apparent meanderings of his mind as he recalls his experiences in the war as a child, early romances, and a traumatic university drama tour in Europe, where another relationship founders. Two thematic clusters are crucial to properly evaluating the text. First is identity formation and second is a sense of underlying ideological contexts. Using the terminology of the literal war that had waged during his childhood, in *Trawl* Johnson positions himself polemically. Rather than seeing him expressing empty and dull rhetorical flourishes, I see in his perspective the suggestion of a sociological critique underpinning many observations: "I now realise the point at which I became aware of class distinction, of differences between people which were nothing to do with age or size, aware in fact of the class war, which is not an outdated concept, as those of the upper classes who are not completely dim would con everyone else into believing it is. The class war is being fought as viciously and destructively of human spirit as it has ever been in England: I was born on my side, and I cannot and will not desert: I became an enlisted man consciously but not voluntarily at the age of about seven" (53). What still makes *Trawl* uncomfortable reading for many is his idea of a class attrition and unfairness directed at the dispossessed by the very class embodied by most readers and potential critics. The mundane material forming Johnson's narrative, so often attacked as inconsequential, contributes to a weighty variant of a retrospective bildungsroman if one accedes to the possibility of a quotidian radicalism from reconceiving the apparently inconsequential. These are the patterns of everyday existence of the victims of such oppresive social dynamics. For Johnson sees some purpose emerging against the odds, unexpectedly. "Nothing there to precipitate it. ·· But everything, building up on this voyage, all the thinking, collectively, accumulatively, must have led to this sudden freedom I feel now, relievedly, relieved of all the thinking" (166). The material works upon him as a mass of perceptual and emotional processing, and in what is almost its dialectical negation, a clarification occurs, albeit a temporary and fragile one. Certainly as Hassam says, Johnson is "questioning at the thematic level but ultimately demonstrating at the level of structure the instability of those generic boundaries by which a culture legitimates and privileges certain forms of discourse" (160). Such discourses for Johnson are mostly embodied in institutions and particular kinds of individuals.

The specific, localized raison d'être for confronting his failed romances and sexual encounters is that Johnson anticipates a significant new relationship and wishes to avoid past error. This is derived from his real-life experience: "this is the best thing she has done for me, Ginnie, that I am more natural now, whatever nature is, but I know what I mean, and for any of the earlier ones, others, I would not have felt this, she releases me, Ginnie" (169). His thoughts are of Virginia Kimpton (later Johnson) who becomes his wife and is also referred to in *See the Old Lady Decently*. Both transition and desire are the underlying motifs of the novel. Johnson maps, coordinates, and charts past failings onto his present narrative of the voyage, offering the reader Johnson's own parallel inner voyage of self-discovery almost as an aesthetic act of contrition.

The aesthetic rendition of everyday life continues in *The Unfortunates* and has attracted similar critical dismissal to that applied to *Trawl*. Of *The Unfortunates* Johnson explains straightforwardly and simply in the Burns interview, "I used to rely on this man, Tony Tillinghurst. He looked at the first two novels and improved them by his suggestions, he acted as a rein of my self-indulgence. He died of cancer and it's all recounted in *The Unfortunates*" (91). However, the most striking issue is the nature of this text as an object. As I explain in *B. S. Johnson: A Critical Reading,* the novel consists of "twenty-seven unbound sections (paginated separately) contained in a box (from which one can infer a reference to funereal rites) that can be shuffled at will (apart from the 'FIRST' and 'LAST' sections, which are fixed points much like birth and death) according to the wishes or choice of the reader. Moreover, it is the first of Johnson's books that concedes a significant other as the focus and axis of both structure and thought. In this sense it can be seen to initiate a new phase and suggests an aesthetic nuance. As a formal object the novel draws attention to itself, intensifying its own presence as if creating a Situationist moment, something seen partially in the devices in previous novels such as *Albert Angelo*" (37). The response to this so-called "book-in-a-box" is hesitant even from his closest associates. Ghose says he argued on the issue with Johnson: "All right, I say, so the loose sheets in the box mirror the idea of randomness but after I've shuffled them and shuffled them and closed the box what there is in my mind is a biography whose form is really no different from *David Copperfield* because after I've read *David Copperfield* what I have in my mind is not a chronological life but a group of random images. Bollocks, he says . . . " (33). Some are hostile. Mackrell concludes that "neither the form nor the material of the novel offers more than a superficial experience of indeterminacy . . ." (55). Nevertheless, perhaps as Tredell indicates "rearrangement and rereading can constantly produce fresh surprises and juxtapositions." (35)

The Unfortunates records an epiphany of sorts during a visit to Nottingham to report on a football match, a mundane experience for him at the time of writing. The text is about memory and guilt, recalling his promise to a dying friend to memorialize him, but until the apparently unconscious and unexpected reminder of past times shared, he has shirked his task. He invokes the initial relationship, Tony's research, his family life, his illness, his death, and the return to selfhood that all these memories entail for Johnson, facing one's egocentric nature. The alternative is an image of death:

But I know this city! This green ticket-hall, the long office half-rounded at its ends, that ironic clerestory, brown glazed tiles, green below, the same, the decorative hammerbeams supporting nothing, above, of course! I know this city! How did I not realize when he said, Go and do City this week, that it was this city! Tony. His cheeks sallowed and collapsed round the insinuated bones, the gums shrivelled, was it, or shrunken, his teeth now standing free of each other in the unnatural half yawn of his mouth, yes, that mouth that had been so full-fleshed, the whole face, too, now collapsed, derelict, the thick-framed glasses the only constant, the mouth held open as in a controlled scream, but no sound. ("FIRST" 1)

The anonymity of the city and Johnson's work pattern are shattered by the specificity of Tony's death. The past is reinvoked by the moment of emergence, a transition; like the city which triggers his memory, his conscious understanding is vulnerable to disintegration marked by the lacunae of whiteness, passages without words or symbols which characterize many of Johnson's works. Clearly, the exit from the station offers both a literal emergence into the urban reality, but represents much more than simply a physical act. Johnson passes through a spatial symbol of constricted (or suppressed) emotion into a literal environment where he must reconfront his past loss and fears. He seeks to defer his unease by patterning his behavior, by identifying a series of signs, which invoke notions of familiarity and constructive solidity. He begins the reconstruction of the present through that of the past itself, which reinvokes the human agency of death, reflecting the mood of the narrator rather than the presence of the city or the past existence memorialized in the narrative of Tony himself with his illness: "Covered courtyard, taxis, take a taxi, always take a taxi in a strange city, but no, I know this city! The mind circles, at random, does not remember, from one moment to another, other things interpose themselves, the mind's   The station exit on a bridge, yes, of course, and the blackened gantries rise like steel gibbets above the midland red wall opposite" ("FIRST" 1). At the exit, as from birth, he is faced with what can be read as symbols and reminders of death.

Johnson memorializes Tony by recording his words on a newly

acquired tape recorder, on the pretext of requiring assistance with an article. This deception conceals a reversal of Tony's role, its negation, since these words, once recorded, retain no intersubjective or genuine purpose. In themselves they convey an awful reality, but less through their literal meaning than through the change in Tony's body and physical abilities. Both the words on the tape *and* those in Johnson's book preserve the contextual truth of Tony's death and confer upon it an awful recognition for the narrator. Having recorded the detail of human frailty, their recovery redefines his memory, constituting an objective record of decline. Through Johnson's mediation, Tony's become a bleak promissory note, a self-negation:

His fingers tampering with the mike, and he kept switching it off, perhaps it was too much for him, the thought I won't be here, perhaps he had this thought inside him, insistently, by now, all hope gone, saying, I won't be here to see this, or that, or whatever, even to see this article we were talking about, perhaps I was too ghoulish, in wanting to have his voice, the reason I had brought the recorder, though I did genuinely want his help with the article, too. Ghoulish, but not now, no, I have the man's voice still, the shake in it that was not there before, the sippings, the pauses, long sighs, I remember so clearly, have played it enough times, his voice, or the last vestiges of it, it's not that clear, a new slur, too, but his voice, his voice I still have, yes, and what he said, what he was. ("Then they had moved" 7)

As if to confirm and emphasize that things can be said in a nonverbal and nonliteral fashion, the narrator reminds himself constantly of the inconsequentiality of most of their shared words. He tries to recall their joint conversations and specifically Tony's utterances. He cannot, even though he recalls that Tony exemplifies the role of literary advisor and appeared happy in his own roles of man of letters, fellow poetry editor, wit, thinker, and critic. All are essentially verbal. Ironically, the substance of the words is lost apart from the bathos of the tape recording. This paradox of the text's relationship with the world of our expressiveness is a chief thematic concern. The loss of words traumatizes Johnson; he is overwhelmed by the recognition of the common desolation of approaching death, a passing away of the power of language. The assertion *"what he said, what he was"* about Tony thus is unconvincing, trailing from the specificity of the incident, of the suppressed emotional responses.

The collapse of discursive form results from the physical effects of Tony's illness, graphically detailed:

His face appeared dry, the skin as if carelessly powdered, in places, his hair had grown suddenly thinner, there was dandruff in great yellow-grey flakes and his teeth were slightly more noticeable, for he had lost weight, a stone or more. His breathing, too, was affected, there were now great pauses in his conversation as he sighed to the limit of his lungs, unnatural pauses, unsyntactical, which gave his words curious emphases and dramatizations, bathos, together with these other pauses when he had to take a drink to moisten his mouth. ("Then they had moved" 3)

The pauses are symptomatic and expressive of life conditions and are not syntactical. Curiously these symptoms satisfy the function of the identification of Tony in a more enduring way than all the words exchanged between the two men and make the impediment of Tony's language capability curiously appropriate despite their representation of personal loss. Embodiment, disease, and death reassert the fundamental boundaries of the material. The box does a similar thing for the text. Words fail them both. For Johnson, the rigmarole of the match report is habitual, stripped of passion, emotion, or any continuing relevance apart from money. It erodes his own creative presence, revived only by this act of memento mori.

Of the relationship with Tony, Johnson records domestic settings to ritualize and solemnize Tony's death. He refuses to sanctify and symbolize any allegory of passing, preferring to create a kind of textual and materialist version of cryptal art. On the occasion of Tony's first London visit, Johnson reflects being unable to resist going beyond the actual to create characterization that distorts the occasion. He refutes this fallacy, parading his own textual transgression to display how the aesthetic urge can deviate from a truthful reflection:

And he would heave himself from that black divan, and wash as much as he thought appropriate, how can I know how much he washed, and he little ate if at all for that breakfast I had prepared for us.   I sentimentalize again, the past is always to be sentimentalized, inevitably, everything about him I see now in the light of what happened later, his slow disintegration, his death. The waves of the past batter at the sea defences of my sandy sanity, need to be safely pictured, still, romanticized, prettified. ("I had a lovely flat then" 2)

The aesthetic tradition and such "prettified" memories represent an aspect of his inability to confront death or understand its nature and significance. Johnson catches himself trying to invest his memory with significance from a reading of the mundane, conjuring a belated wedding present to himself from Tony and June on the occasion of Tony's last visit before his debilitating illness to the Angel, Islington in London. He finds he is unconvinced by his own responses, highlighting a novelistic trap: "It was good, yes, though we did not use it until our electric one failed, but for some uses, in some ways, it was better than the electric one, that's true, handier, as well, how I try to invest anything connected with him now with as much rightness, sanctity, almost, as I can, how the fact of his death influences every memory of everything connected with him" ("At least once he visited us" 1).

The bulk of the text thematizes or supplements the initial transitional movement, with its rupture of the pattern of normality, fractured by Johnson's recognition and reassertion of the past. Johnson as a figure and his memories emerge from the station as if from Tony's mouth, terrified at its own impending dissolution, offering a synthesis of periods of traumatic suppressed emotions. Johnson explains that "the dead past and the living present interacted and transposed themselves in my mind" (*Memoirs?* 24), and the box and sections of the novel rehearse and repeat that movement. Understanding death involves mapping a vast landscape, both of the past and an uncharted territory. Johnson has only the interiority of his present consciousness and a chronicle of past events, a series of transformations in both his own life and that of Tony and his family.

The past is not simply concerned with Tony; as I say in my article "(Re)-acknowledging B. S. Johnson's Radical Realism, or Re-publishing *The Unfortunates,*" "Death runs parallel (something accentuated by the technical trick of these moments passing through each other) with other transitions: of publication, Tony's PhD success, childbirth, and Wendy's infidelity" (47). The implicit guilt in Johnson's narrative is both offset and yet deepened by the nostalgic repetition of the opening movement and feelings. Johnson does this because it is as close as he can come to retrieving Tony, while accepting that his focus still centers on his own past and emotional loss, as it did in his time of knowing Tony. This recurrence displaces periodically the narrative he promised his friend, and yet by doing so, repeats the pattern of their engagement with each other. Johnson recalls the triviality of Tony's illnesses and his suspicion of Tony's hypochondria. Johnson's realization of the severity of his friend's illness offers a paradigm of the guilt underlying his attempt at his friend's recovery in literary terms. Johnson recuperates his own limitations and self-absorption:

The first thing that brought it home to me, was that he was too ill to come down to London for the publication party of my novel, in my flat, the novel which was so much better for his work on it, for his attention to it. It was dedicated to them! This shocked me, I was annoyed, angry even, that he, that both of them, should find any excuse whatsoever for missing something so important, that its importance to me should not be shared by them, it made me think almost that he was backing out of his support for the book, my paranoia again, yes. But they sent a telegram, and a letter the next day, very apologetic, he was ill, but he still had faith in the book. ("Just as it seemed" 4)

Faced with his self-centeredness, Johnson finds that only the physical presence of the city appears to partially unify all elements of his ego, Tony, and the physical conditions of their lives: "Used to go shopping there, underneath the Town House, it is called, with Tony and June, sometimes, could go there again now, on my walking way, in this way, up there, it starts on rising ground, on ground having risen, rather, ha, make my way there, it's an object, it's an objective, it will pass the time" ("Cast parapet" 3). The objective change in people can be charted, but not retained as social space apparently can. Tony loses the power of sustained language and concentration. Tredell notes astutely the transformation in Tony, away from a position where, as an English literary academic, "A large part of his discursive identity is provided by literary criticism" (37). Ironically, of course, this is a position that Johnson scorns.

There is a sense of greater forces. In the novel, nature, which he declares as chaotic, seems to defy the moment of fune*real* celebration and mourning, to resist the chaos of its own arbitrariness; the narrator recalls the departure from the mortuary:

Someone gave us a lift back to the house, I forget who, but it was packed, three or four of us in the back, the car, and as we went away up the hill, over the shoulder of the hill, I looked down and back at the crematorium, sunny but there was still a blue haze, perhaps from the sea, and there was a straight column rising from the chimney of the crematorium, it went straight upwards, as far as smoke can ever be said to move in a straight line, into the haze, the sky, it was too neat, but it was, it was. ("We were late for the funeral" 1)

Johnson's idea of nature and of being seems negated by the regularity of a monumental image reflecting what might be interpreted as a pathetic fallacy.[7] As a narrator he adheres to factuality in a manner that is undercut by his unnecessary repetition that marks the end of the passage above. The factuality of the experiential validates narrative integrity and authenticity, for as Nathalie Sarraute says, "The 'true fact' has indeed an indubitable advantage over the invented tale. To begin with, that of being true. This is the source of its strength of conviction and forcefulness" (63).

The emphasis upon the physical presence of the book reemphasizes the physical presence and effects of language and its failings. The aleatory presence of nature is subverted to provide the partial form of the novel—the shuffleable chapters—resisted by the designated first and last chapters and moreover contained in the box.

Here we conceive of life, death, burial (coffin) in the form or object of the novel, itself a form that absorbs life into the containment of the death it represents metonymically. The box resists the act of narrative and yet opens the way for it; nature involves decay and rebirth. In the process of the limited choice of placing the unbound chapters of the book, passing them into one another, the reader participates in the reenactment of a choice that suggests the transformations by which man attempts to assume a responsibility for his fate. Each can shuffle them about and achieve his own random order. In this way the whole novel reflects the randomness of the material: it is itself a physical tangible metaphor for the randomness and the nature of cancer. "Now I did not think then, and do not think now, that this solved the problem completely. The lengths of the sections were really arbitrary again; even separate sentences or separate words would be arbitrary in the same sense" (*Memoirs?* 25-26). To shuffle is to pass the objective through itself and reorder not only its meaning, but its occurrence. Words and sentences can be set together in different ways. One senses Johnson hopes, but doubts, that they are defined by their place in the currents of space and time, which pass through them. The denial of the reader's possibility of absolute choice in the book's reconfiguration is intentional and significant. It offers a process by which control and order are anticipated and yet frustrated, mirroring the relationship of the subject with nature (of which cancer is an indifferent part multiplying within the subject). Life remains contingent. He describes Tony's move as a postgraduate to a rented house where his research and lifestyle seem ordered, but the surroundings have their own trajectory and disorder. The idea of growth in the garden is both natural and yet uncontained, like the cancerous growths, which destabilize Tony's intellect and Johnson's sanguinity:

The house itself was perhaps mid-Victorian, with a bay window, small, two up and two down, kitchen and bathroom built on half-width at the back, so that there was a common concrete area with the next house and a shared garden, their garden had shoulder-high shrubs and growths of some kind, or higher, unkempt, and Tony and I laughed at the idea of him gardening, as I remember, at the idea of him wanting to impose some order on this overgrowth.   He worked in the front room, had his books around him, did he say for the first time all his books were with him, now they had a house. ("Then he was doing research" 1)

On one level Johnson reminds us that man and thought exist within nature as integral, uncontrolled elements. Rationality and control through knowledge represented by Tony's books offer only an illusion of framing the disorder of nature and its resistance to man, but, like the garden, an ontological truth is undiminished and unmediated by such epistemic thinking as Tony's.

Following his period of confessional prose Johnson ditched the self-evidently autobiographical basis and began what almost constitutes a paradigm shift with *House Mother Normal*. That novel and *Christie Malry's Own Double-Entry* inscribe a world as if painted with broad brushstrokes, verging on comic-book perspective, with exaggerated and yet apparently simplistic characterization. This is a landscape of comic desperation with its sense of human absurdity and helplessness. Nevertheless, as Johnson explains when interviewed by Burns, these narratives were planned while writing his first novel in September 1959: "During that time I had ideas for two more novels which became *House Mother Normal* and *Christie Malry*" (85). The first, *House Mother Normal*, plays with a sparse presentation, turning to dark comedy by narrating successively events at an old people's home from various viewpoints. Johnson explains, "What I wanted to do was to take an evening in an old people's home, and see a single set of events through the eyes of not less than eight old people" (*Memoirs?* 26). The text can only be fully understood on completion and much of the novel's meaning is deferred until that point. Apart from the House Mother, the mischievous and malign matron of the establishment, who introduces the text and concludes with twenty-two pages, each geriatric is featured for exactly twenty-one pages. The narratives—for in a multiperspectival sense they must be regarded as plural in that they are simultaneous experiences of the same episode—of an hour in an evening in an old people's home, are each paginated separately but also sequentially in their bound progression. There is a short introduction and final section of twenty-two pages for the House Mother herself. Together they build and convey both through words and the very pattern of expression on the page surface a contextualized view of the bizarre activities and cruelties of the home, although Mackrell comments that the pensioners "all appear to be concentrating far more on their own past memories than on what is happening around them, and thus to some extent are locked in their own private worlds. These worlds, however, are portrayed with vivid and convincing detail" (56). Bare white lacunary sections represent various conditions: forgetfulness, inattention, sleep, and various stages of senility. Thus Johnson conveys the blankness of their existence. Age awards gravitas despite the present indignities suffered by the elderly inmates: "The dignity of the old people in *House Mother Normal* is partly theirs as members of the generation that fought on the Somme, and who have survived only to face death again in the modern equivalent of the workhouse" (Parrinder 125).

All of the pensioners sing a peculiar song of the House Mother's devising and this appears with alterations (apart from those contingent upon memory lapse or senility and therefore deficient in some form) on the same page in each first-person account. Similarly the accounts end with a reference to the manipulative manager of the home—apart from the case of the accounts of the most senile pair of George Hedbury and Rosetta Stanton—with slightly variable typographical placement indicating real time:

> Listen to her!
> No, doesn't matter. (27, 49, 71, 93, 115, 137)

Each pensioner recalls the particularities of his or her past. Sarah Lamson recalls a First World War Christmas, "Knowing he was for the Front made him depressed, then suddenly he'd be so cheerful, such good company, he made it a wonderful Christmas for all . . ." (12), and life as a widow when she was raped by her master in service, "I might even have enjoyed it, it was two years since Jim had gone, but he was so rough and arrogant with it, he seemed to think because I was a servant he could order me about in anything . . ." (18). Charlie Edwards reminisces of his life as a musician in London: "Like the famous or notorious Mrs Marshall's All-Up Club in Frith Street. All that dust-up in the papers over bribing a police sergeant. They were all taking" (38-39). Ron Lamson, in great physical pain, struggles against memory loss: "I shall try again to remember my first fuck. The first is the one you never forget, they say. They are not right in my case, not for the first time, either" (88). In terms of the present, Charlie ruminates on the menial work he is obliged to undertake and the indignities of sometimes having to be changed like a baby. His belief in reason is almost completely marginalized by his dependency.

The framing tone of voice of the House Mother is insistently comedic and dark. It echoes in the other accounts. So does the gradual emerging picture of her oppressive regime. She makes the pensioners work for her profit, forces them to clear up, conduct a jousting tournament with mop and wheelchairs, and play pass the parcel with "shit" from her dog, Ralphie. She strips before them, and as a finale fornicates with Ralphie, the dog. Surely Johnson takes us beyond recognizably the "liberal" or covertly universal themes such as those Levitt identifies—"the effects of old age, the continuity of memory and experience, the human persistence in the process of dying" (581)—and Johnson moves the novel into a parody of both managerial and bureaucratic expediency that is generated by ego and yet justified on quasi-rational grounds. Society redeems itself by power and practice. As Johnson says, "At the end, there would be the viewpoint of the House Mother, an apparently 'normal' person, and the events themselves would then be seen to be so bizarre that everything that had come before would seem 'normal' by comparison. The idea was to say something about things we call 'normal' and 'abnormal' and the technical difficulty was to make the same thing interesting nine times over . . ." (*Memoirs?* 26-27). The sexual detail is in part to challenge presuppositions about the elderly that desexualizes them and their past. Gloria Ridge recalls, "Careful, I'm always careful, never let them stick it up me without a rubber on, very careful all my life, never had no kids, never!" (100). This contrasts with the virtual blankness of the senility-influenced pages of George Hedbury and Rosetta Stanton. Rosetta's words are particularly painful, offering a glimpse into a version of solipsism and existential despair of quotidian poignancy. In the middle of random Welsh words from her childhood and a silence of five completely blank pages, she summons her complaint:

I am

Terrible, Ivy

Now I can   every
word you say   I am a prisoner in my
self. It is terrible. The movement agonises me.
Let me out, or I shall die   (175-76)

What might be the point of Johnson's devices and form? Certainly, the collective supersedes the individual in the frame of the text and its account of the brutal, revealing, funny, and grotesque experiences at the home. As Ronald Hayman observes, "it is sometimes hard to construe the first eight monologues until their meaning is clinched by the ninth, which comes from the House Mother . . ." (8). Only at the House Mother's prompting is the composite or overall picture of the novel completed. She confirms our suspicion with her sneering account, offering a tableau of ritual humiliations, cheap labor and beatings, all truly Dickensian and yet reconfirmed as contemporary scandals of abuse of the elderly are recognized as not uncommon. Parrinder claims that the House Mother "is an ordinary person and therefore combines various more or less understandable forms of corruption with an energetic habit of self-justification" (123). Certainly passing shit (a detail commented upon by Hayman but elided by most other critics apart from Mackrell) seems a metaphoric pun for the mess of life and its disgust. House Mother says, "I disgust them in order that they may not be disgusted with them-

selves. I am disgusting to them, in order to objectify their disgust, to
direct it to something outside themselves, something harmless"
(197). As Parrinder concludes, "Her monologue has a rhetorical purpose; she is an inveterate liar because she is a deliberate storyteller using her fantasies as a means of subduing and imposing on
others. These fantasies have become an adequate substitute for re-
ciprocal human relationships" (124).

In advance of her pornographic act, she explains the kind of apparently perverted game that she imposes upon her charges:
"Sometimes for a change I have them doing Travel in the form of
bizarre sexual antics" (199). At the end House Mother chides both
the reader and, by implication, her creator when she concludes:

And here you see, friend, I am about to step outside the convention, the
framework of twenty-one pages per person. Thus you see I too am the pup-
pet or concoction of a writer (you always knew there was a writer behind
it all? Ah, there's no fooling you readers!), a writer who has me at present
standing in the post-orgasmic nude but who still expects me to be his
words without embarrassment or personal comfort.   So you see this
is from his skull. It is a diagram of certain aspects of the inside of his
skull!   What a laugh! (203-04)

One can't quite go as far as Parrinder in concluding that for
Johnson "These satisfactions must be perverse because a healthily
sensual individual would not have taken on her job in the first
place; this, at least, is what Johnson seems to imply" (123). Nevertheless, human indignity and the grotesquery of power are assembled almost graphically on the page as intertwined themes. The
individual stories reinforce the performative present of the evening
at the home, adding cultural and individual resonance: Charlie
Edwards's memories of the First World War slaughter; Ivy Nicholl's
memory of a murdered servant and her titled master; Gloria Ridge's
incoherent uncertainty as to whether she had either no children or
eighty; Sioned Bowen's recollection of a Factor who cheats his way
to a fortune; and the almost total absence of significant consciousness from George Hedbury.

Christie Malry's Own Double-Entry offers a further sparse and
playful text based upon another scheme, this one shared by the protagonist. It provides Johnson's most overtly political text. It is simultaneously comic and serious, both analytical and epigrammatic
in style. The tension of these overlapping elements and their very
incongruities provide a sense of transformation. The novel
spatializes itself and the city, using lacunae and italicized thoughts
already familiar as typical of Johnson. His constant reflection becomes a commentary on the architectural and spatial significance

of the social subject. Even Christie's apparently most ridiculous outburst offers a critique of his environment and social conditions. Using another device, Johnson italicizes all of Christie's internalized thought. Christie quizzes himself:

Who made me walk this way? Who decided I should not be walking seven feet farther that side, or three points west of nor-nor-east, to use the marine abbreviation? Anyone? No one? Someone must have decided. It was a conscious decision, as well. That is, they said (he said, she said), I will build here. But I think whoever it was did not also add, So Christie Malry shall not walk here, but shall walk there. If he chooses. Ah! And there I have him / her / them! If I choose so. But my choice is limited by them, collectively. . . . (23)

The almost slapstick characterization helps the polemical intention, as the reader is not drawn into identifying with the paradigms and identifications inherent in conventional narrative realism. Johnson seeks to disrupt inappropriate epistemic identification.

Concerning his protagonist, the narrator addresses his implied reader in a tone of cultural and ideological admonishment: "Nor are his motives important. Especially are his motives of no importance to us, though the usual clues will certainly be given. We are concerned with his actions. A man may be defined through his actions, you will remember. We may guess at his motives, of course; he may do so as well. We may also guess at the winner of the three-fifteen at the next meeting at Market Rasen" (51-52). Clearly events, characters, and things can be reread. Essentially, Johnson evokes Sarraute's insistence that character or personality is a diversion from true relations (8). This strategy prioritizes events, actions, social relations, and political consequences, issues elided by most critics. Hence, the familiar may be reconfigured and imply different interpretative possibilities of the real. The reader recognizes the overall dynamics of Christie's squeeze or repression by very mundane elements, like having a wage increase swallowed by increased social payments. Both the bizarre dimensions of his pathological revenge and the pared-down narrativity are mapped discursively and polemically against the ground of the apprehensible and real. In the novel, in the mouth of the protagonist's mother, Johnson indicates that his narrative *dialecticizes* (a word that is evident from his practice even without its appearance in this novel) in a manner parallel to the tradition of the radical thought influencing this period and which was busy thematizing social and metaphysical process.[8] The brief reference is instructive.

In Christie's scheme of overturning ideas, a negative dialectics, Johnson inverts Nietzsche's placement of justice as responding to the violation of a commonwealth of communal pledge and contract which leads to punishment of the individual; Christie in reverse perceives collective incursions on individual needs expressed by property and appropriation of space (Nietzsche 203-04) as requiring not only an individual demand for freedom, but anarchic action. Note the social, intersubjective constitution of individual rights that Christie sees as constrained. Christie's extreme contestation relies partly on understanding the city critically, with the sort of penetration conveyed when Merleau-Ponty conceives the external world of space as always *already constituted,* resisting its revision by man's habitual *wordless perception* (251-52). Christie articulates mostly such unspoken objections. He critiques the positioning of his subjectivity within the power relations, expressed as limited access and choice. He inverts the normal power relations as described by Nietzsche which attach themselves in spatial terms to the relationship of justice and retribution, being celebrated in the further monumental space of the court and prisons, through the medium of constructed objective space.

Christie prioritizes, however pathologically, communal rather than individual infractions and slights of the individual. Collectivity becomes a matter of culpability, one that reaches its vengeful climax when the protagonist poisons thousands of Londoners for their complicity in the systemic abuse of his rights. Thereby Johnson evokes a series of dialectical qualities and observations that permeate every level of the text itself. Christie's deviance reconfigures the nature of subjectivity in its traditional role of characterization. This cipher demands equivalency, account of value, and free access to the natural world unconstrained. These themes in Nietzsche evoke the origins of modernity and its adaptation of law and subjectivity from the classical mode: "To the question how did the ancient, deep-rooted, still firmly established notion of an equivalency between damage and pain arise, the answer is, briefly: it arose in the contractual relation between creditor and debtor, which is as old as the notion of 'legal subjects' itself and which in its turn points back to the basic practices of purchase, sale, barter, and trade" (195).

Exchange itself is a spatial praxis with outcomes. Christie articulates this in his thoughts. He recognizes that he cannot confront a dead planner or speculator, but he sees a genealogy or succession of culpability and responsibility which defies the facelessness of capitalism, thereby refusing its retreat into facelessness through bifurcations of responsibility, lost in the diffusion of time and successive generations: *"But his successors, heirs, executors, administrators, personal representatives and assigns certainly are, or they would not be here, in business. They are not averse to taking respon-*

sibility for all the money they/he/she left them, so they may conveniently take responsibility for standing this building in my way, too, limiting my freedom of movement, dictating to me where I may or may not walk in this street" (24). Christie cannot perceive his problem in anything but causal terms; most Johnsonian protagonists connect feeling and pain to environment and perception. Spatiality possesses historical roots, as does Christie's predicament. Christie is insistent he inherits rather than either deserves or provokes his containment at the hands of such a viciously indifferent society. As Merleau-Ponty notes, "My personal experience must be the resumption of a prepersonal tradition. There is, therefore, another subject beneath me, for whom the world exists before I am here. . . . Space has its basis in our facticity. It is neither an object, nor an act of unification on the subject's part . . ." (254). Through Christie, Johnson recuperates a sense of individual dislocation as a significant act, rendered as a spatialized "facticity," so that the apparently ordinary, essentially intramundane, environment of city life is transformed into something hostile and fascinating. Everyday things can be reconfigured. Revolution might be suggested in the most familiar of objects, as when Christie learns to make a Molotov cocktail in the satirically entitled chapter 16, "Keep Britain Tidy; or, Dispose of this Bottle Thoughtfully":

Glass bottles are obtainable in their millions. . . . No, by far the best bottle on the market for them has been provided by the soft drinks companies: half an imperial pint capacity, a screw cap of light gauge metal, glass walls of the very minimum thickness, a circumference so snug to the hand as to make accurate throwing relatively easy, and, being non-returnable, of such ready availability as to provoke ironic comment that the forces of conservatism are unwittingly providing the very instruments of their own discomfort. (133)

In practical and symbolic terms, the seeds of revolt are available to subjects who perceive both the injustices and the opportunities for disruption. He posits the personal malaise of any individual as having the potential to reveal the duplicity of accepted norms and experience. Christie goes on to poison hundreds of thousands via their drinking supplies. This reflects in narrative terms an irony implicit in much of the critique of the period offered by thinkers such as Marcuse, who says, for example, "Basic to the present form of social organization, the antagonisms of the capitalist production process, is the fact that the central phenomena connected with this process do not immediately appear to men as what they are 'in reality,' but in masked, 'perverted' form" (70). Christie's account is one form of multiple examples of such "unmasking." Christie heightens such reworking of relations until it becomes a pathological process, thus revealing culture's own underlying and ongoing antagonisms. Despite their extreme nature, Johnson's themes evoke Sarraute's idea of an "emotional commotion that made it possible to apprehend all at once, and as in a flash, an entire object with all its nuances, its possible complexities, and even—if, by chance, these existed—its unfathomable depths" (16-17). His overall position appears to be that alienation derives from its historical circumstances, an outcome of ideological narratives and practice. In a dialogue with Christie, the novel's narrator comments polemically "Politicians, policeman, some educators and many others treat 'most people' as idiots" (166). Christie's campaign is their worst nightmare, but is caused by their attitude toward the mass.

By the stage of his last novel *See the Old Lady Decently,* Johnson transforms the dialectic of the disorganized and of reduced potential explored in *Albert Angelo;* such reductions or contractions determined by the shift toward order and control in the later novel are extended beyond their impact upon the immediacy of the individual or the specific group and are now perceived in terms of quite how such epistemological tyrannies shape the cultural and social process in a broader context of language and discourse. Much of his mother's experience is woven into the enigmatic, complex, and yet fragmented narrative, originally intended as the first part of the planned *Matrix* trilogy to be based on their relationship. The titles were to read across the spine of the books: *See the Old Lady Decently, Buried Although,* and *Among Those Left Are You.*

Johnson develops multiple parallel themes that are represented or intertwined in a formally complex manner. The novel is the most apparently informal, deconstructive, and experimental of novels. Yet the book depends upon an elaborate process or organizing principle, one that defers and partially reroutes the conventional narrative form and process. Johnson brings together a series of fragmentary elements using a both random and erratic schema, combining different periods and themes represented by different kinds of lettering as titles. The scope is various: he reflects on the process of attempting to write, the central narrative of recovering his deceased mother's life, but there are some striking sections that chart the creation of a narrative of empire and power that he fragments and undermines, literally. Using the example of the First World War, he attacks the process of order and domination, but the curious power of narrative is expressed through his BB (or Broader Britain) sections. These appear to be imperial narratives reflecting places and environments under imperial rule. However, Johnson bowdlerizes them, removing both place names and whole sections of sentences, making the narratives oddly formal and incomplete. From what should or might suggest itself as nonsense, the hegemonic qualities and assumptions of superiority of cultural voice come through, vaguely absurd, yet threatening. In "BB4,"

The largest of geysers a native close to riddled with thermal of various cook your in one, take a delicious in and be scalded to in the third throws up it, column of steaming from a cone of siliceous all about seethes and hisses under your head foremost into a mud-hole or boiling if you in the vicinity you feel the rising from the ground your finger beneath feels hot enough to boil and they even bury their dead in a life of ease and luxury on the income derived from Government rents this marvellous land from the natives and a fixed scale of charges for showing has been drawn. (61)

The foreign, the Other, becomes objectified by the passage as a site of wonderment and strangeness. The Eurocentric eye and voice creates cultural and literal capital; it appropriates the scene, its signification, and literally possesses both the land and the experience despite its clearly incomplete and partial nature reflected in the style and structure of the passage itself. The more impressionistic and fragmentary, the more dismissive of Otherness the voice becomes: "Perhaps the most situated town in all the, how is it that it is clearly not further?   It is due to the mixture of.   They are lethargic and unprogressive.   The descendants of slaves brought by the are without energy and leave as much work as possible to be done by the women" (62). By not naming in specific terms, through using lacunae and imprecision, Johnson conveys the effectiveness of the male discourse of colonialism, its resistance and adaptability, and its contempt for variation. Michael Bakewell quotes Johnson in his untitled introduction to the novel, "The GB and BB bits are intended to involve the reader—he has to supply information himself—what he knows of the Empire" (10); they make clear Johnson's disapproval of these ideological and historical influences. The excisions serve much like the disruptions within the type of postcolonial poetry described by Bhabha and categorized through its effect on the reader that could be equally applied to Johnson's novel: "That disturbance of your voyeuristic look enacts the complexity and contradictions of your desire to see, to fix cultural difference in a containable, *visible* object. The desire for the Other is doubled by the desire in language, which *splits the difference* between Self and Other so that both positions are partial; neither is sufficient unto itself" (50). Johnson foregrounds what remains unsaid by a strategy making evident the *invisibility* of absent words. This makes evident the inadequacy of the partiality that a centered egocentric, traditional literary narrative depends upon and its broader applications in language's broader political contexts. In these sections fragments rework the efficacy of language, because what is unexpressed often reveals with clarity the imprint of concrete historical oppressions.

Johnson moves from the traditional discourse of his mother's time, her own early experiences from school to work as a skivvy in a hotel where she is distressed at an encounter—"there she saw her first black man, there he was, in the washing-up galley, his back to her, what fierce features he must have, she thought, a black man like one of those in the Glorious British Empire books we had at school!" (18)—on toward his own ironic critique of the process in "BB1": "Greater, ever greater, broader too, not Empire, not Imperial, but by linguistic extension part of ourselves, our Broader Britain" (32). Of an unnamed place, Johnson demonstrates the coordinates of linguistic and spatial patterning and appropriation:

Was named in after by Governor, and laid out and the streets named at the same period.   The streets are built at right angles to one another, and the principal thoroughfares are intersected by smaller streets bearing the name of the great thoroughfares with the prefix "Little."   On two hills.   Along its course stand the chief clubs, insurance offices, banks, and the Town Hall.   In eighteen there were thirteen buildings: three weatherboard, two slate, and eight turf huts. (33-34)

The anonymity suggests the replication of the ordering, the ideological core at the heart of the process itself. The aestheticization and its traditions are neither immune to nor separate from this discourse and symbolic and literal configuration. Johnson creates the image of responding to natural forces, which are then coerced into the vision of value, worth, and purpose by which nature is suborned: "Generations of enthusiastic have left few expressions of admiration worth.   Mankind is dumb before such a.   Not only are words inadequate to, but is the last thing anyone thinks of turning the mind away to abstractions, to God and articulate expression, the roar of cannon too convincing to be inspiring, a feast for the senses and a source of dumb awe, always something besides a sublime" (47). That the aesthetic can appeal to a supposed dumbness or quality of the sublime makes it suspect. As Freire says "Self-sufficiency is incompatible with dialogue. Men who lack humility (or have lost it) cannot come to the people, cannot be their partners in naming the world" (79). Naming cannot be imposed since it ultimately must be continually re-created and depends upon collectivity rather than coercion. Moreover, as Freire insists, "Dialogue requires an intense faith in man, faith in his power to make and remake, to create and re-create, faith in his vocation to be more fully human" (79). In every sense this is completely opposite to the dynamics that emerge in Johnson's novel in terms of another nameless environment that is featured in the lacunary style of "BB3," where in spite of the lack of specificity and reference, one senses the power to subvert faith both within the subjected themselves by denying faith in them as a categorial notion: "Long since ceased to live according to their lawless fancy, placed under the charge of superintendents appointed by the authorities of the, and amply supplied with all the modern machinery of education, nothing but their inherent incapacity prevents their attaining complete equality with the.   But the disability exists, and all that the most philanthropic can hope for the natives is their gentle diminution, followed by their peaceful extinction." (50-51).

Johnson knows well how to convey the inhumanity of the imperial/colonial processes, incorporating a critique or critical intervention similar to Freire's comment on a class that refuses dialogue because it "start[s] from the premise that naming the world is the task of an elite and that the presence of the people in history is a sign of deterioration, thus to be avoided . . ." (78-79). By extracting the signifiers of any particularities, in this last novel Johnson savages the generalizing rhetoric of colonial destruction through its own assertive vocabulary and voice, its appeal to "Englishmen who had founded their idea of the upon the romances of and his followers . . ." (51), being a cultural dynamic and ideology. Colonialism is a world of claims such as "A successful experiment in culture was made in the Municipality, from English spawn.   Four members of the House are Natives, attracted by Nicholson, as the fort used to be called . . ." (71). Nevertheless, both his text and the historical realities from which they implicitly draw, in order to represent some level of comprehensibility, serve to determine quite how liminal the process of power can appear, powerful enough to articulate its threat without naming or detail or historical rootedness. Language can, as a fringe activity, evoke subliminally a discourse that is effective and threatening. Its appeal and efficacy is demonstrated in parallel by Johnson's horror at the stupidity of the appeal to war and the mass killings of the First World War. Reality haunts the rational concept of things as an often unwritten, obscured form.

The collocation of the BB commentary is increasingly incoherent, its fragmentation showing the centrifugal quality of power, but implying the persistence through timelines of its effects. Power, ambition and oppression persist. The passages could be of any period, quaint in phraseology, destructive in effect, and myopic. "BB7" commences with a typical Western dismissive colonial voice: "The natives are very low down in the scale of humanity, and yet they use a which has puzzled the wisest mathematicians of.   The is not such a mysterious engine as the, but the skill with which they use it is astonishing" (81). Without the specifics, together the BB sections imply the totalizing quality of colonial discourse, the separation of cultural values from factuality. Imperial force and the colonial impulse constitute an ideological force that is a cluster of effects and attitudes that subvert both legitimate meaning and freedom. In his strategy Johnson demonstrates how removal of content markers leaves the coordinates of a mediating structure that in some senses stands alone, formally and ideologically, as an incursive frame. This is similar to what Habermas outlines as a method for an effective ideological critique of modernity, "a 'decentered understanding' in an environment, an 'unscrambling' of 'contexts' of meaning and reality, when internal and external relationships have been unmixed . . . cleansed of all cosmological, theological, and cultic dross [revealing] . . . that the autonomy of validity claimed by a theory (whether empirical or normative) is an illusion because secret interests and power claims have crept into its pores" (115). This serves to describe Johnson's demythologising of imperial/colonial discourse through its own words in numerous BB sections, those literary and cultural processes that Johnson parodies and invokes. This formal conception of lacunary expression serves as much more than a structural or generic device. For on one level, in a narrative sense, Johnson challenges any *autonomy of validity* that might have been understood to have somehow attached itself to imperial/colonial theories and structures, or crucially in their residuum in texts and accounts; and on another level Johnson reminds his reader of the danger of the palpably absurd appeal to the prejudicial and conspiratorial secretions of power. His critique is indicated by the realization that a central truthfulness can be recovered from such accounts themselves once, in Habermasian terms, this *"unmixing"* and *"cleansing"* by Johnson has been undertaken. Significantly, the BB sections conclude with an admission of their own genocidal tendencies, which provides the reader the moral necessity for critical readings of social discourse, a moral pricking of consciences. Johnson's strategies leave these colonial, hegemonic discourses with the baldly disingenuous and yet plainly disturbing declaration toward the end of the novel: "There are no aborigines now left in the island" (116). Sense and structure that have been confused, deconstructed, and mixed together reassert themselves in an admission of the full horror of method and intention. Johnson demonstrates in narrative something that resembles Bhabha's recognition that "Postcolonial critical discourses require forms of dialectical thinking that do not disavow or sublate the otherness (alterity) that constitutes the symbolic domain of psychic and social identifications" (173). As Levitt comments, "The technical complexity and inventiveness of *See the Old Lady Decently* undermines the customary line between subject and object. In its self-reflexive use of author as character, it is intensely personal; yet the apparatus of reflexiveness serves as a screen against subjectivity: author and character remain separate as long as the author can keep them separate, as long as we recognize that life and art, however interconnected, are not quite the same" (585-85). As I have argued repeatedly, Johnson's ambition for life and art is dialectical, for everything is concurrently universal and disparate, not bound by any division between fictional and life-world categories.

Coda

The 1985 *Review of Contemporary Fiction* featured Johnson, including a variety of readings of his life and work. A handful of other scattered academic papers exist, but overall critical appraisal of Johnson is still patchy. Often his writing is misinterpreted or undervalued. My monograph, *B. S. Johnson: A Critical Reading,* is in part both intended to challenge and expand previously underdeveloped aspects of the analysis. In the literary tradition of Woolf and Beckett, Johnson continues a highly innovative and often unique form of development of the novel. For this alone he deserves fuller attention. As I have demonstrated, his thematic and critical originality ought further to confirm his reputation in his own right. Johnson suffers from a regressively class-bound critical establishment in Britain, and it seems that it is time to set aside such prejudices. I find grounds for optimism in the ongoing publication in the United States by New Directions of his novels and this journal's commitment to his oeuvre. Hopefully, the growing body of critical work on his novels will give academics the confidence to include his books on course lists and in their own scholarly work. I have merely scratched the surface. Concerning Johnson there is so much more that needs to be said. Perhaps America can find more words.

NOTES

[1] The major prose work consist of an early joint collection of short stories with Zulfikar Ghose, *Statement Against Corpses*; a section of *Penguin Modern Stories 7* also featuring Anthony Burgess, Susan Hill, and Yehuda Amichai; six novels published over approximately ten years: *Travelling People* (1963); *Albert Angelo* (1964); *Trawl* (1966); *The Unfortunates* (1969); *House Mother Normal* (1971); *Christie Malry's Own Double Entry* (1973);

the once influential semitheoretical prose collection *Aren't You Rather Young to Be Writing Your Memoirs?* (1973); and, the final posthumous, highly fragmentary seventh novel, *See the Old Lady Decently* (1975). This last was published apparently in unaltered form from a completed manuscript, about which his publisher had expressed reservations.

[2] For *The Unfortunates* since each section is paginated separately, the first few words of each section is included for identification of any quotations.

[3] For these allusions to Tristram Shandy's chair and the use of blackening pages to signify Maurie's initial illness and later death, see *Travelling People* 11-12, 211-13, 224-26.

[4] For this counter paradisical theme also see Kanaganayakam 91; and Tew, *B. S. Johnson* 18-20, 93-94.

[5] Interestingly, Butor's novel shares some of the postcolonial consciousness and commentary that I perceive in *Albert Angelo,* and this has been noted. See Spencer 83-85. Clearly both novels intervene into the school context with a strong notion of the ideological form of all levels and phases of society.

[6] Authorized B. S. Johnson biographer Jonathan Coe revealed to me in conversation in the British Library on 27 January 2000 that his archival research had revealed that the pupil essays that constitute part of *Albert Angelo* are almost unchanged transcriptions of the actual material from weekly essays—of the type referred to in Brathwaite's *To Sir, with Love*—collected from the pupils Johnson himself taught in north London while a supply teacher. Only the names have been altered in the main. Johnson was apparently not the most successful of teachers.

[7] Identifying emotion in inanimate objects, as if some harmony of subject-object were available aesthetically; Johnson scorned such a position in the main.

[8] Much in the manner of figures such as Vaneigem, Merleau-Ponty, Sartre, Lefebvre, Marcuse, and so forth in texts far too numerous to cite. Nevertheless such discourse is rare as the primary and conscious function of a novel itself, particularly a British one.

WORKS CITED

Bakewell, Michael. Introduction. *See the Old Lady Decently*. By B. S. Johnson. London: Hutchinson, 1975. 7-14.

Bergonzi, Bernard. Unpublished transcript BBC radio interview broadcast on 26 March 1968, "B. S. Johnson: Interview by Bernard Bergonzi: Novelists of the Sixties" [Study Session on Radio 3]. Caversham: BBC Written Archives, 1968. 1-17.

Bhabha, Homi K. *The Location of Culture*. London: Routledge, 1994.

Bourdieu, Pierre. *The Rules of Art: Genesis and Structure of the Literary Field*. Trans. Susan Emanuel. Cambridge: Polity, 1996.

Bowker, Gordon. "Remembering B. S. Johnson." *London Magazine*

October-November 2000: 45-54.

Braithwaite, E. R. *To Sir, with Love*. London: Four Square, 1962.

Burns, Alan. "B. S. Johnson: Interview." *The Imagination on Trial: British and American Writers Discuss Their Working Methods*. Ed. Alan Burns and Charles Sugnet. London: Allison & Busby, 1981. 83-94.

Butor, Michel. *Degrees*. Trans. Richard Howard. London: Methuen, 1962.

——. *Second Thoughts*. Trans. Jean Stewart. London: Faber & Faber, 1958.

Davies, John David. "The Book as Metaphor: Artifice and Experiment in the Novels of B. S. Johnson." *Review of Contemporary Fiction* 5.2 (Summer 1985): 72-76.

Depledge, David. "Author with a Bold Device: Interview [of Johnson] with David Depledge." *Books and Bookmen* June 1968: 12-13.

Figes, Eva. "B. S. Johnson." *Review of Contemporary Fiction* 5.2 (Summer 1985): 70-71.

Freire, Paulo. *Pedagogy of the Oppressed*. Trans. Myra Bergman Ramos. New York: Continuum, 1970.

Ghose, Zulfikar. "Bryan." *Review of Contemporary Fiction* 5.2 (Summer 1985): 23-34.

Goodman, Jonathan, ed. *The Master Eccentric: The Journals of Rayner Heppenstall 1969-81*. London: Allison & Busby, 1986.

Gordon, Giles. *Aren't We Due a Royalty Statement? A Stern Account of Literary, Publishing and Theatrical Folk*. London: Chatto & Windus, 1993.

Habermas, Jürgen. *The Philosophical Discourse of Modernity: Twelve Lectures*. Trans. Frederick Lawrence. Cambridge: Polity Press, 1990.

Hassam, Andrew. *Writing and Reality: A Study of Modern British Diary Fiction*. Westport: Greenwood Press, 1993.

Hayman, Ronald. *The Novel Today 1967-1975*. London: Longman, 1976.

Johnson, B. S. *Albert Angelo*. London: Constable, 1964; New York: New Directions, 1987.

——. "Anti or Ultra?" *Books and Bookmen* May 1963: 25.

——. *Aren't You Rather Young to Be Writing Your Memoirs?* London: Hutchinson, 1973.

——. *Christie Malry's Own Double-Entry*. London: Collins, 1973; London: Penguin, 1984.

——. *House Mother Normal*. London: Collins, 1971; Newcastle upon Tyne: Bloodaxe Books, 1984; New York: New Directions, 1987.

——. *See the Old Lady Decently*. London: Hutchinson, 1975.

——. *Travelling People*. London: Constable, 1963; London: Transworld, 1964.

——. *Trawl*. London: Secker & Warburg, 1966; London: Panther, 1968.

——. *The Unfortunates*. London: Panther, 1969; rev. ed. Intro. Jonathan Coe. London: Picador, 1999.

——. Unpublished typewritten letter: Johnson to Miss Pughe, from his parent's residence in Barnes. 11 November 1959. Caversham: BBC Archives.

——. Unpublished letter: Johnson to Miss Pughe, from his parent's residence in Barnes. 15 December 1959. Caversham: BBC Archives.

——. Unpublished letter: Johnson to Miss Pughe, addressed 34, Claremont Square, London, N1. 9 April 1961. Caversham: BBC Archives.

——, and Zulfikar Ghose. *Statement against Corpses*. London: Constable, 1964.

——, and Julia Trevelyan Oman. *Street Children*. London: Hodder & Stoughton, 1964.

Kanaganayakam, C. "Artifice and Paradise in B. S. Johnson's *Travelling People*." *Review of Contemporary Fiction* 5.2 (Summer 1985): 87-93.

Levitt, Morton P. "The Novels of B. S. Johnson: Against the War against Joyce." *Modern Fiction Studies* 27 (1981-1982): 571-86.

Mackrell, Judith. "B. S. Johnson and the British Experimental Tradition: An Introduction." *Review of Contemporary Fiction* 5.2 (Summer 1985): 42-64.

Marcuse, Herbert. *Negations: Essays in Critical Theory*. London: Allen Lane, 1968.

Merleau-Ponty, Maurice. *Phenomenology of Perception*. London: Routledge and Kegan Paul, 1962.

Nietzsche, Friedrich. *The Birth of Tragedy and The Genealogy of Morals*. Trans. Francis Golffing. New York: Doubleday, 1956.

Parrinder, Patrick. *The Failure of Theory: Essays on Criticism and Contemporary Fiction*. Brighton: Harvester, 1987.

Robbe-Grillet, Alain. *Snapshots and Towards a New Novel*. Trans. Barbara Wright. London: Calder and Boyars, 1965.

——. *The Voyeur*. Trans. Richard Howard. London: John Calder, 1959.

Sarraute, Nathalie. *Tropisms and The Age of Suspicion*. Trans. Maria Jolas. London: John Calder, 1963.

Spencer, Michael. *Michel Butor*. New York: Twayne, 1974.

Sterne, Laurence. *The Life and Opinions of Tristram Shandy*,

Gentleman. New York: Penguin, 1967.

Tew, Philip. *B. S. Johnson: A Critical Reading*. Manchester: Manchester UP, 2001.

———. "Chaos and Truth: B. S. Johnson's Theoretical and Literary Narratives." *Focus: Papers in English Literary and Cultural Studies*. Ed. Maria Kurdi, Gabriella Hartvig, and Andrew C. Rouse. Pecs: U of Pecs P, 2000. 38-54.

———. "Contextualizing B. S. Johnson (1933-73): The British Novel's Forgotten Voice of Protest." *Anachronist* (Eötvös Loránd University, Budapest) Winter 1998: 165-92.

———. "(Re)-acknowledging B. S. Johnson's Radical Realism, or Re-publishing *The Unfortunates*." *Critical Survey* 13 (2001): 37-61.

———. Unpublished interview with Zulfikar Ghose (Tufnell Park, London). 5 January 1999.

Tredell, Nicolas "Telling Life, Telling Death: *The Unfortunates*." *Review of Contemporary Fiction* 5.2 (Summer 1985): 34-41.

White, Glyn. "Recalling the Facts: Taking Action in the Matter of B. S. Johnson's *Albert Angelo*." *Hungarian Journal of English and American Studies* 5.2 (Autumn-Winter 1999): 143-62.

A B. S. Johnson Checklist

Travelling People. London: Constable, 1963; London: Transworld, 1964.

Albert Angelo. London: Constable, 1964; New York: New Directions, 1987.

Statement against Corpses. London: Constable, 1964 (with Zulfikar Ghose).

Trawl. London: Secker & Warburg, 1966; London: Panther, 1968.

The Unfortunates. London: Panther, 1969; rev. ed. Intro. Jonathan Coe. London: Picador, 1999.

House Mother Normal. London: Collins, 1971; Newcastle upon Tyne: Bloodaxe Books, 1984; New York: New Directions, 1987.

Christie Malry's Own Double-Entry. London: Collins, 1973; London: Penguin, 1984.

Everybody Knows Somebody Who's Dead. London: Covent Garden Press, 1973.

Aren't You Rather Young to Be Writing Your Memoirs? London: Hutchinson, 1973.

See the Old Lady Decently. London: Hutchinson, 1975.

Italo Calvino

Alan Tinkler

When Italo Calvino died in 1985 at the age of sixty-two, he was working on a series of six essays to be delivered at Harvard University under the auspices of the Charles Eliot Norton Lectures. Calvino completed only five of the essays, which have been collected under the title *Six Memos for the Next Millennium*. In his introduction to the lectures, Calvino writes: "My confidence in the future of literature consists in the knowledge that there are things that only literature can give us, by means specific to it" (1). Calvino realized that in order for literature to probe epistemological as well as ontological concerns, literary experimentation was necessary; thus he continuously refashioned himself as he explored ways of examining the human condition.

In 1956, when Calvino published *Italian Folktales: Selected and Retold by Italo Calvino,* he included an introduction in which he establishes the value and ability of each storyteller: "Therein lies, for us, [the art of storytelling's] real moral: the storyteller, with a kind of instinctive skillfulness, shies away from the constraint of popular tradition, from the unwritten law that the common people are capable only of repeating trite themes without ever actually 'creating'; perhaps the narrator thinks that he is producing only variations on a theme, whereas actually he ends up telling us what is in his heart" (xxxi). The individual storyteller, by taking control, by making it her own tale, manages to convey the knowledge of what is in the heart. Even as Calvino theorizes about the importance of the storyteller and the associative importance of structure, he is first and foremost an artist; therefore, he engages theoretical concerns in order to achieve aesthetic works. Martin McLaughlin argues that the "critic's first job, in Calvino's own words, is to discern the different layers of writing beneath the uniform surface of art" (xi). Calvino vigorously criticized his own work, and the virtuosity of his experimentation is inextricably linked to this self-criticism.

Like many prolific writers, Calvino often worked on more than one piece at a time. While he was writing his influential work *If on a winter's night a traveler,* he was also crafting *Mr. Palomar,* a work that would not be published for another eight years. McLaughlin, after examining early drafts of *Mr. Palomar,* attributes the delay to Calvino's search for the appropriate structure. He notes: "For

Calvino structure was an integral part of the meaning of a literary text" (x). Without structural integrity, a work simply was not complete. Calvino offers the following on structure: "I do not consider any literary operation concluded until I have given it a sense and a structure that I can consider definitive" (qtd. in McLaughlin x). Part of the creative process is linking the purpose with the design, and different structures are needed for different purposes. The resulting variety of Calvino's creative works is astonishing, from the neorealistic *The Path to the Spiders' Nests* to the experimental *If on a winter's night a traveler*.

Throughout his career, Calvino argued for the dismantling of interdisciplinary barriers: "We will not have a culture equal to the challenge until we compare against one another the basic problematics of science, philosophy, and literature, in order to call them all into question" (*Uses of Literature* 45-46). The resulting scope of Calvino's aesthetic inquiry was broad. In his early novel *The Baron in the Trees*, Calvino tackles Enlightenment philosophy. Regarding the eighteenth century, Calvino finds: "the eighteenth century remains one of the historical periods that fascinate me most, but this is because I find it increasingly rich and many-faceted and full of contradictory ferments that are still going on today" (*Uses of Literature* 35). The multiplicity of modes of examination during the Enlightenment as well as the fundamental interest in epistemology during the period explains Calvino's compulsive interest. Along the same lines, Calvino's admiration of the fantastic stems from his interest in contradictory modes of representation; Calvino believes, "literature in the *fantastique* tradition was relaunched by the Surrealists in their struggle to destroy the barriers between the rational and irrational in literature" (*Uses of Literature* 47). Throughout his career, Calvino questioned assumptions, particularly those aligned with institutions such as universities and the Catholic Church.

Calvino was born on 15 October 1923 in Santiago de Las Vegas, a suburb of Havana, Cuba, where his parents, both professors, conducted research in botany and tropical agronomy. By 1925 the Calvino family had returned to its native Italy, Italo's namesake. They settled in San Remo, close to the Calvino ancestral home in San Giovanni. Not surprisingly, the landscape of the Italian Riviera, Calvino's childhood playground, seeps into many of his works. Even though his parents were antifascist and freethinkers, Calvino attended a Protestant elementary school before attending a state-run high school. In order to please his parents, Calvino matriculated at the University of Turin, intending to study agriculture. By this time, however, Calvino was already interested in literature and writing, which, he admits, came naturally to him. In a short autobiographical essay, "By Way of an Autobiography," Calvino writes, "I set my hand to the art of writing early on. Publishing was easy for me, and I at once found favor and understanding" (*Uses of Literature* 340-41). Though publishing came easy for him, Calvino recognized, given his life experiences during the war, the fragility of peace and personal security—"peace and freedom is a frail kind of good fortune that might be taken from me in an instant" (340).

Calvino's discomfort was well founded, "Having grown up in times of dictatorship, and being overtaken by total war when of military age" (340). Calvino and his younger brother, Florio, joined the Italian Resistance when the Germans occupied northern Italy in 1943. At one point, their parents were briefly held by the fascists. Until 1945, Italo was a partisan who fought in the Ligurian mountains with the Garibaldi Brigades. His war experience would inform his neorealist novel, *The Path to the Spiders' Nests,* which won the prestigious Riccione Prize. The novel exposes the activities of partisan fighters through the eyes of a young boy. Calvino's war stories firmly established his reputation as a short-story writer in Italy. Two of his famous war stories, "Going to Headquarters" and "The Crow Comes Last," were initially published, like many of his shorter works, in journals, such as *Il Politecaico.* The war stories were subsequently collected, in translation, in *Difficult Loves* and *Numbers in the Dark and Other Stories.*

During 1947, Calvino, having returned to university, received his degree in English Literature after defending his thesis on Joseph Conrad. With a successful first novel and an already strong reputation as a short-story writer, it is little wonder that he landed a job at the Einaudi Publishing House in Turin where he started in the publicity department before becoming an editor, a job he would hold until 1984. When reflecting on his publishing house experience, Calvino writes, "Working in a publishing house, I spent more time with the books of others than with my own. I do not regret it: everything that is useful to the whole business of living together in a civilized way is energy well spent" (*Uses of Literature* 341). Sara Maria Adler in her book *Calvino: The Writer as Fablemaker* further qualifies Calvino's experience at Einaudi; the publishing house, she argues, was an intellectual cauldron: a "meeting place for historians and philosophers" (3). In fact, Calvino throughout his career was a voracious reader who concerned himself with literary and scientific trends, both past and present, and his literary production attests to the fact that his interests were wide-ranging.

Calvino's great strength was his intellectual versatility. Even though the political remained a concern, Calvino effortlessly shifted from the political after *The Path to the Spiders' Nests* to attend to the literature of fancy, initially folktales. While some of Calvino's interest in folktales can be understood by way of his ideological interest in the literature of the people, he was also clearly interested in recording Italian folktales as a literary project, along the lines of the Grimm collection of German folktales. In his introduction to *Italian Folktales: Selected and Retold by Italo Calvino,* Calvino writes, "I was unexpectedly caught in the spiderlike web of my study, not so much by its formal, outward aspect as by its innermost particularities: infinite variety and infinite repetition" (xvii-xviii). Calvino's own literary project would use this premise as a foundation: "infinite variety and infinite repetition." In fact, some critics, such as Adler, use the fable as a moniker for Calvino's entire literary production, suggesting that "The key to a comprehensive perspective of Calvino lies in the fact that he portrays the world around him in the same way it is portrayed in the traditional fable" (121). While this may be reductive, it is generally useful to keep in mind elements of fantasy while reading Calvino.

Fantasy, for Calvino, is not removed from reality; fantasy simply represents another performance of reality. Twenty years after finishing his Italian trilogy, *The Cloven Viscount, The Nonexistent Knight,* and *The Baron in the Trees,* Calvino writes in his essay "Levels of Reality in Literature," "Different levels of reality also exist in literature; in fact literature rests precisely on the distinction among various levels, and would be unthinkable without an awareness of this distinction" (*Uses of Literature* 101). Throughout his career, even when he becomes seemingly more interested in the structural complexity of fiction, Calvino always teases with representations of reality. Once Calvino exhausts a mode, say neorealism, he shifts to another manner of aesthetic expression, such as the fantastical tale, in order to keep his investigation fresh. After the fantastic tales, Calvino shifts to the experimental tale. Even as Calvino transforms his inquiry, he never loses sight of his creative underpinnings; he never forgets his neorealistic foundations, nor does he, when exploring science, leave fantasy behind. Each phase simply becomes amalgamated into his larger aesthetic vision. Critics, as a result, tend to focus on one element or another. McLaughlin, for instance, concentrates on structural elements, while Adler pursues the fantastic. In Calvino's collection of short stories *Numbers in the Dark,* which includes works from throughout his career, readers witness the shifts within one collection.

Calvino valued multiplicity enough to devote a section to it in his Harvard lectures. In the essay he focuses attention on the writings of Carol Emilio Gadda and Robert Musil. Calvino values Gadda's distortion of representation: "the more the world becomes distorted before his eyes, the more the author's self becomes involved in this process and is itself distorted and confused" (108). Calvino fundamentally distrusts the simple since the uncomplicated lacks the necessary density to explore the world. Returning to the eighteenth century's fascination with encyclopedic knowledge, Calvino finds that the novel, like the encyclopedia, is a "network of connections between the events, the people, and the things of the world" (105). Calvino seeks ways in which to understand the network of connections. His interest in Musil stems from Musil's delving into complexities of philosophic discourse. Calvino finds: "For Musil, knowledge is the awareness of the incompatibility of two opposite polarities. One of these he calls exactitude—or at other times mathematics, pure spirit, or even the military mentality—while the other he calls soul, or irrationality, humanity, chaos" (110). Calvino similarly recognizes that opposites cohabitate the same space at the same time; polarities are mutually present.

When Calvino moved to France in 1964, he found that living in a foreign land stimulated his awareness of his surroundings: "The ideal place for me is the one in which it is most natural to live as a foreigner" (*Uses of Literature* 341). He also befriended Raymond Queneau while aligning with Oulipo: Ouvroir de litérature potentiellé or Workshop for Potential Literature, founded by Queneau and the mathematician François Le Lionnais. The workshop, Beno Weiss explains in *Understanding Italo Calvino,* "explored the 'infinite potential of language for new forms' in order to 'determine how arbitrary limitations work as aesthetic principles, how, for example, restraints generate innovations' " (90). The heightened attention to structure represents the theoretical underpinnings for most of Calvino's subsequent narrative projects. While it is not necessary to explicate fully the formal intricacies of Calvino's works to enjoy reading them, careful consideration of the structures provides another layer of complexity while illuminating Calvino's exploration of epistemological and ontological structures.

While many critics suggest that Calvino's move to Paris represents a fundamental turning point in his creative career, it is more useful to consider his participation in Oulipo as a continuation of established interests. Before moving to Paris, Calvino published *Marcovaldo,* a book of interconnected stories. The structure of *Marcovaldo* is similar in many respects to his prototypical structural novel, *Invisible Cities.* In both books there is a fragmentation of place and memory that empowers the exploration of the respective protagonists. The fundamental difference rests in the explicitness of the fragmentation in *Invisible Cities*. *Marcovaldo* represents a bridge from his earlier writing and his later writing, a bridge that exists prior to Calvino's association with Oulipo. The fact that the Oulipo inquiry was consistent with Calvino's creative project is confirmed by *Marcovaldo*. Calvino was, not surprisingly, already aware of Queneau's work prior to moving to Paris. In 1947 Calvino wrote a review of Queneau's *Pierrot mon ami*, and once in Paris he translated Queneau's complex work *The Blue Flowers* into Italian. While in France, Calvino wrote three of his most significant works: *Cosmicomics, Invisible Cities,* and *If on a winter's night a traveler*. His work with Oulipo affirmed his use of self-imposed rules on his writing. When discussing why Georges Perec, a famous member of Oulipo, imposed rules, Calvino suggests, "In order to escape the arbitrary nature of existence, Perec, like his protagonist [in his novel, *Life A User's Manual*], is forced to impose rigorous rules and regulations on himself, even if these rules are in turn arbitrary" (*Six Memos* 122). Calvino's entire aesthetic and philosophic project can be thought of in terms of his examination of the arbitrariness of existence as well as the arbitrariness of rules.

Before moving to a discussion of each work, I should delineate a few of the broader critical trends, as there has recently been a heightened critical interest in Calvino. McLaughlin represents a strand of criticism that pays acute attention to the structural complexities of Calvino's texts. Calvino's earlier works become apprentice pieces when placed beside his subsequent structurally complex works. Weiss, on the other hand, focuses his attention on the phenomenology of Calvino's texts by examining the role of the reader (or perceiver) throughout the works. Weiss suggests that the structural games provide a potential barrier: "when readers are no longer fully appreciative of what the artist is offering, when they fail to respond properly to the text, then something has surely gone awry" (203). Even as Weiss admits that some readers find Calvino's later works frustrating, he defends Calvino because even in the more difficult works he "never totally loses sight of man's irrepressible humanity" (205). Sara Adler represents a third trend in Calvino criticism which highlights the fable as well as Calvino's links with Jorge Luis Borges. Other critics, particularly the Italian critics, focus on his earlier works, the works expressly linked with the Italian postwar experience. Not surprisingly, many of these critics are aligned with Marxist criticism. Lucia Re, for instance, examines how Calvino breaks with "traditional bourgeois art" (18). Given Calvino's creative versatility and his interest in and production of criticism, it is not surprising that there has been extensive critical interest in Calvino. With the arrival of the new millennium, the critical interest has only accelerated as Calvino is now being judged as one of the most important writers of the twentieth century.

The Path to the Spiders' Nests (1947)

In 1964 Calvino added an introduction to his first novel, exploring in detail his attachment to the school of neorealism that was popular among young Italian writers during the postwar period. Calvino admits that the neorealistic project was less artistic than pragmatic, stemming from "a physical, existential, collective need" (7). As a result, Calvino along with other neorealist writers focused primarily on content, specifically the compromises individuals made during and after the Second World War. Until recently, critics, particularly Italian critics, considered *The Path to the Spiders' Nests* as the archetypal neorealist novel. Many critics now question the novel's realism as the novel tends to subvert the didacticism that is a fundamental attribute of neorealism; the story simply does not provide the necessary committed message. Instead, the novel responds to fascism by employing the tradition of Dickens, Stevenson, Twain, and Swift—writers who are obviously not cornerstones of neorealism.

The novel explores fascism by way of a child observer, Pin. Pin's character provides Calvino with the perfect vehicle to consider the bizarre verisimilitude of the resistance movement. By using a child, Calvino is able to balance innocence with brutality. In the final scene of the book Pin gives a fellow resistance fighter the P38 pistol that he had earlier stolen from a German officer who was visiting his sister, a prostitute, so that the resistance fighter can execute a traitor. The traitor is Pin's sister, who by the end of the novel is an SS informer.

The Path to the Spiders' Nests begins with Pin in a village bar where a group of men are deciding whether or not to form a small partisan resistance group, G.A.P. Pin, a cantankerous child with a quick wit, boasts about being able to steal the pistol of a German officer who frequents his sister. The men dismiss him, saying that until he gets the pistol he cannot be a member of the group. By the time Pin has stolen the pistol and put himself in danger, the men have forgotten about the pistol—they had simply set the challenge to quiet Pin. The pistol, which Pin conceals within a riverside spiders' nest, becomes one catalyst for the narrative: "Pin decides that he will keep the pistol himself and not give it to anyone or tell anyone that he has it. He'll just hint that he possesses a terrible power, and everyone will obey him" (51).

Once the German officer realizes the theft, the occupying Germans track down Pin who has kept the holster even after hiding the gun. After being carted off to a villa-turned-prison, Pin meets the notorious partisan Red Wolf, who plans a successful escape from the prison with Pin in tow. Though he leaves Pin to his own devices so as not to place a boy in harm's way, Pin falls in with an infamous band of mountain partisans led by the inept and cowardly Dritto. The band consists solely of outcasts, as an experiment by the commander of the brigade, Kim, who wants to test the powers of the proletariat. Communism, according to the party line, will be successful because each man, including the weakest, is able to carry his own weight. So, while Dritto is eventually castigated as an ineffectual and cowardly leader, the band holds its ground in conflict, thus winning approval.

The episodic movement within the book allows Calvino to explore human nature, specifically by way of social interactions. Pin steps to the background as Kim, the commander of the brigade, defends the notion that "partisan warfare is as exact and precise as a machine; he has taken the revolutionary impulse matured in factories up into the mountains . . ." (132). Calvino in his introduction addresses the Kim episode: "To satisfy this need for the ideological component, I adopted the expedient of concentrating all the theoretical considerations into a chapter which is different in tone from the others, Chapter IX, the one containing the reflections of the commissar Kim, which almost constitutes a preface inserted in the middle of the novel" (12). Calvino's admission that *The Path to the Spiders' Nests* is a form of "committed literature" does little to affect the validity of the aesthetic project. While *The Path to the Spiders' Nests* does have ideological moments, the strength of the novel stems from Calvino's acceptance of the constraints of rendering an aesthetic work. The disjuncture of the Kim episode, in fact, emphasizes the dominance of aestheticism over didacticism.

Intermixed within the chain of events is wonderful prose that overshadows the party line. Calvino stylizes the novel so that he can explore the intricacies of boyhood imagination as it contrasts with the world. Pin, while in the German prison, meets a boy who spits blood: "And he spits out a reddish froth on to the ground. Pin looks at him with interest; he has always had a strange admiration for anyone who manages to spit blood, and always liked to see someone with tuberculosis spitting" (62). Pin is not only a childhood observer; Pin is a child. And Calvino's success at rendering Pin's point of view is nothing less than brilliant. In the end, it is this narrative success that moves the novel beyond the pejorative tag often given to ideological literature. Calvino is aware of the neorealist conventions and uses Pin's character to subvert them in order to produce work of lasting importance.

Difficult Loves
(stories written during the 1940s and 1950s)

Calvino's initial reputation in Italy was as a short-story writer. In fact, some critics suggest that had Calvino not written any longer pieces, he would still be revered in Italy for his short works. "Going to Headquarters" and "The Crow Comes Last" established Calvino's reputation. Many of the stories collected in *Difficult Loves* were published in small journals such as *Il Politecaico,* and all the stories were published in one of two Italian collections, *Ultimo viene il corvo* and *I racconti.* Many of the stories that were not included in *Difficult Loves* are included in the recently released collection *Numbers in the Dark and Other Stories.*

Difficult Loves is divided into four sections: "Riviera Stories," "Wartime Stories," "Postwar Stories," and "Stories of Love and Loneliness." The first three sections include stories written between 1945 and 1949 while the last section represents stories written during the 1950s. While non-Italian critics tend to focus attention on Calvino's longer works, his short stories are splendid. The short stories demonstrate Calvino's mastery of the form; they also show that even at the earliest moments of his career, he was acutely interested in both the structure as well as the art of storytelling.

In "Going to Headquarters," two men walk through "a sparse wood, almost destroyed by fire" (87). An armed man is leading an unarmed man to headquarters. While it is apparent to the reader that the unarmed man will be shot as a traitor, the unarmed man is strangely casual about the potential danger, asking: "Then will they let me go?" (87). He is told, yes; he will be let go after having his name entered on the rolls. As the walk continues, the unarmed man asks about the headquarters, which elicits the response: "one can't say headquarters is in any place or area. Headquarters is wherever it is" (89). The armed man's job, he claims, is simply to escort the unarmed man. Even as the unarmed man gives the impression of perfect indifference, he demonstrates his awareness. When referring to other fascists who have been taken to headquarters, he says, "I just wondered, since they'd never come back" (90). The two men are both complacent throughout their walk, and their fates are mutually bound. The end comes when the unarmed man asks the armed man whether or not he thinks he is a spy: " 'If we thought you a spy,' said the armed man, 'I wouldn't do this.' He snapped back the safety catch of the gun. 'And this.' He put it to his shoulder and made a motion as if about to fire at him" (93). Just before the armed man opens fire, the unarmed man thinks: "There . . . He's not firing" (93). And, the story ends: "So he remained, a corpse in the depth of the woods, his mouth full of pine needles. Two hours later he was already black with ants" (94).

The wide-ranging collection includes the comedic as well as the erotic. In "Theft in a Pastry Shop," a comic piece, a group of children break into a pastry shop to eat delicacies. After they chase the children away, the police remain, eating the remnants. In "The Adventure of a Soldier," a story of love and loneliness, a soldier is alone in a train compartment until a woman sits beside him. She sits there even though there are other seats available; throughout the journey they are silent partners. As the train journey progresses, the soldier gradually works his hand to her knee where "the train cradled it in a rocking caress" (189). After becoming skittish, the soldier continues, allowing his hand to ascend her thigh. In order to aid him, she places her jacket over his hand. "But when, finally, a first stirring ran through the widow's softness, like the motion of distant marine currents through secret underwater channels, the soldier was so surprised by it that, as if he really supposed the widow had noticed nothing till then, had really been asleep, he drew his hand away in fright" (193). After removing his hand, decorum is reestablished. The subtlety of the story is devastating as is the tenderness. Calvino, of course, is aware that one consequence of war is the loss of sexual partners.

When considering Calvino's short stories, Martin McLaughlin divides them into five categories: war, peacetime memories, child-centered or nature tales, postwar low life, and political allegories (17). It is not surprising that Calvino's subsequent longer works can be divided into similar categories. While McLaughlin discusses Calvino's short stories, he notes: "Calvino establishes himself as a fine craftsman of short stories, helped often by being a rigorous self-critic—indeed even if he had written no novels at all, Calvino would have remained a major exponent of this favorite Italian genre" (17).

The Italian Trilogy: *The Cloven Viscount* (1952), *The Baron in the Trees* (1957), and *The Nonexistent Knight* (1959)

The novels that are collectively referred to as the Italian Trilogy reveal Calvino's shift from the neorealistic to the fantastic. These three works follow Calvino's collection of *Italian Folktales,* which was published in 1956. In fact, the genesis of *The Cloven Viscount* comes from the fairy tale "The Cloven Youth," which is included in the collection of folktales. While there is no specific genesis for *The Baron in the Trees* or *The Nonexistent Knight,* they clearly represent an extension of his interest in narrative possibilities of folktales.

In *The Cloven Viscount* the Viscount Medardo of Terralba travels from Italy to join the crusades. During his first battle, he is cleaved in half. When Medardo returns to Terralba by way of a litter, he pays the bearers half of what they deserve as he is only half a man. The implication is that Medardo has been cleaved into a good half, which was left behind, and a bad half. The narrator, Medardo's nephew, becomes one of the first targets of Medardo's pernicious actions. As Medardo wanders the forest he cleaves everything in half, including the poisonous mushrooms he has given his nephew as a gift. Medardo's attendants save the nephew, warning him against eating the mushrooms. Medardo's attendants, however, are fighting a losing battle. As Viscount, Medardo wields significant power, including presiding as judge. When he adjudicates, he does so with viciousness, sending criminals who would typically be granted clemency to the gallows. He also sends twenty lackadaisical constables to the gallows. Around the countryside, Medardo earns the following monikers: Bereft One, Lame One, Maimed One, Sideless One, Bad 'Un, among others.

Once Medardo's errant half has been rendered, the Good 'Un returns, having hobbled from the battlefield in Turkey to Italy. To compensate for his evil half, the Good 'Un wanders the countryside, attempting to make right the actions taken by the Bad 'Un. It doesn't take long to realize that the actions of the good half are almost as destructive as the actions of the bad half. Love, in the end, becomes the unifying force. Each half falls independently in love with Pamela, and after both halves separately marry her, the two halves as a matter of honor agree to a duel. The duel reopens the wounds, allowing Dr. Trelawney to reattach the two halves, making Medardo whole again. "So my uncle Medardo became a whole man again, neither good nor bad, but a mixture of goodness and badness, that is, apparently not dissimilar to what he had been before the halving. But having had the experience of both halves each on its own, he was bound to be wise. He had a happy life, many children and a just rule" (245). When considered allegorically, Calvino examines the existential nature of humanity, suggesting balance is required. When considered in terms of the political climate, Calvino represents a Germany divided.

The whole, be it Germany or Medardo, only comes by way of union. The maturation of Medardo falls within the realm of the ontological. In an early section of the tale when Medardo arrives in Turkey, the narrator conveys: "My uncle was then in his first youth, the age in which confused feelings, not yet sifted, all rush into good and bad, the age in which every new experience, even macabre and inhuman, is palpitating and warm with love of life" (146). As Calvino's first foray into a novella-length tale of fancy, it is not surprising that the tale remains largely allegorical, particularly given its association with an existing folktale. Calvino in his introduction to *Italian Folktales* argues: "natural cruelties of the folktale give way to the rules of harmony" (xxix). Importantly, for Calvino, "The tendency to dwell on the wondrous remains dominant, even when closely allied with morality" (xxx). Folktales are a form uniquely suited for exploring the human condition.

While *The Nonexistent Knight* is not explicitly based on a retold folktale, the novella reflects Calvino's continued interest in folktales, particularly the importance of the storyteller. As Calvino researched folktales, he found that women usually narrate the tales, so it is not surprising that in *The Nonexistent Knight* a nun named Sister Theodora narrates the tale. In addition to the tale itself, the narration also includes a significant amount of discourse on the writing of the tale. This heightened attention to narratology moves Calvino into a new space. From this point forward, each project in one way or another draws attention to the writing or to the structure. For *The Nonexistent Knight,* Calvino's research on folktales provided him with the necessary latitude: "A regard for conventions and a free inventiveness are equally necessary in constructing a folktale" (*Italian Folktales* xxxi). Calvino would pay close attention to conventions as well as inventiveness throughout his career.

The Nonexistent Knight, however, is more than a discourse on narrative; the tale also scrutinizes questions of identity. The nonexistent knight, Agilulf, is absent on two fronts. Not only is he lacking physical form, as he is just a shell of armor, the validity of his knighthood is questioned when the suggestion is made that the virgin he rescued from ravishment was not a virgin. He leaves Charlemagne on a quest to find the truth. The question of identity is also examined by the inclusion of an important minor character, Gurduloo. Gurduloo takes on a seemingly infinite number of identities, and names, throughout the tale. While never conflicted, Gurduloo takes his identity from his surroundings, so when he climbs into a pear tree, Charlemagne chortles, "Look, he's being a pear" (27). When Gurduloo comes across ducks and starts mimicking them, a little peasant girl says, "He thinks the ducks are him" (25). Gurduloo gains his identity from the self he witnesses in other objects, be they sentient or not. Charlemagne, exposing the irony, pairs Agilulf and Gurduloo, making Gurduloo Agilulf's servant:

"That's a good one! We have a subject who exists but doesn't realise he does and there's my paladin who thinks he exists but actually doesn't. They'd make a great pair, let me tell you!" (28). The allusion to Cervantes is unavoidable, particularly since before being banished, Agilulf, though nonexistent, was the consummate knight. Calvino's acute attention to the nature of storytelling suggests that Calvino is as concerned with the art of telling the tale as with notions of identity. This imaginative pairing becomes fully realized in *The Baron in the Trees*.

The germination for *The Baron in the Trees,* Calvino admits, came from his own childhood. Italo and his brother Florio played in trees while young. The tale, which examines the Enlightenment, is set in the late eighteenth century, and by the end of the story, the narrator's worldview has changed: "I HAVE no idea what this nineteenth century of ours will bring, starting so badly and getting so much worse" (213). Even though there is an expressed concern for the changing social, political, and economic environment, *The Baron in the Trees* is a fairy tale at its core.

The parameters placed on action are articulated early in the tale. Cosimo escapes to the trees when his father chastises him for refusing to eat the fare, "snail soup and snails as the main course" (11), cooked by his sister. As he has dressed for dinner, Cosimo ascends to the land of trees as a child learning to be a proper Italian gentleman. Biago, Cosimo's brother and the narrator of the tale, suggests: "Life at our home was like a constant dress rehearsal for an appearance at court, either the Emperor of Austria's, King Louis', or even the court of those mountaineers from Turin" (5). When he climbs into the trees, Cosimo says, " 'I'll never come down again!' And he kept his word" (13). One strength of the work is the compelling rendering of what it would be like to live in trees.

Once Cosimo climbs into the trees, he becomes a philosopher. By the end of the tale, Cosimo becomes an icon who is visited by the important philosophers of the day, including Voltaire. Cosimo questions the philosophy of the Enlightenment, particularly in Italy where effects are absent: "In fact, all the causes of the French Revolution were present among us too. Only we were not in France, and there was no revolution. We live in a country where causes are always seen but never effects" (194). This topsy-turvy positioning of cause and effect is also witnessed in the relative value placed on the lives of the nobles: "All of them lived a pleasant life visiting each other and hunting. Life cost little" (54). Cosimo, in order to confront the fissures, creates a life in the trees that is both physically as well as philosophically rewarding. So while Cosimo originally climbs the tree in rage, he remains to cultivate a rewarding life that operates in constant dialogue with Enlightenment principles.

Marcovaldo or The seasons in the city (1963)

With *Marcovaldo or The seasons in the city,* Calvino balances his earlier interest in neorealism and the fantastic. In this short novella which reads more like a series of interrelated short stories, Calvino explores by way of his protagonist, Marcovaldo, the contemporary city life of a man whose work includes shoveling snow during the winter, carting plants around the city during the summer, and dressing as Santa Claus at Christmas. As the secondary title suggests, the novella marches through a series of seasons, starting with spring. In addition to touching on Marcovaldo's experiences as a poorly paid laborer for Sbav and Company, the stories also attend to Marcovaldo's disparate city existence. Not surprisingly, Marcovaldo maintains dynamic fantasies about rural life, particularly given the city's pollution. As is generally the case for those with nostalgia for the rural existence, Marcovaldo has little understanding of the realities of rural life.

In the first story, "Mushrooms in the city," Marcovaldo is excited when he discovers some mushrooms that are just about to surface on a small plot of ground by his bus stop. He relishes this knowledge, waiting desperately for the rains necessary to push the mushrooms above ground. His cache is exposed as the street cleaner, Amadigi, witnesses him exploring the hidden treasure. The morning after the rain, Marcovaldo harvests his plot quickly only to find out that Amadigi has found a more substantial field of mushrooms down the road. In order to circumvent Amadigi's desire to keep his trove a secret, Marcovaldo announces to everyone he sees where Amadigi's mushrooms can be found. The story closes in the hospital where Amadigi and Marcovaldo share adjacent hospital beds after having had their stomachs pumped: the mushrooms were poisonous. The rural is foreign to Marcovaldo; he is unable to differentiate a poisonous mushroom from an edible one.

One recurring theme throughout *Marcovaldo* is urban pollution. Pollution comes in many forms: neon lights exploding through the night, blue paint tainting rivers, chimneys expelling smog, and refuse stinking up the air, to name a few. In "Moon and GNAC" Marcovaldo is in the difficult position of teaching his children about the stars as a neon sign flashes on and off. The interval is unending, unnerving, and unvarying at twenty seconds. The entire rooftop sign reads: SPAAK-COGNAC. Not only does he have to wait out the illumination before attempting to locate constellations with his children, he also has to deal with a surprisingly logical question from them: "What company put up the moon then?" (73).

In a story near the end of the collection, "Marcovaldo at the supermarket," Marcovaldo and his family visit a "self-service supermarket," ostensibly to shop, but in reality to gawk at the consumer goods. Initially each member of the family pushes a cart through the supermarket, simply looking longingly at the goods lining the shelves. Then, Marcovaldo, having instructed his wife and children not to touch anything, makes a rapid turn at one of the intersections to elude his family. Once out of sight, he places goods in his cart; he wants to experience the pleasure of satisfying his desires if only for ten minutes. Like Marcovaldo, his wife and children peel off down different aisles, collecting their desirables. This story, like many of the stories in the collection, does not remain reified in the realm of realism. The story ends with the reunited family pushing their carts circuitously up a construction ramp and onto the roof where suddenly the jaws of a crane open, allowing Marcovaldo and his family to dump the goods into the distended jaws.

While the integrity and desirability of food represents a dominant leitmotif throughout the collection, another interesting recurrence is the search for solitude in an environment that affronts the senses at every moment. In "Park-bench vacation" Marcovaldo, after sighting an isolated park bench under some trees, attempts to find solitude by sleeping on the bench. Marcovaldo thinks to himself, "Oh, if I could wake just once at the twitter of birds and not at the sound of the alarm and the crying of little Paolino and the yelling of my wife, Domitilla!" (5). When he returns in the evening to the bench, Marcovaldo has to wait to gain the bench as a couple sits upon it quarrelling. Once the couple leaves, Marcovaldo is first disturbed by the flashing street lamps before having to conceal himself from the night watchman only to find the night noises bothersome. Once he figures that his level of exhaustion is so great that he could not but fall asleep, he is kept awake by the stench of passing garbage trucks. At some point, Marcovaldo falls asleep, and the story ends with jets of water from sprinklers waking him in time for him to rush to work.

This collection is not a diatribe against the drab conditions of an industrial city as the stories relate with uncanny humor the verisimilitude required to live and work in an industrial city. There is awareness rather than despair. The stories represent a fantastic portrayal of life in a drab city, and the collection is, at times, self-referential. In "The Forest on the superhighway" Marcovaldo's son reads a collection of fairy tales. The reference to fairy tales as well as the form makes it clear that the narrative represents a fantastic imaginative exploration which is a different type of imaginative effort than the more traditional neorealist novel, *The Path to the Spiders' Nests*. *Marcovaldo* is an example of how Calvino continuously reinvents himself, adapting his narratives to suit particular narrative needs.

Cosmicomics (1965)

In *Cosmicomics* and *t zero* Calvino, by way of a timeless protagonist, Qfwfq, explores foundational scientific traditions, including the big bang theory and the disappearance of the dinosaurs. His renewed focus on science stems not only from his participation in Oulipo but also from his interest in George De Santillana, who, while traveling through Italy in 1936, argued that scientific myths generate from scientific hypotheses. The commingling of the mythic and the scientific suits Calvino, and this generative association explains Calvino's interest in the Enlightenment, as was seen in *The Baron in the Trees*.

The title *Cosmicomics* also conveys another union of compelling interests; *Cosmicomics* is a neologism derived from cosmic and comic, and the stories satisfy both concerns. While Oulipo and Santillana provide the dialogic backdrop, Calvino devises his own direction. In this case the examination of science and of myths is not sufficient, hence the inclusion of the comic, which Calvino aligns with myth. On the whole, *Cosmicomics* is concerned with models of perception and the usefulness of models. When the universe expansion theory becomes problematic, another hypothesis steps into its place: one hypothesis replaces another. At the level of myth, however, both myths remain even as the most recent myth, in this case big bang, maintains a certain privilege.

Each story in the collection starts with a selection from a significant historical text. The widely anthologized "All at One Point" has the following epigraph: *"Through the calculations begun by Edwin P. Hubble on the galaxies' velocity of recession, we can establish the moment when all the universe's matter was concentrated in a single point, before it began to expand in space"* (43). Then, the narrative begins: "Naturally, we were all there,—*old Qfwfq said,*—where else could we have been?" (43). Qfwfq, a polymorph, is always present, if not as a physical entity, at least as a sentient one. In this story Calvino constructs a setting that realizes the myth/hypothesis of all matter concentrated in a single point.

Later, in "The Dinosaurs," Qfwfq is the last dinosaur. Given that perceptions have changed, Qfwfq is not seen as a dinosaur even though his physical characteristics are consistent with those of a dinosaur. In this story Qfwfq is more reflective than in the other stories, saying at one point, "I knew the life of the Dinosaurs from within, I knew how we had been governed by narrow-mindedness, prejudice, unable to adapt ourselves to new situations" (104). The New Ones have their own mythic understanding of the Dinosaurs, which is vastly different from the perception of the last dinosaur, Qfwfq.

"The Distance of the Moon" is also widely anthologized. The story's epigraph: *"At one time, according to Sir George H. Darwin, the Moon was very close to the Earth. Then the tides gradually pushed her far away: the tides that the Moon herself causes in the Earth's waters, where the Earth slowly loses energy"* (3). Qfwfq then tells the story about how the moon's elliptical orbit used to bring it close to the earth, so close in fact that Qfwfq and others were able to jump across from the surface of the earth to the surface of the moon. "My cousin, the Deaf One, showed a special talent for making those leaps. His clumsy hands, as soon as they touched the lunar surface . . . suddenly became deft and sensitive" (5). The monthly moon visits end when the "sea's surface, instead of being taut as it was during the full Moon, or even arched a bit toward the sky, now seemed limp, sagging, as if the lunar magnet no longer exercised its full power" (11). The next visit would be that of Armstrong's. While writing *Cosmicomics*, Calvino was undoubtedly aware that the space program was in overdrive. The space program interested Calvino not only because of the scientific merits but also because of its association with the cold war. As in *The Cloven Viscount*, the omnipresence of the contemporary social and political milieu is realized in the text.

t zero (1967)

Like many of Calvino's works, *t zero* simultaneously looks back over his oeuvre as well as projects forward to arenas of future interest. *t zero* is comprised of three sections: "More of Qfwfq," "Priscilla," and "t zero." In the first section Qfwfq continues to be concerned with cosmic issues. In the second section the focus is reproduction. In the final section Calvino makes a dramatic departure by writing three stories that function by way of strict adherence to the constraints of deductive reasoning. A similar pattern is employed in Calvino's seminal work, *If on a winter's night a traveler*.

In the first section there are four stories: "The Soft Moon," "The Origin of the Birds," "Crystals," and "Blood, Sea." These four stories are similar to the concluding stories in *Cosmicomics*, where the focus is on the biological rather than the universal. The premise of

"Blood, Sea," for instance, is that the sea has become internalized as blood. Rather than understanding evolution as movement away from the ocean, evolution more accurately represents the carrying of the ocean within. To borrow from the story's epigraph: *"The sea where living creatures were at one time immersed is now enclosed within their bodies"* (40). With this initial premise, Qfwfq not only discusses evolutionary concerns, but also, and more importantly, contemporary mechanical society, specifically automobiles. In the final scene of the story, a Jaguar strikes a tree, and the story ends, "the sea of common blood which floods over the crumpled metal isn't the blood-sea of our origin but only an infinitesimal detail of the outside, of the insignificant and arid outside, a number in the statistics of accidents over the weekend" (51). The elevated, theoretical discourse has been brought down to the real, the statistical. The reader can seek an actuarial table to find the frequency of accidents.

Before the first reproduction story, "Mitosis," Calvino provides seven epigraphs that deal with both the creation of life as well as conceiving death. The first epigraph, from George Bataille, concerns asexual reproduction: "In asexual reproduction, the simplest entity which is the cell divides at a point in its growth" (55). In "Mitosis" Calvino explores this relatively simple premise, relating it to notions of existence, in general, and of love, in particular. Mitosis provides interesting parameters when considering existence; after all, in mitosis the progenitor cell does not exist after it divides into two cells. The biological becomes psychological, "the moment when wrenching yourself from yourself you feel in a flash the union of the past and future" (74). Given that the story is also an exploration of love, there are interesting implications of manifesting love in such a singular society that requires the division of self. In "Meiosis" and "Death," the object of affection, Priscilla, is the opposing reproductive cell. Again, the action at the cellular level becomes conflated with the action of beings, and the action of beings can be understood in terms of genetic heritage where the individual becomes marginalized. In fact, agency rests not with the individual but with the gene pool.

"t zero" and the following three stories represent a shift in Calvino's narrative project. Each of the stories is the deductive manifestation of a constraint. In "t zero" the predicament is one in which a lion is in the midst of a leap at the narrator who is shooting an arrow in defense. The arrow, dipped in venom, may or may not strike the lion. At this moment, t zero, the moment when various outcomes conceptually exist, the inquiry becomes one of results. While Calvino explores the two dominant possibilities, he leaves available the infinite number of nonarticulated possibilities. The story also explores the possibility of remaining at t zero, remaining trapped within the present moment when all possibilities remain, when time no longer moves forward or backward. The narrator, in the end, values an existence that involves the movement of time. To be trapped within one temporal moment removes "meaning" from the equation of life, making life not worth living. Besides, if the arrow does strike the lion then the future does not look so bad; it is only if the arrow misses that the predicament becomes dire but still unknown. While Calvino leaves the question open about what will happen after the moment of t zero, he returns to this temporal quandary in subsequent works, such as *If on a winter's night a traveler*.

The Castle of Crossed Destinies (1969)

In *The Castle of Crossed Destinies* Calvino explores storytelling by way of images, specifically tarot cards. The collection is divided into two parts: "The Castle of Crossed Destinies" and "The Tavern of Crossed Destinies." Each section contains eight stories, and in each of the two sections, Calvino uses a different deck of tarot cards to propel the story forward. Calvino admits in an end note that the prose within each story simply tries to "reconstruct and interpret" (123) the stories told by the images. Each deck of cards is laid out in a geometric pattern, and each story moves through the cards vertically, horizontally, or diagonally. While the geometric possibilities allow for an infinite number of stories, each section is limited to eight.

Calvino also writes in the end note that he "thought of constructing a kind of crossword puzzle made of tarots instead of letters, of pictographic stories instead of words" (126). Calvino stipulates the importance of the rules: "But I felt that the game had a meaning only if governed by ironclad rules; an established framework of construction was required, conditioning the insertion of one story in the others. Without it, the whole thing was gratuitous" (127). Once Calvino establishes the rules, he proceeds. Though Calvino considered buying a third deck of tarot cards, he decided to publish the project once he satisfied himself with the two renderings that make up this collection of stories. Calvino admits: "I went no further than the formulation of the idea as I have just described it. My theoretical and expressive interests had moved off in other directions. I always feel the need to alternate one type of writing with another, completely different, to begin writing again as if I had never written anything before" (129). So when Calvino writes earlier in the endnote that "I publish this book to be free of it: it has obsessed me for years" (126), we can take him at his word.

In the final analysis, the stories within the collection do not hold the same type of resonance as Calvino's other works. In fact, most of the segments are quickly forgotten even as the conceptual frame remains firmly imbedded within the mind of the reader. So while the concept is compelling, particularly the notion that the tarot cards are telling their own stories, the end result is a little flat.

The Watcher and Other Stories (1971)

Three of Calvino's superb novellas appear in *The Watcher and Other Stories:* "The Watcher," "Smog," and "The Argentine Ant," published in 1963, 1958, and 1952, respectively. Since these stories are relatively early, they deal with the transformations affecting Italy during periods of rapid change. The three novellas investigate the political system and the impact of rapid industrialization as well as the tenacity of human nature. "The Watcher" pays particular attention to the influence of the Catholic Church in a shifting political environment where the Communist Party is unsympathetic to the Church's views. In "Smog" Calvino explores an environment that is burdened by enormous quantities of industrial pollution. And in "The Argentine Ant" Calvino examines how a relocated family deals with living in a community where there is an ant infestation that escapes solution. While Calvino has admitted that there are some essayistic characteristics to the stories, the stories are nevertheless compelling.

In "The Watcher" Amerigo Ormea, a left-wing poll watcher, is assigned to observe the polling operations setup within Turin's famous "Cottolengo Hospital for Incurables." Amerigo's motivating premise is rather simple: "In politics, as in every other sphere of life, there are two important principles for a man of any sense: don't cherish too many illusions, and never stop believing that every little bit helps" (4). So even though the hospital is a haven for the Christian Democrats, Amerigo is optimistic that his function as opposition poll watcher will bear fruit.

The Cottolengo Hospital is a seemingly endless labyrinth: "Amerigo knew all these stories [of the inmates] and he felt no curiosity or amazement at them; he knew that a sad, nervous day was ahead of him; as he wandered in the rain, looking for the entrance number marked on the little card from City Hall, he felt he was stepping over the frontier of his world" (6). Amerigo, throughout the story, examines not only the frontier of the hospital; he also examines the frontiers of his mind. Amerigo finds that the hospital, like the government, is outdated and in need of "repair." He also finds that the Church is manifestly complicit in the archaic establishment. When he realizes the fate of the hospital and the Catholic Church, he wonders whether or not communism will experience a similar end: "would it happen with Communism, too? Or was it already happening?" (14). Communism, as an institution, comes to experience similar forms of corrupted reification.

In "Smog" the resolution also comes at the end. The premise of "Smog" is that the entire city is trapped under a perverted cloud of industrial pollution. The organizations that are supposed to work for the eradication of the smog are purposefully ineffectual as they do not wish to cause their own demise. The magazine *Purification,* which the protagonist of the story writes for, only exists because purification is necessary. There is relief, however; relief exists in a pastoral rural setting. The narrator/protagonist of the story witnesses the laundry carts being pulled through the streets, and in the evening they return with clean laundry. The protagonist decides one day to follow the carts: "I wandered through the fields white with hanging laundry, and I suddenly wheeled about at a burst of laughter. On the shore of a canal, above one of the locks, there was the ledge of a pool, and over it, high above me, their sleeves rolled up, in dresses of every color, were the red faces of the washerwomen, who laughed and chattered; the young ones' breasts bobbing up and down inside their blouses, and the old, fat women with kerchiefs on their heads" (136). And the epiphany: "It wasn't much, but for me, seeking only images to retain in my eyes, perhaps it was enough" (137). Just knowing that the sensual rural exists enables the protagonist to continue.

In the final story, "The Argentine Ant," Calvino tackles human nature by exploring individual tenacity when faced with obstacles, even if the obstacles are only tiny ants. When a couple moves to a new town, they casually recollect references that ants are endemic to the region, but they dismiss them since jobs are available there. The couple remembers the infestation when their baby wakes, screaming because it is covered with ants. Instead of moving, the couple simply participates in the community-wide effort to eradicate the ants, and the inventiveness of their neighbors is uncanny. Not surprisingly, given the precedent established in "Smog," there is an agency that ostensibly helps to exterminate the ants, but there are myths about whether the agency, "The Argentine Ant Control Corporation," is helping to solve the problem or whether it is aggravating the problem in order to remain a viable entity. While the couple never considers moving from their new home, there is a haven—the sea: "The water was calm, with just a slight continual change of color, blue and black, darker farthest away. I thought of the expanses of water like this, of the infinite grains of soft sand down there at the bottom of the sea where the currents leave white shells washed clean by the waves" (181).

Invisible Cities (1972)

Even though *Invisible Cities* is less widely known than *If on a winter's night a traveler* and *Cosmicomics,* it is a recognized masterpiece, winner of the prestigious Reltrinelli Prize. While the table of contents delineates the complicated structure, the narrative is not held hostage to it. In fact, because of the strength of the narrative voice, the narration is fluid. A character named Marco Polo, a Venetian traveler, tells a series of tales to Kublai Khan. When Marco Polo first starts telling the tales, he does so with gestures, as he is not familiar with the language: "Marco Polo could express himself only with gestures, leaps, cries of wonder and of horror, animal barkings or hootings, or with objects he took from his knapsacks— ostrich plumes, pea-shooters, quartzes—which he arranged in front of him like chessmen" (21). Marco Polo quickly becomes the Great Khan's favorite storyteller. Even after Marco Polo learns the language, the Great Khan remembers each city by the antecedent gestures.

As it turns out, the cities, each given wonderfully arcane feminine names, turn out to be the same city: Venice. So Marco Polo is simply narrating his memories. When the Great Khan starts to recognize the similarities, Marco Polo suggests that "Cities, like dreams, are made of desires and fears, even if the thread of their discourse is secret, their rules are absurd, their perspectives deceitful, and everything conceals something else" (44). After admitting, however, that the city is Venice at the start of the sixth chapter, the reader plays witness: " 'Memory's images, once they are fixed in words, are erased,' Polo said. 'Perhaps I am afraid of losing Venice all at once, if I speak of it. Or perhaps, speaking of other cities, I have already lost it, little by little' " (87). *Invisible Cities* becomes a magnificent exploration in memory, language, and the art of storytelling.

In order to survey Venice, Calvino devotes five subchapters to each of the following themes: "Cities and memory," "Cities and desire," "Cities and signs," "Thin cities," "Trading cities," "Cities and eyes," "Cities and names," "Cities and the dead," "Cities and the sky," and "Hidden cities." While the titles provide the operating parameters within each subchapter, the collection remains strong because the storytelling is not subjugated to the structure; the structure enhances the story. *Invisible Cities* is a fluid whole. In fact, the structure enhances the story as the various avenues of view more fully develop the reader's impression of Venice. The narration also toys with the notion that even as each piece is accumulated, there is more that remains unrealized: "At every point the city offers surprises to your view: a caper bush jutting from the fortress' walls, the statues of three queens on corbels, an onion dome with three smaller onions threaded on the spire" (90).

The strength of *Invisible Cities* rests with the mounting description of Venice: "The city of Leonia refashions itself every day: every morning the people wake between fresh sheets, wash with just-unwrapped cakes of soap, wear brand-new clothing, take from the latest model refrigerator still unopened tins, listening to the last-minute jingles from the most up-to-date radio" (114). The city Marco Polo describes is the modern Venice, and it is well rendered and familiar: "This was the first time I had come to Trude, but I already knew the hotel where I happened to be lodged . . ." (128). Importantly, the city is not only a city of the past, but also a city of the future.

If on a winter's night a traveler (1979)

If on a winter's night a traveler, probably Calvino's best known work, came after a six-year publishing hiatus and represents the pinnacle of Calvino's exploration of narrative construction. This novel about novels provides ten different beginnings in twelve chapters. By exploring the notion of narrative construction, Calvino scrutinizes the process of writing and reading novels in a manner that is wonderfully self-referential. The reader is implicated, and a reader is the protagonist of the novel. The novel begins, "You are about to begin reading Italo Calvino's new novel, *If on a winter's night a traveler*. Relax. Concentrate. Dispel every other thought. Let the world around you fade" (3). These introductory instructions are framed with the end of the novel: "Just a moment, I've almost finished *If on a winter's night a traveler* by Italo Calvino" (260). The intermediate 257 pages, however, provide an expansive narrative experiment.

An unnamed reader is the protagonist of the novel who, after purchasing Calvino's new novel, finds the text is corrupted. Because of a production error, the pages begin repeating. The mystery that the protagonist is reading is about a traveler who is suddenly in possession of a piece of luggage which he knows nothing about. He is caught, like in "t zero," within a temporal quandary: "This is what I mean when I say I would like to swim against the stream of time: I would like to erase the consequences of certain events and restore an initial condition" (15). *If on a winter's night a traveler* raises repeatedly this question of erasing and restoring. With each new beginning, the reader is acutely aware of the narrative impulse that moves the story forward. The momentum inevitably propels the reader through the multiplicity.

Given that the protagonist is so enthralled with the mystery, he cannot wait to trade the book for an uncorrupted copy. As it turns out, the novel begun was not the new Calvino novel but rather a novel by Bazakbal, a Polish author. So instead of purchasing the Calvino novel, the reader decides to buy the Bazakbal novel. The reader explains, "I started the Polish one and it's the Polish one I want to go on with" (28). The bookseller sells the reader the book after mentioning that a young lady, whom we learn to be Ludmilla, has also bought the Polish novel after returning the repeating Calvino mystery. Once the protagonist starts the second novel, he realizes immediately that the story is different. As he is enthralled with the new novel, he keeps reading. Ludmilla also becomes en- trapped in the quandary. Ludmilla's sister, Lotaria, provides an al- ternative perspective, as she believes many readers simply want to clarify the problem. Lotaria identifies her sister as one who "reads one novel after another, but she never clarifies the problems," which Lotaria feels is "a big waste of time" (44).

In the penultimate chapter, the reader comes across other un- named readers who provide alternative perspectives. One reader argues, "If a book truly interests me, I cannot follow it for more than a few lines before my mind, having seized on a thought that the text suggests to it, or a feeling, or a question, or an image, goes off on a tangent and springs from thought to thought, from image to image, in an itinerary of reasonings and fantasies that I feel the need to pursue to the end, moving away from the book until I have lost sight of it" (254). Another reader suggests, "Every new book I read comes to be a part of that overall and unitary book that is the sum of my readings" (255). Throughout *If on a winter's night a traveler,* various interpretations are given. Not surprisingly, the valuation of these readings follows closely Calvino's considerations of the practice of reading: " 'I, too, feel the need to reread the books I have already read,' a third reader says, 'but at every rereading I seem to be read- ing a new book, for the first time' " (255).

As in *Invisible Cities,* the interrupted beginnings of *If on a winter's night a traveler* are framed with a unifying narrative, spe- cifically the relationship between Ludmilla and the unnamed pro- tagonist. Since each new beginning ends at a compelling moment, *If on a winter's night a traveler* sustains itself by the interlocking frames, and the interlocking frames continue to implicate the actual reader of the novel. At the beginning of chapter 7, for instance, "Your mind is occupied by two simultaneous concerns: the interior one, with your reading, and the other, with Ludmilla, who is late for your appointment" (140). As readers read, Calvino implies, they have other things on their mind. Regardless of what the author intends, the actual reading experience is different for each reader since each reader has his or her own concerns that affect the process of reading.

Calvino is also concerned with authorial corruption. While Marana, a translator who is the agent of the false starts, never appears as a character, he is culpable for the labyrinth. Marana, the reader learns, is a "representative of the OEPHLW of New York (Organization for the Electronic Production of Homogenized Literary Works)" (122). Marana not only produces false translations as well as forgeries; he also provides access to the strategy for *If on a winter's night a traveler:* "he will break off this translation at the moment of greatest suspense and will start translating another novel, inserting it into the first through some rudimentary expedient; for example, a character in the first novel opens a book and starts reading. The second novel will also break off to yield to a third, which will not proceed very far before opening into a fourth, and so on" (125). Even with the overt disclosure of the narrative strategy, the novel is successful in the manner in which it expands to include the fragments.

By raising issues of structure and reading as well as authorial practice and intention, Calvino suggests the subjective importance of the practice of both reading and writing. Lotaria reminds the protagonist that "a suitably programmed computer can read a novel in a few minutes and record the list of all the words contained in the text, in order of frequency" (186). For Calvino, this represents a horrific way to approach a text. Reading the text cannot be replaced with a tabulation of word frequency. Even with the imposition of structures, Calvino never forgets the human element nor the aesthetic element. Both writing and reading are manifestations of what it means to be human. For Calvino, reading is not simply "the recording of certain thematic recurrences" (186) as Lotaria claims, but an active process of engagement with the text.

Mr. Palomar (1983)

When thinking about *Mr. Palomar,* we need to consider that Calvino started the piece while he was working on *If on a winter's night a traveler,* particularly since the two texts nicely mirror each other.

While *If on a winter's night a traveler* is a hypernovel that pays acute attention to the structure and language of a novel, *Mr. Palomar* swings in the other direction: *Mr. Palomar* is a book about observing and imagining the world. One interesting characteristic of *Mr. Palomar* is the position of the index which explicates the structural strategy. The index is located at the end of the book, effectively concealing the structure from the reader until after she has finished the novel.

The book is divided into three chapters, and within each chapter there are three subchapters which are then divided into three parts. In all, there are twenty-seven sections. The thematic progression is based on the following three concerns: "Those marked '1' generally correspond to a visual experience . . ."; "Those marked '2' contain elements that are anthropological, or cultural in the broad sense . . ."; and "Those marked '3' involve more speculative experience, concerning the cosmos, time, infinity, the relationship between the self and the world, the dimensions of the mind" (128). The first section of the first chapter, titled "Reading a wave," is 1.1.1. The second section of the first chapter, titled "The naked bosom," is 1.1.2, and so on. The last section of the ninth chapter completes the pattern and is titled "Learning to be dead." Unlike *If on a winter's night a traveler,* where the structural element is unavoidable, *Mr. Palomar*'s lexicon is concealed within the prose and is not readily apparent. In other words, the story works itself out without relying on an overt declaration of the structure, though unlike in *Macovaldo,* where the sections are fundamentally interchangeable, the order in *Mr. Palomar* is crucial for the work, as it would be unfitting to place "Learning to be dead" anywhere except at the end. It is fitting for the structure to be both seamless and elemental in Calvino's last novel.

In the first paragraph of the first chapter, the narrator explains what Mr. Palomar is doing as he observes a wave—"it is not 'the waves' that he means to look at, but just one individual wave: in his desire to avoid vague sensations, he establishes for his every action a limited and precise object" (3). Palomar makes discrete observations in order to gain an understanding of the world around him. The narrator explains that Palomar is a "nervous man who lives in a frenzied and congested world," who "tends to reduce his relations with the outside world" (4). He tries, through his observations, to gain control: "to defend himself against the general neurasthenia, he tries to keep his sensations under control insofar as possible" (4). Palomar is not always successful, and when he loses control, he "goes off along the beach, tense and nervous as when he came, and even more unsure about everything" (8).

The reader gains a progressively better understanding about how Palomar perceives the world as each slice of Palomar's life is narrated. When observing his garden in "The infinite lawn," Palomar considers that it would be best to isolate a square meter of lawn and count "how many blades of grass there are, what species, how thick, how distributed" (31). He recognizes the futility of the project. Even if he properly cataloged each component, Palomar has done little to understand the lawn.

When considering how to formulate a model of experiencing the world, the narrator makes overt one of the seminal conflicts in the work, namely, how does the individual fit in the world? "Deduction, in any case, was one of his favorite activities, because he could devote himself to it in silence and alone, without special equipment, at any place and moment, seated in his armchair or strolling. Induction, on the contrary, was something he did not really trust, perhaps because he thought his experiences vague and incomplete" (109). In the final chapter, "Learning to be dead," Palomar "decides that from now on he will act as if he were dead, to see how the world gets along without him" (121). Palomar, like characters throughout Calvino's novels, lives in a mortal world, and as in his other works, Calvino explores the value of human existence. Though mortality is a certainty, how life is lived is of great consequence.

Under the Jaguar Sun (1988)

In 1972 Calvino started to write a book using the trope of the five senses. While he never completed the work, Esther Calvino released the collection of three stories in 1986, the year following Calvino's death. Esther includes a quotation from a note written by Calvino a few days before he became ill. In the note, Calvino discusses the importance of frames: "Both in art and in literature, the function of the frame is fundamental. It is the frame that marks the boundary between the picture and what is outside. It allows the picture to exist, isolating it from the rest; but at the same time, it recalls—and somehow stands for—everything that remains out of the picture. I might venture a definition: we consider poetic a production in which each individual experience acquires prominence through its detachment from the general continuum, while it retains a kind of glint of that unlimited vastness" (85-86). Even though the five stories were not fully integrated, Esther believed the three stories to be publishable, as they were "written in different periods of his life" (86), not to mention the fact that each of the stories is a rewrite of previously published material. In the stories Calvino uses sensory perception as an avenue to ask broader questions about human nature.

In "A King Listens" a king receives instructions on how to remain on the throne. As it turns out, the king is bound to the throne. In order to remain in control of his castle, which is a labyrinth, the king develops an acute sense of hearing in addition to establishing a network of informers. There is also an awareness of counteragents, which is reminiscent of *The Path to the Spiders' Nests:* "Perhaps all the agents in your pay work also for the conspirators, are themselves conspirators; and thus you are obliged to continue paying them, to keep them quiet as long as possible" (39). The infrastructure of state is supported by networks of eavesdropping. This raises the question of hearing versus listening; to hear is not the same as to listen. And the quandary of listening drives each new king into a paranoid state with the end result being—"you realize that being king is of no use for anything" (56).

In "The Name, the Nose" Calvino investigates the sense of smell and the social constructions that result from olfactory responses. This story is contemporary to science's recognition that smells play a vital role in behavior. In "The Name, the Nose" the correlation between the animal kingdom and humans is made explicit: "In our herd, our nose tells us who belongs to the herd and who doesn't; the herd's females have a smell that is the herd's smell, but each female also has an odor that distinguishes her from the other females" (71-72). The narrative includes three scent-induced pursuits. For each pursuit, the historical period shifts. In the second quest, which is set in France while the czars still ruled Russia, the protagonist says, after entering a perfumery, "What I am looking for is not the perfume suited to a lady I know. It is the lady I must find! A lady of whom I know nothing—save her perfume!" (70). As each quest continues, the olfactory sensibility indicates looming mortality. When noticing the sense of smell in herds, for instance, the narration recognizes that "danger—everything is first perceived by the nose, everything is within the nose, the world is the nose" (71). The quests however are futile as each search ends with the woman's death: ". . . I recognize the base, the echo of that perfume that resembles no other, merged with the odor of death now as if they had always been inseparable" (81). The smell of mortality is endemic.

In the title story of the English edition, "Under the Jaguar Sun," taste becomes conflated with religious as well as sexual desire. A man and a woman, who are traveling through Mexico, devour various indigenous cultures (Zapotecs, Olmecs, and Mixtecs, specifically). The couple is initially awed by a painting of an "abbess and her confessor for thirty years" (4). When the priest represented in the painting died, the younger abbess, twenty years his junior, died within twenty-four hours. The devotion of the abbess to the priest is quickly couched in terms of food. As it turns out, the nuns of noble lineage would spend hours searching "for new blends of ingredients, new variations in the measurements" since "whims of gluttony" were the "only craving allowed them" (6). The couple's investigation into Mexican culture includes not only the cultural but also the culinary. So after visiting another church, Olivia, the partner to the unnamed man, desires *"chiles en nogada"* (8). While the menu doesn't offer her first choice, it does offer her *"guajolote con mole poblano"* (8). As desires build, there is a mounting of sexual tension as well, resulting in a consummation of sexual desires.

A twist is introduced with the exploration of indigenous religious ceremonies. The suggestion is cannibalism. As the couple leaves a religious site, the protagonist looks at Olivia: "And as you try to read a person's thoughts in the expression of his eyes, so now I looked at those strong, sharp teeth and sensed there a restrained desire, an expectation" (16). Later the cannibalistic urges become absolutely explicit: "It was the sensation of her teeth in my flesh that I was imagining, and I could feel her tongue lift me against the roof of her mouth, enfold me in saliva, then thrust me under the tip of her canines" (23). The religious rites, however, are not simply rendered in terms of cannibalism, as the story also explores the dynamics of sacrifice. The couple's guide, Salustiano, explains: "It could be the victim himself, supine on the altar, offering his own entrails on the dish. Or the sacrificer, who assumes the pose of the victim because he is aware that tomorrow it will be his turn. Without this reciprocity, human sacrifice would be unthinkable. All were potentially both sacrificer and victim—the victim accepted his role as victim because he had fought to capture the others as victims" (26). With this realization, the protagonist reconsiders his relationship with Olivia: "my mistake with Olivia was to consider myself eaten by her, whereas I should be myself (I always had been) the one who ate her. The most appetizingly flavored human flesh belongs to the eater of human flesh. It was only by feeding ravenously on Olivia that I would cease being tasteless to her palate" (26). The story ends with the protagonist imagining what it would be like to be cut open and devoured.

The Road to San Giovanni (1993)

Before Calvino died in 1985, he told his wife that he intended to write twelve more books before quickly amending his plan: " 'What am I saying?' he added. 'Maybe Fifteen' " (vii). One of the works was a series of autobiographical "memory exercises." Esther collected five of the pieces to include in *The Road to San Giovanni*. She felt, however, that she couldn't use his working title, *Passaggi obbligati,* since "he meant to write others . . . since it seems that many of the passages are missing" (vii). The five pieces included in the collection were written between 1962 and 1977.

Given Calvino's interest in the temporal and the spatial, it is not surprising that the collection deals in great part with movements through space and time. The first piece, "The Road to San Giovanni," starts: "A general explanation of the world and of history must first of all take into account the way our house was situated, in an area once known as 'French Point,' on the last slopes at the foot of San Pietro hill, as though at the border between two continents" (3). With the establishment of this border, Calvino establishes both his father's destination, toward the ancestral home at San Giovanni, as well as his own, down the hill toward literary pursuits. While his father trudges up hill to his fields where he both studied agriculture as well as worked the family fields, Italo locates the world differently. Calvino moves down the hill to the city.

The Road to San Giovanni is not simply an autobiographical work, as Esther's introduction suggests. As Calvino explores his memory, he also explores the narrative requirements of such a rendering. When, for instance, he considers his father's language, he finds himself unable to remember the Latin (i.e., scientific) names of the regional plants, so Calvino makes up nonsensical monikers: "Photophila wolfoides," "Crotodendron indica," and "Ypotoglaxia jasminifolia," to name three. Calvino admits that he is "inventing the names" since he "never learned the real ones" (12). He readily accepts the limitations of memory: ". . . I could perfectly well have looked up some real names, instead of inventing them, and maybe rediscovered what plants my father had actually been naming for me; but that would have been cheating, refusing to accept the loss that I inflicted on myself, the thousands of losses we inflict on ourselves and for which there is no making amends" (12). This narrative project obviously combines Calvino's interest in memory and language.

The second story, "A Cinema-Goer's Autobiography," situates Calvino in the world down the hill from the family's estate. Calvino would sneak from home to the various cinemas in order to enter the world of the film. While he recognizes that such a positioning enters the realm of cliché, he situates his cinema experience as wrapped up in the concerns that would interest him throughout his life: "it satisfied a need for disorientation, for the projection of my attention into a different space, a need which I believe corresponds to a primary function of our assuming our place in the world, an indispensable stage in any character formation" (38). Calvino also explores his interest in narrative form by way of his cinema experience. Italian cinema-goers, he relates, are notorious for entering late and exiting early from films, and he was no exception. If his departure from home was delayed, he would still go even if the film had already started, or, if he had to make it home at a particular time, he would leave the film early. As a consequence, many films had gaps that would need to be filled: "even today, after thirty years—what am I saying?—almost forty, when I find myself watching one of those old films—on television for example—I'll recognize the moment I walked into the cinema, the scenes I watched without understanding, and I'll retrieve the lost pieces and complete the puzzle as if I'd left it unfinished only the day before" (41). Two other peculiarities about his early cinema experience stayed with Calvino. The first deals with dubbing. Calvino recollects that most films were dubbed poorly into Italian, and more interestingly, during the war the fascist censors would dub away scenes that were offensive by creating a dialogue that had no relationship with the events on the screen. The second peculiarity deals with the gap between film rolls. For some inexplicable reason, the projectionists were not able to seamlessly effect the reel changes, resulting in a delay. The gap would force Calvino to recall that he was not in San Francisco or some other exotic location, but in provincial Italy.

Throughout the collection, Calvino interrogates his surroundings and his memory. When considering his participation in the resistance movement, he chooses to recount the day a compatriot died. In the short piece "Memories of a Battle," Calvino desperately attempts to reconstruct the events of a battle, figuring that if he gets the morning right, he'll be able to remember the rest of the day. Regaining memory, particularly memory of traumatic events, Calvino finds, is both difficult and necessary: "This imagined memory is actually a real memory from that time because I am recovering things I first imagined back then" (88). Memory works by way of imagination both at its inception as well as in its recollection. When Calvino and his comrades think that the battle is over, they enter the city to join the celebrations. As they enter, however, they realize that the victory song being sung is not the song of the resistance but rather the song of the fascists. Cardù is killed as they retreat back into the hills. Calvino imagines the fascists discovering Cardù's body: "one of the *bersaglieri* turns over a body on the ground and sees the reddish-brown mustache and the big chest torn open and says, 'Hey, look who's dead,' and then everybody gathers round this dead man who instead of being the best of theirs had become the best of ours, Cardù who ever since he had left them had been in their thoughts, their conversation, their fears, their myths,

Cardù who many of them would have liked to emulate if only they'd had the courage, Cardù who carried the secret of his strength in that calm bold smile" (88-89).

Numbers in the Dark and Other Stories (1995)

Given the international interest in Calvino's work, it is not surprising that Esther collected some of his earlier works for publication in English. The pieces in *Numbers in the Dark and Other Stories,* ordered chronologically, were written as early as 1943 and as late as 1984. Most were previously published, but some, particularly some early fables, appear for the first time. The collection is divided into two sections. The first, "Fables and Stories," contains works from 1943-1958, and the second, "Tales and Dialogues," contains works from 1968-1984. No explanation is given for the ten-year gap. In her preface Esther, when discussing Calvino's habits of writing, says that from 1945, "there was never a period when Calvino was not writing. He wrote every day, wherever he was and in whatever circumstances, at a table or on his knee, in planes or hotel rooms" (1). Esther closes with a qualification: "texts that may seem unconnected to the main body of his work are part of projects that Calvino had clearly developed in his mind but did not have time to finish" (3). Regardless of the validity of Esther's stipulation, the collection provides English readers with a variety of previously unavailable works.

Since Calvino had no input in the selection of the stories for the collection, it makes sense to view each story independently, as there was no structural plan for the collection. The stories, though, provide interesting insights into Calvino's works. On the one hand, the stories affirm the general movement of his oeuvre that has been explored up to this point, but the stories also dismantle some of the linearity previously established. Even though Calvino's first novel, *The Path to the Spiders' Nests,* falls within the scope of neorealism, his earliest writing, after playing with theatrical writing, was fables. This explains more fully Calvino's interest in Italian folktales.

Throughout the collection, one of the dominant characteristics is playfulness, particularly with the political writings. "The Black Sheep" starts: "There was a country where they were all thieves" (23). The black sheep is the only honest man in the village, and he dies of hunger. The notion of thievery shifts once some thieves become rich. The rich thieves start hiring others to steal for them, hence the rise of the divide between the rich and the poor. The penultimate paragraph explains the divide: "So it was that only a few years after the appearance of the honest man, people no longer spoke of robbing and being robbed, but only of the rich and the poor; but they were still all thieves" (24-25).

In the title story, "Numbers in the Dark," the son of a housecleaner helps his mother do odd tasks as she cleans an office building. The boy, Paolino, is prophetic, recognizing that machines will make redundant many of the accountants who order numbers. As Paolino wanders the labyrinth, he finds a lone accountant who sits "in the very last cubicle, bent over an old adding machine" (86). The old man, who will be replaced by efficient machines, tells Paolino that things are "All wrong" (87). When Paolino questions whether or not the machines make mistakes, the old man qualifies his answer by telling Paolino, "No, from the start. It was wrong from the start" (87), before leading him into the basement where the old account books are kept. The old man has found a mistake in one of the ancient account books which he has obsessed about: "Over all these years, you know what that mistake of four hundred and ten lire has become? Billions! Billions!" (88). What troubles the man more than the error is his belief that the accountant who manufactured the error did it intentionally. This early story, finished in 1958, provides another child protagonist's view of the world, not unlike Pin's in *The Path to the Spiders' Nests*.

When reading the collection, we naturally look for connections with Calvino's other works. In the last story of the collection, "Implosion," for instance, Qfwfq returns. While it is difficult to know whether or not Calvino planned another work along the lines of *Cosmicomics* or *t zero,* it is interesting to realize that he continued to toy with the epistemological inquiry of science as late as 1984. Qfwfq muses: "To explode or implode . . . that is the question" (260). Of course, Qfwfq explores the difference by way of his unique perspective: "You explode, if that's more to your taste, shoot yourselves all around in endless darts, be prodigal, spendthrift, reckless: I shall implode, collapse inside the abyss of myself, towards my buried center, infinitely" (261). The story is a strangely concise explication of life's choices. His insights into human nature as well as his mastery of prose and his narrative experimentation assure that Calvino will be read for years to come.

WORKS CITED

Adler, Sara Maria. *Calvino: The Writer as Fablemaker*. Potomac, MD: José Porrúa Turanzas, S.A., 1979.
Calvino, Italo. *The Baron in the Trees*. Trans. Archibald Colquhoun.

New York: Harcourt Brace, 1977.

——. *Cosmicomics*. Trans. William Weaver. New York: Harcourt Brace, 1968.

——. *The Castle of Crossed Destinies*. Trans. William Weaver. New York: Harcourt Brace, 1977.

——. *Difficult Loves*. Trans. William Weaver, Archibald Colquhoun, and Peggy Wright. New York: Harcourt Brace, 1984.

——. *If on a winter's night a traveler*. Trans. William Weaver. New York: Harcourt Brace, 1981.

——. *Invisible Cities*. Trans. William Weaver. New York: Harcourt Brace, 1974.

——. *Italian Folktales: Selected and Retold by Italo Calvino*. Trans. George Martin. New York: Harcourt Brace, 1980.

——. *Marcovaldo*. Trans. William Weaver. New York: Harcourt Brace, 1983.

——. *Mr. Palomar*. Trans. William Weaver. New York: Harcourt Brace, 1985.

——. *The Nonexistent Knight and The Cloven Viscount*. Trans. Archibald Colquhoun. New York: Harcourt Brace, 1977.

——. *Numbers in the Dark and Other Stories*. Trans. Tim Parks. New York: Vintage, 1995.

——. *The Path to the Spiders' Nests*. Trans. Archibald Colquhoun with revisions by Martin McLaughlin. Hopewell, NJ: Ecco, 1998.

——. *The Road to San Giovanni*. Trans. Tim Parks. New York: Vintage, 1994.

——. *Six Memos for the Next Millennium*. Trans. Patrick Creagh. Cambridge: Harvard UP, 1988.

——. *t zero*. Trans. William Weaver. New York: Harcourt Brace, 1969.

——. *Under the Jaguar Sun*. Trans. William Weaver. New York: Harcourt Brace, 1988.

——. *The Uses of Literature*. Trans. Patrick Creagh. New York: Harcourt Brace, 1986.

——. *The Watcher and Other Stories*. Trans. William Weaver. New York: Harcourt Brace, 1971.

McLaughlin, Martin. *Writers of Italy: Italo Calvino*. Edinburgh: Edinburgh UP, 1998.

Re, Lucia. *Calvino and the Age of Neorealism: Fables of Estrangement*. Stanford: Stanford UP, 1990.

Weiss, Beno. *Understanding Italo Calvino*. Columbia: U of South Carolina P, 1993.

An Italo Calvino Checklist

Fiction

The Path to the Spiders' Nests. Trans. Archibald Colquhoun. New York: Random House, 1956; revised trans. Martin McLaughlin. Hopewell, NJ: Ecco, 1998.

Italian Folktales: Selected and Retold by Italo Calvino. Trans. George Martin. New York: Collier, 1961; New York: Harcourt Brace, 1980.

The Nonexistent Knight and The Cloven Viscount. Trans. Archibald Colquhoun. New York: Random House, 1962; New York: Harcourt Brace, 1977.

Cosmicomics. Trans. William Weaver. New York: Harcourt Brace, 1968.

The Baron in the Trees. Trans. Archibald Colquhoun. New York: Random House, 1969; New York: Harcourt Brace, 1977.

t zero. Trans. William Weaver. New York: Harcourt Brace, 1969.

The Watcher and Other Stories. Trans. William Weaver. New York: Harcourt Brace, 1971.

Invisible Cities. Trans. William Weaver. New York: Harcourt Brace, 1974.

The Castle of Crossed Destinies. Trans. William Weaver. New York: Harcourt Brace, 1977.

If on a winter's night a traveler. Trans. William Weaver. New York: Harcourt Brace, 1981.

Marcovaldo. Trans. William Weaver. New York: Harcourt Brace, 1983.

Difficult Loves. Trans. William Weaver, Archibald Colquhoun, and Peggy Wright. New York: Harcourt Brace, 1984.

Mr. Palomar. Trans. William Weaver. New York: Harcourt Brace, 1985.

Under the Jaguar Sun. Trans. William Weaver. New York: Harcourt Brace, 1988.

The Road to San Giovanni. Trans. Tim Parks. New York: Pantheon, 1993; New York: Vintage, 1994.

Numbers in the Dark and Other Stories. Trans. Tim Parks. New York: Vintage, 1995.

Nonfiction

The Uses of Literature. Trans. Patrick Creagh. New York: Harcourt
  Brace, 1986.
Six Memos for the Next Millennium. Trans. Patrick Creagh. Cam-
  bridge: Harvard UP, 1988.

Ursule Molinaro

Bruce Benderson

On 10 July 2000 the writer Ursule Molinaro passed away at her home in downtown Manhattan. She had been bedridden for about two weeks after a traumatic stay in hospital, against her will. Aside from numerous manuscripts, literary magazines, and published books—for which I have become the literary executor—she left little behind. The effects of Ursule Molinaro, including her archives, now total one ingeniously crammed storage space about the size of a small bathroom, maintained by her daughter Isabelle Molinaro, around the corner from her former apartment on East Second Street. Her age and place of birth are still shrouded in the mystery she imposed upon them. Her career as a prolific fiction writer, playwright, painter, and translator of French, German, and Italian is now relatively obscure, despite a prodigious output and a small band of enthusiastic colleagues, readers, creative-writing students, friends, and publisher Bruce McPherson—all of whose lives and crafts were irremediably influenced by her.

Like Nabokov, Molinaro was a European transplant to America who made the decision to put herself through the arduous process of learning to write in her new language. She came to the United States in 1946, probably around the age of thirty, from Paris, to work as a French language proofreader for the newly formed United Nations. At that time, she had published one book of poetry in French, called *Rimes et raisons* (1946). Due to a passion for language as well as an education in Germany, Italy, France, and England, she was already astonishingly multilingual, to the extent that she could speak the languages of all these countries fluently with no discernable accent. Another small book of prose with six illustrations by Léon Kelly, *Petit manuel pour la circulation dans le néant,* was published two years later.

Molinaro's literary roots were decidedly international and modernist, based on her rich education and her travels and her proficiency in languages. She admired Baudelaire, Goethe, Faulkner, Beckett, Giraudoux, Cocteau, and Tennessee Williams. She deeply disliked literature she felt was based on gossip, and for that reason was known to skewer with great contempt the work of Proust, who she thought was a deplorable stylist, badly in need of editing. She also was a deprecator of Anglo-Saxon naturalism, holding up

Dickens as an example of the type of literal-minded writer one should not aspire to be. She was more likely to evince a passion for the decadent writer Huysmans, and she admired Lorca and D'Annunzio. Of course, she was able to read all of these writers in their original language.

At some point in the 1950s, presumably after Molinaro had made the switch from writing in French to writing in English, influential literary agent Georges Borchardt decided to represent her. This association would prove fruitful in the 1960s and early 1970s, when her novels would be published by Harper & Row and New American Library in the United States and Julliard and Grasset in French, but it would dry up by the late seventies, when Molinaro began to seem unmarketable to the Borchardt agency and began to receive less and less attention from them.

The first people to publish Molinaro in the States were Cecil Hemley of Noonday and Themistocles Hoetis, who was editor of *Zero*. One of the Molinaro stories from Cecil Hemley's magazine *Prism*, "The Insufficient Rope," would later be included in the 1963 anthology *Best American Short Stories*. Starting in 1958, Molinaro was co-founder and fiction editor of the *Chelsea Review*, which began to publish some of the most innovative and avant-garde work on the international scene, including hers. However, she gave up that editorship in 1965, partly because of increasingly negative relations with the magazine's moneyed benefactor and co-editor Sonia Raiziss, with whose young adopted son, Peter St. Mu, Molinaro had fallen deeply in love. By 1964, with the publication of her first novel, *The Borrower,* in a French translation of her original English version, she already had emerged as an important playwright on the off-off Broadway scene and a noted short-story writer.[1] This must have been the time when the fully formed persona of "Ursule Molinaro, American writer" emerged. This new persona was, in part, a miraculous disappearing act, an attempt to excise not only her voice as a French writer, but many of the painful memories of her European childhood and her incarceration during the German occupation of France. Although she rarely provided details about her upbringing, in the 1990s she did write a book-length text, still unpublished, which she playfully described as a memoir, although she never revealed how factual or imaginary it was. It describes an extremely alienated little girl, brought up by a widowed mother in a high-bourgeois or perhaps aristocratic, provincial European household of mostly unsympathetic adult relatives, including a sadistically hostile grandmother. Molinaro's later flight throughout France in an attempt to evade occupation authorities and her subsequent imprisonment during the occupation, presumably for hiding a Jewish couple in her home, are alluded to in several stories and plays, and they obviously became a devastating focus for her ideas about the cruelty of the human species and the tyranny of nationalism.

These traumatic events form in part the basis of her literary rebellion against family values, nationalistic hegemony, and the literary tradition of biography. Henceforth she would never associate herself with any family history or single ethnicity in her conversations. It was as if she had exiled all the disagreeable facts of her biography—especially those dealing with progeny and nation—to the realm of fiction, where, rather than repressing them, she was free to take a kind of revenge upon them—to rework them into satirical, philosophical, or political metaphors. Once Molinaro became established as an American writer, her origins and age—her entire past—would be a matter of speculation. The only clues to these were in her fiction. Few photos of her from the past or present ever appeared—she accused photography of stealing the surface while betraying the inner life—and interviewers often left frustrated in their attempts to draw the "story" of her life from her.

In her rebellion against the biographical tradition, as well as family and ethnic history, Ursule Molinaro eventually cast herself into a universe of one. Her obstinate honing of individuality would continue for four more decades of writing mostly fiction and plays. Her literary contacts would become less mainstream as time passed. Often working alone in a cultural vacuum, with little community support, Molinaro the ideologue and artist had only one strength upon which to rely—her prodigious literary craft. In a version of the Nietzschean superwoman, she had invented herself and her world. It was a world of social judgments and political values, but it has turned out to be no easy ally of that fusion of sociology and psychoanalysis we call new historicism or that blatant political activism in the world of literary scholarship that thinks of fiction as a minor platform. Molinaro's texts elude such analyses because they are obstinately and saliently eccentric. They are the crowning achievements of an individuality, loaded with her penchants, commonsense wisdom, multicultural tidbits, occult notions, and word play. Her character portrayals are always antipsychoanalytic (as was she), adhering more to pre-Freudian ideas of innate character, the interplay of humans and nature, existential choices, and even astrology than to formulas of early childhood experience.

Despite these eccentric characteristics, from the late 1970s, Molinaro's writing was often described as feminist. It is true that her fiction and plays show a pronounced concern with the injustices of social power. She is most at home when dealing with the mentalities or behavior of oppressed women as well as minority races, gays, and animals. Of course, such a perspective comes as no surprise. She grew up feeling oppressed in her own childhood home. In conversations with me she often expressed deep dissatisfaction with the roles available to women in her lifetime. She was, from a fairly early time in the twentieth century, an advocate of sexual freedom who enjoyed two husbands and affairs with several men and, most probably, some women. Although she had one daughter, she rejected the conventional role of motherhood, and her daughter spent most of her early years not with Molinaro but with Molinaro's mother. In her life, then, she resembled her characters: renegade women who insist upon libidinal freedom and authority. In addition, Molinaro's dissatisfaction with women's roles took blatant form in her novel *The Autobiography of Cassandra, Princess & Prophetess of Troy,* an attempt to rework the myth of the fall of Troy as a feminist parable.

However, Molinaro's unrelenting individuality as a writer forces us to question whether she should really be thought of as a feminist in the contemporary sense of the word—especially in the current context of materialist feminism or theoretical feminism. It's true that her retellings of Greek myths all stem from her notion that these stories are really about the struggle between a defunct preclassical matriarchy, which she prefers, and the new male order in which we continue to live. Still, such theses are always eclipsed by her own canny ahistorical intuitions, her cultured, quirky asides, her delight in the sensualities of language and her vivid and extremely perverse imagination. Her revamping of Greek myth in a feminist context is also a purposefully anachronistic retelling of it. She exploits the time-worn tales of Cassandra, Jocasta, Iphigenia, Circe, and others to create new tensions and new mentalities. Polemic, if it exists at all in a narrative by Molinaro, becomes its least interesting aspect, and feminist ideology takes a back seat to the delicious, icy ironies about human foibles that Molinaro fabricates with witty, linguistically rich prose. Her Grecian tales strike me as resembling the self-made antiquity of a Pierre Louÿs or the classical reconstructions of a Giraudoux; but her liberationist attitudes do, in fact, bring her closer to the surrealist tradition in its championing of imagination and creativity as the preeminent tools of spiritual and political transformation. Moreover, the preponderance of perfumes, hues, patterns of light, and other sensory elements in many of her texts in some central way connects them to Catholic or Latin sensibilities, setting them against the often unadorned preoccupations of certain Anglo-Saxon writers who have been known to focus on gender politics. Finally, Molinaro actually was quite interested in some of the libidinal manifestations of "machismo," which she thought turned some men into enticing sexual objects. More than a feminist, I would rather describe her as a female adventurer.

Molinaro's first novel, *The Borrower,* appeared in translated French with Julliard (*L'un pour l'autre*) in 1964, but was not published in the United States until 1970, by Harper & Row. It wasn't translated by her. Once she had learned to write in English, she felt qualified only to translate *into* that language, rather than from it. She once told me that, since this was a first novel, "I wanted to put in it virtually everything I knew." Consequently, this is her longest novel: 230 pages. (As someone who had honed her mastery of four languages to a perfect precision, she saw no greater sin than wordiness and was a champion of brevity and economy.) *The Borrower* establishes, perhaps ironically, a theme that would become a preeminent obsession for Molinaro, the theme of identity. It is the story of an American scholar of German who visits the Harz Mountains, which are linked in literary history to Goethe and Heine. In the snow, on the corpse of an unknown man, is a shoebox containing a manuscript, which the American steals, translates, and presents as his own work. The novel takes place thirty-three years later, when the American returns to the mountains in an attempt to shed the identity of the manuscript-bearing corpse, which has now practically engulfed his own. The idea of an identity with which one is born being totally supplanted by a fictional one, through the medium of literature, is of course very appropriate, given Molinaro's own identity development; but in this case, the persona is achieved by borrowing (stealing) and the thief of identity becomes trapped in an artificial construction.

Critics and fellow writers were highly impressed (or in some cases perplexed) by Molinaro's labyrinthine tale, chock full of cultural allusions, psychological insights, and rather hilarious situations, all presented like a kind of postmodern detective story. In an undated letter about *The Borrower,* Joseph McElroy places the book in a tradition that goes "way back through *Pale Fire* and Henry James and the *Tempest* to God knows where: an affirmation of the mind's imaginative power to know itself." In a letter that might have been a response to a solicitation for a blurb from Molinaro's publisher, novelist Kay Boyle comically observed, "I have read the book like one bewitched. I am convinced that *The Borrower* is a deliberate stratagem conceived by the C.I.A. (or some other iniquitous government agency) to keep the minds of our citizens off the burning questions that beset our society. Once under its spell, one doesn't care who wins the election." Various French critics, such as Pierre Brodin[2] and Michel Gresset, linked this new "American" writer to the French nouveau roman or at least to the European tradition. This comes as no surprise considering Molinaro's familiarity with the nouveau roman. She would later translate Claude Ollier's *Law and Order* and co-translate Philippe Sollers's *Event* with me for Red Dust, the groundbreaking publishing company of avant-garde literature, owned by Joanna Gunderson. Molinaro was an acquaintance of Alain Robbe-Grillet and an admirer of his work, dining with him occasionally at the home of her agent, Georges Borchardt. She was also one of the first translators of Nathalie Sarraute, in the *Chelsea Review*.

However, Molinaro's link to European tradition would eventually do her career more harm than good. It is true that her career was launched right around the time of the French nouveau roman's visit to America, just as Beckett was winning a lot of attention and when Latin American novelists such as Manuel Puig and Adolfo Bioy Casares were about to be presented to American audiences. All these writers had revived the Faulknerian emphasis on the portrayal of internal consciousness through linguistic innovation. But this modernist, utopian ideal—the capture of thought rather than action by language—would generate a smaller and smaller readership as media began to depend more and more on the visual—and the portrayal of the visual, of action—instead of the portrayal of language or thought. This is not to say that Molinaro was not also a superb storyteller, capable of narrating compelling action scenes, but her growing interest in capturing thought and speech patterns in a prose graphically tailored to these faculties put off some readers and critics.

For her, the ultimate level of her texts resided in their linguistic know-how, which unlocked magical worlds. The social world we live in may be askew, but Molinaro felt that language could remake that world—or at least saturate it with the internal logic of her narratives. Over the years, she developed a crystalline style that invented her own linguistic architecture.

Loosely, her narrative style has two elements. There is the major thrust of the story, often described by a third-person narrator who presents the action as well as the probable thoughts of the characters. But this main narrative is embroidered upon (a reason why Molinaro published a story called "Needlepoint") by parenthetical digressions that Molinaro described as "islands of afterthought" and that serve an auxiliary role of deepening and enlarging the story. These islands of afterthought are hooked to the main text by the use of 2-em spaces, ampersands, dashes, or sentence fragments and sometimes interrupt the story in ways similar to how we think, amassing digressions and enumeration as we stick principally to our main idea. This technique is evident in a passage from her novel *Sounds of a Drunken Summer*:

The captain lived on the island all year round. With an arthritic cocker spaniel. & two tall white birdhouses on a green-velvet lawn.

& resented the painter. For having knocked at his blue kitchen door   at the beginning of that summer. To ask if his impeccably white   much more cheerful   house was perhaps for rent.

Before he began resenting the painter   after the painter became his neighbor   for attracting the old white tail-less cat to the proximity of his birdhouses. But feeding it. Twice daily. (13)

Molinaro's use of the ampersand for *and* and blank spaces for commas and other natural pauses encourages the reader to experience her texts as a flow of thought or speech rather than as mere description. It was a technique that would enchant some and leave others feeling less enthusiastic; and some critics, who felt that style should be transparent to show off the story, faulted her for it. In a review of her novel *Green Lights Are Blue,* in the *New York Review of Books,* Bernard Bergonzi complained, "Miss Molinaro is a tireless and engaging punster, and goes in, less happily, for endless typographical tricks, being particularly and pointlessly addicted to parenthesis signs and numerals. Her playing around with these merely goes to show how limited are the technical resources of the avant-garde novelist as compared to the innovator in music or the visual arts, who can completely abandon traditional materials if he wishes" (37-38).

Just as they had attempted to do to Gertrude Stein, some publishers tried to close up the eccentric spacing of Molinaro's texts, but Molinaro insisted upon it, telling them that if they read her texts out loud, the innate logic of her spacing would become easily apparent. She felt that digression and repetition were essential aspects of life and looked at her rambling descriptions as something akin to a relief map of consciousness with more salient elevations and flatter areas. That is exactly what they were: deft tracings of the meandering human mind. These "tropisms" were in the tradition of Woolf, Beckett, and Sarraute.

In a piece she wrote about her style called "Why Speak Ill of the Surface? Only the Void Has None,"[3] which is published for the first time in this issue, Molinaro complained about the waning reputation of the word and the increasing hegemony of the image:

Even though the word is said to have been with us since the beginning, it has as bad a reputation as the biblical serpent.

When a thought is expressed inadequately, or an image poorly rendered, it is the word that gets blamed, not the perhaps-not-clearly-enough-thought-out thought, or defective image.

The piece was in part a response to a critic whom she said had compared the typographic style of her novel, *Positions with White Roses,* to "a balking mule." And she added rather acerbically that this critic's attempt to imitate her spacing was itself quite unsuccessful. As further explanation of her style, she added, "As the eyes are forced to pause, the reader's breath cadence becomes synchronized with the rhythm of the story, whose tension—apathy—anguish—humor—etc. communicate themselves at the intended speed, with the intended inflection."

Molinaro's preoccupation with linguistic form also occasionally exposed her to accusations of superficiality. This was, primarily, an American complaint. French and Italian and Latin American critics seemed to find experiments in the conveyance of information just as profound an activity as the content that was being conveyed could ever be; indeed, they deeply believed that form and content were inextricably overlapped. There was, for example, in the eyes of most French critics, no such thing as a Marxist narrative that employed conventional capitalist structures of narration. The form had to change with the content. Conversely, many American critics felt that word play, sentence fragmentation, and other unconventional linguistic experiments could subtract from innovative content, which they associated with the story and the explicitly stated ideas. They accused linguistically oriented writers of being dense and elitist, and thus, in a sense, reactionary.

In a mostly favorable review of Molinaro's comic novel *Green Lights Are Blue* in the *New York Times* in May 1967, Eliot Fremont-Smith called the book "great fun, mildly bawdy, quite ridiculous, very stylized and less campy than delightfully, yearningly nostalgic. Inconsequential, as said, and nice for May. If you like that sort of thing." And he did like it, but did not, it appears, take it very seriously.

Other critics, such as Marie-Claude de Brunhoff, in *La Quinzaine littéraire,* who reviewed *Green Lights Are Blue* in conjunction with Jane Bowles's *Two Serious Ladies,* interpreted Molinaro's quirky style as coming from "une palette 'fauve' " (a fauvist palette). American writer and scholar Kenneth John Atchity called Molinaro's style a successful attempt to re-create the cinematic technique in narrative structure and praised her highly for it.

Green Lights would be followed by another novel two years later:

Sounds of a Drunken Summer (1969). *The Borrower* would be published by Harper & Row in 1970. However, by the mid-1970s, Molinaro was rarely published by large mainstream houses (an exception being *A Full Moon of Women,* published by Dutton in 1990). I believe this was due partly to a waning vogue for linguistically focused fiction (the Latin American boom was just ending) and partly to her refusal to market her biography for publicity purposes (the customary vehicle for obtaining Warhol's fifteen minutes of fame). She was almost perversely averse to self-promotion, feeling that it was the job of agents and publicists and not that of an artist. She also did not wish to be questioned about her past. Countless times, she alienated media people who might have promoted her by acting disdainful or disinterested, preferring instead to dote on those with whom she could identify—friends and colleagues whose perverse humor or alienation greatly entertained her but annoyed establishment figures. She was, for example, an early habituée of the trendy New York hangout Elaine's in the 1960s, and Elaine ranked among one of her closest friends. However, when journalists, playwrights, and actors who frequented Elaine's began to make disparaging comments about her much younger lover, St. Mu, Molinaro rejected that world in favor of her relationship. The networking of Elaine's sixties crowd helped propel many of its hangers-on to national attention, but Molinaro simply thought personal relationships and emotional authenticity were more important. Fortunately for her, there were still intriguing venues for her prodigious output of stories and novels in the 1970s, eighties, and nineties, which included respected literary anthologies such as *New Directions* as well as innovative publishers McPherson & Co. and the Fiction Collective.

Molinaro also fit badly into her work environment at the United Nations. Although she made some lifelong friends during her several years of service as a bilingual proofreader there, she does not seem to have exploited those international "connections" that some of today's writers might have. Nor did she seek advancement in position. She merely waited for each day to end so that she could go back to what she considered her real life as a writer. This wasn't easy. She once told me that it took several hours of good reading each evening to decompress from her job so that she could start writing.

Shortly after working at the United Nations, Molinaro published some of her early fiction in the men's magazine *Oui.* A former colleague saw one of her stories in an issue someone had abandoned in the subway and was appalled to see his respectable friend's name next to images of naked women flaunting enormous breasts. Molinaro was highly amused by what she considered his stupidity.

Another aspect of Molinaro's work that may have alienated the mainstream was her value judgments about characters. In her fourteen novels, four collections of short fiction, eighteen one-act plays, and hundreds of published stories, there are no wise fathers, happily married, sensual wives, or golden childhoods. There are, instead, philandering, bathetic husbands or macho sex objects; unhappy, rebellious, or gleefully adventurist women; and misunderstood children, many of whom have minds one usually associates with adults. Her texts are most distinguished by their vivid, unconventional, and sometimes victimized heroines. These heroines sometimes sport a striking physical characteristic (such as the hoofed girl in her novel *Angel on Fire* or the sister with the deformed spine in the novel *Positions with White Roses*). They have a dramatic disregard for the exigencies of their social situation, often transgress it dramatically and suffer royally as a result. Their social "martyrdom" usually places them at the sidelines of the conventional world, a fate that gives them the privileged position of the sibyl from which to evaluate the other members of their species. And they are always rewarded by an increase of wisdom and perspective.

In the novel *The Autobiography of Cassandra, Priestess & Prophetess of Troy,* the prophetess relates her own doom from the privileged psychic level of a person who is dead. What she offers us in a rather elegant and deadpan manner becomes not only the story of power robbed from women by men but also a rant against the shoddy treatment smug civilizations inflict upon the visionary, who is often an artist. In the comic novel *Fat Skeletons,* a translator,[4] weary of serving unappreciative publishers, thinks of passing her own work off as a translation and then is shocked to receive a book to translate that tells the story of her own life. Her subservient position as a translator of work that is often inferior to her own dovetails wittily with the other injustices in her life, including having had to put up with a colorful, narcissistic literary mother and a talentless but hilariously talkative writer friend—who tortures her with endless pronouncements about his nonexistent career. All of these oppressions have detached the translator from "the game," which, again, gives her the special objectivity of the disqualified from which to perceive the foibles of others. Likewise, in the novel *The New Moon with the Old Moon in Her Arms,* Molinaro chooses to martyr a patrician poetess of ancient Greece, who scandalizes her proper and unimaginative parents by offering herself to the mob as a religious sacrifice and by striking up an affair with a fisherman. Everything that happens to her in this brief novel is seen from the perspective of her last moments on Earth before she allows herself to be stoned to death, and this device lends a "last-word" finality and objectivity to her perceptions and judgments. Also, Molinaro names the poetess's sensual fisherman-lover Odysseus, casting him in a position of pleasure-service to the doomed though intellectually superior poetess, and thus, erotically, puts Homer in contemporary perspective by "emasculating" his much-revered macho myth.

The majority of the characters in Molinaro's entertaining and insightful narratives can be divided into two types. The first resemble the heroines mentioned above and also resemble Molinaro herself—fierce independents whose entire identity has been self-created by an exercise of will, usually with a flouting disregard for convention or tradition. These are usually, but not always, women. In *A Full Moon of Women*[5] Molinaro's portrait of Simone Weil—the Christian philosopher of Jewish origins, who died, perhaps by choice, of starvation during World War II and whom Molinaro has termed the "Jewish saint"—becomes a prime example of this characterological type. Weil's desire to choose spirituality as a kind of rebellion against parents and the events of wartime Europe takes on an almost willful perversity, reaching the point of self-starvation as an expression of Christian principle.

The second type of Molinaro character is comprised of those women and men who are comically mired in their own pasts and in social convention, a fact that often turns them into laughable, self-righteous clichés. This type of ridiculous character often serves as a foil for the first, from whose point of view it is hoped the reader will experience the narrative. The main female character, April, in the novel *April in Paris,* a provincial, racist American, fits into this category. She is, on the whole, comic and harmless, but when conventional foils such as she are placed in a position of authority and especially in a position of parenthood (such as the narrator's mother in Molinaro's unpublished memoir), their stupidity becomes monstrously oppressive. "May you never have a child who is a saint" ("Have You Asked" 87) is all Simone Weil's mother seems to have to say to a biographer, after her illustrious daughter's death; and "an embarrassment, especially to my father" (2) is how the poetess in *The New Moon with the Old Moon in Her Arms* describes her relationship to her parents, which is partly what prompts her father to remark that she is "behaving like one of the slaves" (1).

Conversely, when conventional characters are there mostly for comic relief (like April in *April in Paris* or the central male character in the novel *Saint Boy),* they provide entertaining evidence of the obnoxious humdrum world of convention that Molinaro's preferred characters have been given the right to flout.

In lieu of this it is interesting to note that Molinaro's literary characters served her quite effectively as social weapons. She used them throughout her life not only to reveal the failings of human society but as an exorcism of those who had disappointed her. She had only two defenses, her writing and her rather intimidating persona. Almost to the end she was an attractive, highly stylish woman. As must be evident by now, form and style for her were the essential vehicles of meaning, and she proved it in her appearance as well as her writing. She often favored all black clothing, and until the last years of her life, wore black polish on elegantly manicured nails. Her jewelry was ostentatious and hieratic, reflecting her interest in the occult. She preferred dramatically high heels, even when encroaching cardiovascular problems made it difficult for her to walk. She promoted smoking as the best of the contemplative tools and loved fine white wine. Her speech was severely correct and could be witty and trenchantly penetrating, sometimes to the distress of the listener. She deplored any kind of foreign accent. I give these details to show what a formidable person she appeared to be. Her iciness and sophistication intimidated some people, and she used them to protect an extremely nonviolent nature that had been subjected to extreme violence during her months of incarceration during the war. It and her writing were her weapons.

When a close friend hurt her irrevocably, that friend was apt to end up part of a composite as a not-altogether-agreeable character for a novel. Two trenchant examples of this deadly word warfare are the novels *Saint Boy* and *Positions with White Roses*. The first novel was partly an extended revenge-exorcism of a friend she had had for at least thirty years, but whose indiscretion about her and consequent lack of remorse led to their breakup. She used the figure of Saint Boy to deride what she saw as his sanctimoniousness and family values. Their breakup was permanent. Molinaro suffered from the loss, but her revenge novel, which also proved to be a wonderful parody of American mores, was her consolation. The wife in *Positions with White Roses* is partly based on a translator whom Molinaro had worked with and considered too competitive and who listed a credit for a co-translation of theirs in a theater program without including Molinaro's name. Molinaro had known both the woman and her husband, and each had given different stories about the other's abuse. Molinaro incorporated a version of these stories into the plot of *Positions* as an essential part of the family structure she portrays in that book. The portrait of the wife in this book is not overly contemptuous, but the fact that Molinaro felt no compunction using this friend as material meant that their relationship was permanently over.

Unlike many feminist writers, Molinaro in her work often relies upon nature as a measure of human behavior. For her, nature is not a cultural construction but an instructive reality. Several of her works, such as *Sounds of a Drunken Summer,* describe the brutality with which animals are treated not only by humans but by other animals. Life had been brutal for Molinaro in the past, and she felt compelled to explore the meaning of that brutality. She was deeply interested in distinguishing animal aggression, which she saw as a viable feature of the natural order and an allegory of existence, from human aggression, which she saw as artificial and contaminated by petty power trips. She was a devoted animal rightist, and perhaps that is why she was apt to interpret human life as finding ultimate sense in sociobiology. She thought that deep human truths could be plainly deciphered in the animal world or that animal behavior might offer a prescription for human behavior. Her insistence upon the purity of the atavistic consciousness could be read as a kind of conservative Darwinism, but instead it became subversive, utopic, and a source of magical meaning in her writing. Unlike many feminist writers who have questioned our preconceived notions about what is natural, Molinaro strove to overturn our assumptions about moral human behavior by the use of striking, sometimes morbid, examples from nature. If, for example, she wanted to illustrate her deep belief in euthanasia as an enlightened social practice, she was more apt to describe how a sick animal is hunted down and killed by members of its pack than to write a prosaic essay listing the practical or compassionate benefits of such a practice. To offer a feminist lesson in abortion rights in the much-published story "The Hanging of My Maid Mildred Mulligan and the Circumstances That Led Up to It," Molinaro concocted a tale of self-abortion and the cannibalism of a fetus in the American historical past. And in her chilling story "The Sin Eater," an Appalachian woman with no other recourse eats her fetus as some cats are wont to do.

In the spirit of nature as preeminent, Molinaro was apt to populate many of her stories with natural metaphors whose beauty, grace, and striking visual characteristics mesmerize us into believing that they are the locus of advanced levels of the meaning about our lives. Thus the nude body of a woman is defined as "a full-blown peony" in the story "A Late-Summer Stranger to Herself." In "Rites of Non-Requital" the female protagonist, who fancies younger men of a lower social status than herself, finds herself "kneeling with condescension to luminous skin or butterfly eyelashes, for spans of requited ecstasy that lasted as long as she could stay on her knees." And to drive home a feeling of hopeless frustration, Molinaro crafted the disturbing but visually fascinating image of a pigeon trapped in an airshaft between an apartment house (hers) and a church in Manhattan in the story "Pigeon in a Pit."

In keeping with Molinaro's approval of the sensory world of nature, her dynamic female characters usually see sexual appetite as a given and not as an oppressive political construct. Rarely is sexuality an excuse for male domination, but, more regularly, a medium of adventure in which female characters learn to express their autonomy.

Liberated female sexual behavior occurs in Molinaro's writing, however, no more frequently than lighthearted, even affectionate portrayals of the male sexual adventurer. In the novels *The Borrower, Encores for a Dilettante,* and *Power Dreamers,* as well as in the unpublished novel *The Curse of Endless Living* (in which the main character, a Sibyl, is found hanging upside down in a fig tree in modern times after being cursed with immortality by Apollo), the male "skirt-chaser" plays a prominent role. At times he is ridiculous and oppressive; but quite often this silly chauvinist is unthreatening, sometimes entertaining, a sex object himself (if he is young) and, at worst, boring, unimaginative, or presumptuous. It's true that her chauvinist Apollo in *The Autobiography of Cassandra* is a scoundrel, who spits in Cassandra's mouth to rob her of credibility, but he is brought back later in *The Curse of Endless Living* as an entertaining Italian playboy with a sports car who foolishly and flashily comes on to the centuries-older Sibyl. In many cases these younger male personae become the worshipers, pets, decorative adjuncts, or even dupes of female characters, who, themselves, rarely need to lose their traditional erotic trappings or feminine attributes to exercise their power. However, these women are not femmes fatales; they are merely liberated, sensual, and logical women, eager to profit from the treasures of the human body. They express their sexual tastes freely, and often this free behavior is presented as an acute criticism of the bourgeois dyad.

Conversely, one of the most ludicrous character types in Molinaro's fiction and plays is the physically unattractive older (that is, paternal) male who feels that his gender status, education, or upbringing gives him a right to assert his desire for younger women or even for the women of his generation. Rather than being threatening, his desire becomes contemptible and is met with haughty derision by a female character who has superior taste, intelligence, and allure, regardless of *her* age. A supreme example of this situation occurs in the story "Rites of Non-Requital,"[6] when an aging teacher is faced with her oldest student—perhaps a couple of years younger than she—who starts coming on to her. She "notices nothing beyond his skinny hair, & a reddish-glazed complexion attributable to broken capillaries."

Molinaro's fictional sexual couplings—which can involve hetero-sexual, homosexual, sadomasochistic, or fetishistic behavior—are more often than not liable to mock conservative conventions of mar-riage, fidelity, the family, and, especially, motherhood. There have been numerous attempts to salvage motherhood as a source of strength in the writing of today's feminists, as well as attempts to reclaim female identity through the portrayal of generations of women linked emotionally and culturally by the fact of birth. Some feminist writers have presented motherhood as a biological power that cannot be taken away from the most abused individual. How-ever, Molinaro, who, one must remember, preferred the animal world to the world of humans, saw little advantage or transcendent meaning in the preservation of the human species by the process of procreation. She also detested the social limitations of the maternal role. For her, the prison sentence known as "family" that puts un-likely inmates—mothers, daughters, aunts, uncles, and fathers—in the same space is almost always one to be escaped. Reflecting upon family produced for her rueful, yet often comic, insights; and if her characters chose motherhood, this choice was usually presented as a mistake.

Sometime in the 1990s Molinaro published a poem-postcard called "A Family Alphabet." Entries F-I read:

F Family, *n.* - a group of at least 3, held together by friction

G Grand-, *prefix* - *with:* mothers, fathers, uncles, aunts, pianos, etc. Pieces of furniture in a family room

H Home, *n.* - euphemism for a place of detention

I Individuality, *n.* - a disease functioning families manage to eradi-cate

As one can see, she took impish delight in indicting the family with her mordant wit. In fact, in an unpublished novel she completed in October 1999, called *Beginnings in Black and White,* her protago-nist goes so far as to profess an allergy to children in order to counter a request from a father in a restaurant to put out a ciga-rette so that he and his baby can sit near him. In this scene the per-fection of individual pleasures is promoted over mere familial con-cerns in an ideology reminiscent of Baudelairean dandyism—the absolute importance of enjoying the perfect cigarette as the ideal tool for meditation or savoring the subtle flavor of a glass of wine to escape the nauseating odors of childhood and the family scene.

Molinaro's best characters have a wide experience of cultural and linguistic variety, which further places them outside the hemmed-in mentality of the nuclear family. In fact, one of her cen-tral themes is the uselessness of inscribing one's consciousness within any nationalist identity at all. She once explained to me that a native speaker of French who wants to speak English but who touches a wall and thinks *mur* before translating it into English will always use the word *wall* with a feeling of unfamiliarity and will always have an accent. And since she believed that all reality is accessible through the medium of language, she believed that the person with a half-developed language can only see the shadows of things. Breaking language barriers was part of Molinaro's philosophy. Her challenge was to master and familiarize herself with the linguistic environment she was depicting no matter how exotic its origin.

No matter what Molinaro wrote about, it was never a tale of "olden times" in a "faraway country." Instead, she strove to discover truths she felt lay beyond the social and the historical but were accessible to her craft, intellect, or daring. And she never resorted to Dickensian naturalism—which she saw as an accumulation of paint-by-number details meant to give a "realistic" feeling of the setting. She chose instead the judicious placement of spare, sensuous details that enhanced the peculiar consciousness of her protagonist; and it is the consciousness of Molinaro's characters that is mostly responsible for startling evocations of setting. Thus Molinaro exploited different times and places in her fiction but never tried to construct paper-and-paste reproductions of them. She just did not believe in the concept of the tourist.

So grotesque did Molinaro view the "ra-ra" call to patrimony that in her narratives its consequences sometimes became Grand Guignol. The short story "Merdica" is the surreal fable of a tennis pro who must endure an inhumane country through an accident of birth. The mythical country of Merdica (from the French word *merde,* meaning *shit,* and an Indonesian word meaning *freedom),* reminiscent of Germany during World War II, was the perpetrator of a cannibalistic holocaust. To escape his patrimony and his family, the tennis pro flees to America. He leaves his past behind and creates a new identity for himself. However, increasing fame as a tennis pro leads to research that links him to the old fatherland. Although he is innocent of any war crime, the association is too much for him. He resorts to a "final solution" to escape the chagrin that such a connection causes him by climbing into a pot at a restaurant so that he will be boiled to death.

One other important facet of Molinaro's fiction may stem from her misanthropy. A strong distaste for the quotidian made her seek answers in phenomena that were located as far away from it as possible. For several decades she developed an interest in astrology, numerology, and certain doctrines of Eastern religion. As an occultist, who wrote two serious books on astrology and numerology,[7] she sought a way to view existence as a journey that extends beyond a single circumscribed ego and beyond the confines of generations and genetics. This approach to existence was related to her support of euthanasia, for she felt that death was not an absolute ending, but merely the end of the circumscribed ego. Such a worldview takes on importance in several of her novels, including *Encores for a Dilettante,* where the character's various past lives become as multifarious and important as his sexual affairs, or in *Power Dreamers,* where the hermaphroditic seer Tiresias embraces the spectrum of gender differences, leading to a kind of wisdom. Molinaro used occult devices to extend the meaning of her characterological portraits—to make them transcend individual sociological or psychological realities so that they would have metaphysical implications. It was a solace to her that the indignities suffered at the hands of family, country, and other sacrosanct institutions would, eventually, be seen in their irrelevance from larger perspectives, other realms. But her occult devices also worked as an adjunct to her strong aesthetic sense. Her occult worlds were often worlds of glistening mirrors, magical colors and plants, caves for sexual rites (such as those in *Positions with White Roses),* and out-of-body experiences that had a precise, stylish excitement to them. Additionally, as I've already hinted, Molinaro saw preeminent meanings in the world of animals and plants, and, together, these elements gave some of her stories and novels the feeling of ritual—ornate and elegant processes reminiscent of some of the rituals of the Catholic Church.

There is, in addition, a certain asceticism and fatality about Molinaro's occultism. She was firmly convinced that the human species is far from the most aesthetic, perceptive, moral, consistent, or compassionate life form. That is why she was interested in the Cathari, who had renounced procreation and whom she discusses in *Positions with White Roses*. She even asked me once if any animal could look more grotesque than the human when giving birth (I couldn't think of one). Certainly, she found the "normal" world no ideal environment for intellectual or artistic pursuits. That is part of the reason why she depicted those who struggle aggressively, i.e., heroically, to survive in their environments as actually fighting a losing and often inane battle, and why she preferred sacrificial geniuses like Simone Weil and the protagonist of her novel *The New Moon with the Old Moon in her Arms,* who sacrifices herself to a religious ritual involving stoning and thus avoids being the usual Western hero whose value comes from a kind of athletic opposition to the powers of oppression. So little did Molinaro glorify survival struggles that she wrote several texts about the dignity and logic of suicide as a vehicle for escaping a meaningless or illness-ridden life. One of the most memorable is the very humorous story "Dr. Arnold Beidermeier's Suicide Parlors," a futurist parody that posits a psychotherapist's New Age business offering elaborate suicide scenarios to discouraged customers. Biedermeier's "parlors would offer not only a humanitarian solution, but a compensation. Something to look forward to: a personalized death, wish-designed to accommodate every conceivable ego image & fantasy" (71). Molinaro uses the shocking proposition of suicide brilliantly here and elsewhere to challenge that bourgeois value that enforces survival as a "duty" to one's country, family, or self.

In the 1980s and 1990s Molinaro found work as a professor of creative writing at various universities, including the University of Hawaii and Virginia Polytechnic Institute. Her teaching was immensely successful, and she was invited to extend her contract to several years at the University of Hawaii. Meanwhile, her tireless literary efforts continued until just a month or so before her death in 2000. In 1990 she published *A Full Moon of Women: 29 word portraits of notable women from different times and places + 1 void of course*. It is a collection of clipped, often removed or ironic portraits of Charlotte Corday, Joan of Arc, Hypatia, Adèle Hugo, Clara Schumann, and other female historical figures, many of whom had spent their lives playing second fiddle to a more prominent person. The book was quirkily revisionist. It makes the reader wonder not only why some of these women did not become more well known but about what potential there is in the study of history to salvage, even rework, wasted lives or unappreciated minds. And the book is, yet again, a retort to mainstream scholarship because of its insistence upon minor historical details and some supposedly minor personae, casting scorn on revered paternalistic literary figures like Victor Hugo and on official versions of historical events. In retrospect, I now realize that Molinaro herself could have been a character in *A Full Moon of Women,* for like many of the women in her book, her talents were often underappreciated, and her only reward for her determined behavior was a sense of developed individuality. A review of the book in the *New York Times Book Review* called "Wife of, Mother of, Daughter of," praised the writing in this "spirited new collection of short fiction"—with some reservations: "As in her longer fiction, Ms. Molinaro displays a poetic eye for detail in these short sketches—deftly showing us, for example, Marat's copper tub and Charlotte Corday's ebony-handled knife. Yet occasionally such details vie with the book's rhetoric. Ms. Molinaro uses varieties of syntax—fragments, ellipsis, parenthesis—to suggest the discontinuity of experience. But, while often clever, this style can also distract."

That same year, Molinaro's classical novel *The New Moon with the Old Moon in Her Arms* was published by the Women's Press in London. Colin Greenland, a reviewer for the *London Times,* took much more kindly to her style than the *New York Times* reviewer of *A Full Moon of Women* had, maintaining that, "Molinaro's eccentric punctuation is perfectly logical; much simpler, in fact, than what we are used to in print. It's an ideal form for transcribing personal reflections, halfway between internal monologue and a letter to a good friend."

Also in the 1990s Molinaro's comic novel *Fat Skeletons,* about a dissatisfied translator suddenly come upon her own life story signed by someone else, was published by Serif in London in 1994. It was translated into French in 1998. McPherson & Co. republished *The New Moon with the Old Moon in Her Arms* and *Fat Skeletons,* which had already been published in England. McPherson also published new works of Molinaro's: *Power Dreamers: The Jocasta Complex* and *Demons and Divas: Three Novels* (1999). Molinaro was reluctant to publish three novels in one book, because she detested thick books, but in the end she relented.

What was extraordinary about this prolific decade was the fact that she accomplished all of this in the context of severely failing health and dwindling funds. Her income was more or less dependent upon her social security checks and a small monthly annuity from some devoted European friends. Her body was failing and she rejected the usual contemporary therapies for it. She detested the new American vogue for physical exercise, which she associated with the noncontemplative life and the dreaded "heroic" sensibility. She was finding it increasingly difficult to walk. She abhorred doctors and hospitals, and for the last two or so years of her life, due to cardiovascular problems and possibly arthritis, was constantly in pain; although, with the help of friends, she still made appearances at her favorite restaurants, films, or literary events. And of course, she never gave up her treasured Gauloises cigarettes or Macon Villages wine. It was almost as if the decline of her body were freeing her from any distraction from her voice as a writer. During some nights of insomnia due to pulmonary problems, she actually produced complete texts which she sat composing in her head. Some of her best work was done during this period, and in this work there are allusions to aging that reveal her struggle with her physical decline, her attempt to conceive of it as a movement toward another plane or reality and even a certain exultant feeling about the triumph of the spirit over the body.

The last year and a half of Molinaro's life was fraught with physical drama. She maintained a firm belief in homeopathic medicines and Chinese herbs all the while her health was failing. However, having come nearly to the brink of death with edema, she finally allowed distraught friends to convince her to see a doctor. Medication controlled her heart failure and gave her approximately a year more of functional health, but then she began to decline again and was taken to the hospital against her will after she fell in her apartment. For her, the stay in hospital was reminiscent of her sojourn in prison during the war, and she vowed never to enter another institution again. *Survivor* was a word she viewed with the utmost contempt. For her it spelled *ego* and was the sign of a truly narcissistic personality. Once back from the hospital, she saw very little appeal in the idea of home health care or a home for the aged. With an astonishing lack of sentimentality, she began to say farewell to this life.

Molinaro's sudden death a couple of weeks later struck most of her friends as entirely appropriate. It was almost like the reasoned act of will by a woman who had always wanted more than anything else to fashion her own destiny. She was that rare breed of artist whose life and work showed total consistency. In the end her self-constructed persona triumphed over everything and will always be articulated in the work she has left behind.

NOTES

[1]This article is about the fiction of Ursule Molinaro. She was also a playwright of prodigious output, but these texts will not be dealt with here.

[2]Brodin was a long-time friend of Molinaro's. Both of them participated in the overseas L'Ecole Libre Des Hautes Etudes, founded in New York as a French school and cultural center for war exiles in 1941.

[3]Papers of Ursule Molinaro, in the possession of Isabelle Molinaro.

[4]Although Molinaro did not begin life as a native speaker of English, for many years she translated into English from French, German, and Italian, including works by Ollier, Sollers, Audiberti, Buto, Uwe Johnson, Hesse, Sarraute, Christa Wolf, and others. She also wrote English subtitles for films by Godard and Edouard Molinaro.

[5]*A Full Moon of Women* lies somewhere between biography and fiction. Molinaro bases her tales on the lives of real women who have been neglected or misrepresented by history but takes poetic license in imagining the details of their lives and consciousnesses.

[6]"Rites of Non-Requital" and the stories cited in the remainder of this article were probably published in literary magazines or anthologies that have not yet been located in the archives of Molinaro. However, all were read to me by Molinaro shortly after she had written them, as was our custom, and were recently rediscovered by me in the collection of manuscripts that exists in her archives.

[7]*The Zodiac Lovers* (1969) and *Life by the Numbers* (1971).

WORKS CITED

Bergonzi, Bernard. Rev. of *Green Lights Are Blue,* by Ursule Molinaro. *New York Review of Books* 24 August 1967: 37-38.

Boyle, Kay. Letter to "Miss Carruth." 22 October 1970.

Brunhoff, Marie-Claude de. Rev. of *Green Lights Are Blue,* by Ursule Molinaro. *La Quinzaine littéraire* 2 May 1969: PAGE #s.

Brodin, Pierre. Rev. of *L'un pour l'autre,* by Ursule Molinaro. *France-Amerique* 15 April 1965.

Fremont-Smith, Eliot. Rev. of *Green Lights Are Blue,* by Ursule Molinaro. *New York Times* 3 May 1967: 47.

Greenland, Colin. Rev. of *A Full Moon of Women,* by Ursule Molinaro. *London Times* May 1990.

Gresset, Michel. "Une imposture sincere." *Le Nouvel Observateur* 31 December 1964.

Johnson, Alexandra. "Wife of, Mother of, Daughter of." Rev. of *A Full Moon of Women,* by Ursule Molinaro. *New York Times Book Review* 2 September 1990: 24.

McElroy, Joseph. Letter to "Jane." Undated.

Molinaro, Ursule. "Dr. Arnold Beidermeier's Suicide Parlors." *Thirteen Stories*. Kingston, NY: McPherson, 1989.

———. "Have You Asked the Leper if He Wants Your Kiss?" *A Full Moon of Women*. New York: Dutton, 1990. 87-91.

———. *The New Moon with the Old Moon in Her Arms*. Kingston, NY: McPerson, 1993.

———. *Sounds of a Drunken Summer*. New York: Harper & Row, 1969.

An Ursule Molinaro Checklist

Fiction

Green Lights Are Blue. New York: New American Library, 1967.
Sounds of a Drunken Summer. New York: Harper & Row, 1969.
The Borrower. New York: Harper & Row, 1970.
Encores for a Dilettante. New York: Fiction Collective, 1977.
The Autobiography of Cassandra, Princess & Prophetess of Troy.
   Danbury, CT: Archer, 1979; Kingston, NY: McPherson, 1992.
Positions with White Roses. Kingston, NY: McPerson, 1983.
Thirteen Stories. Kingston, NY: McPherson, 1989.
A Full Moon of Women. New York: Dutton, 1990.
The New Moon with the Old Moon in Her Arms. London: Women's
   Press, 1990; Kingston, NY: McPherson, 1993.
Fat Skeletons. London: Serif, 1993.
Power Dreamers: The Jocasta Complex. Kingston, NY: McPherson,
   1994.
Demons & Divas: 3 Novels. Kingston, NY: McPherson, 1999.

Nonfiction

The Zodiac Lovers. New York: Avon, 1969.
Life by the Numbers. New York: William Morrow, 1971.

Why Speak Ill of the Surface?
Only the Void Has None.

Ursule Molinaro

Even though the word is said to have been with us since the beginning, it has as bad a reputation as the biblical serpent.

When a thought is expressed inadequately, or an image poorly rendered, it is the word that gets blamed, not the perhaps-not-clearly-enough-thought-out thought, or defective image.

The word is even accused of inadequately translating allegedly inadequate expressions of thought or descriptions of image from one language into another (*traduttore — traditore*).

Perhaps this down-grading attitude stems from the recognition that any expression,   verbal or otherwise,   is subject to the restriction of its form.__Although other forms of human expression: painting/sculpture/dance/music/least of all the self-congratulatory sciences, seem exempt from accusations of inadequacy.__Therefore, using form as an active part of verbal expression seems to enhance the thought, or image, while making an honest word out of the traitor.

Yet, writers who work with an unexpected form to mirror what they wish to say, in word arrangements not conventionally expected to say it, are often accused of letting their style get in the way of their story.

A personal example of the to-be-expected reaction to an unexpected form is a not-unfriendly review which preceded the publication of my latest novel, *Positions with White Roses,* some 18 months ago. It compared my writing to "a balking mule," but added with surprise   that "the device nonetheless works."

It did, however, not work in the imitation of my spacing which the review used to describe it.

Rather than the random sentence breaks used in the review, the spaces used in the novel are a typographical translation of the story's rhythm, isolating islands of afterthought or additional information about a situation, or a character.

As the eyes are forced to pause, the reader's breath cadence becomes synchronized with the rhythm of the story, whose tension—apathy—anguish—humor—etc. communicate themselves at the intended speed, with the intended inflection.

The purpose of the spacing becomes quite evident when the text is read aloud. When the mule does not only balk   when intended   but also dance   slither   trip   catch itself   carry the story, & indulge in passions with the impunity of creatures who, like mules or fictional characters, are their own living end.

Book Reviews

John Barth. *Coming Soon!!!: A Narrative.* Houghton Mifflin, 2001. 396 pp. $26.00.

Coming Soon!!! opens with a variation on the classic message-in-a-bottle motif employed by Barth throughout his career: the discovery by Ditsy, a transgendered *progger*, of a computer disk, waterproofed inside three Ziploc bags, containing an e-novel, which has washed ashore on a Chesapeake Bay marsh. To *prog*, Barth quickly informs us, means "to pick and poke about, to scavenge and to scrounge," in search of nothing in particular, a kind of wetland *dérive*. *Progging*'s aleatory nature provides a clue to the structure of Barth's narrative, which records the probative unfoldings of three works-in-progress: "Coming Soon!!!," the latest postmodern novel by Novelist Emeritus (NE), a character not-so-loosely based on Barth himself; "Coming Soon!!!," the post-PoMo hypertext Ditsy finds, written by Aspiring Novelist (AN) Johns Hopkins "Hop" Johnson, NE's tutee and friendly rival; and "Coming Soon!!!," the potential title of a PoMo or possibly post-PoMo showboat-musical adaptation of the various musical adaptations of Edna Ferber's novel *Showboat,* on which NE and AN collaborate. As veteran readers of Barth's fiction may suspect, *Coming Soon!!!* only imitates aleatory fiction. At his formalist best, Barth is firmly in control here, leaving little to random chance. Similarly, though the novel mimics hyperfiction, its pages sometimes emulating a computer screen, Barth remains self-consciously moored to print, providing his readers no real options for reassembling the novel's narrative strands. Indeed, the old Maestro's bravura orchestration of the multiple components of his latest opus provides one of this text's chief pleasures.

In many respects, *Coming Soon!!!* serves as a companion piece to Barth's 1994 novel *Once upon a Time: A Floating Opera,* which Barth proclaimed was his "Last Book." Like that earlier book, *Coming Soon!!!* is a meditation on last things, among them the century, the millennium, the Novelist Emeritus's career and, soon enough, his life, postmodernism (whose "smoke-and-mirror tricks" Barth's latest mocks, honors, and extends), and the "noble genre of the Novel" itself, which will not die, Barth maintains, so much as it will diminish, along with all print literature, into a coterie pleasure ("like poetry, archery, opera-going, equestrian dressage"). "Stock-taking" novels, both books revisit Barth's first work, *The Floating Opera,* published forty-five years ago, but also manage, through allusion or recycled characters, to evoke everything Barth has written throughout a prolific career (*Coming Soon!!!* is Barth's thirteenth work of fiction and his fifteenth book, its appearance marking the sixth consecutive decade in which he has published). But whereas *Once upon a Time,* a self-described "memoir bottled in a novel," looks backward, *Coming Soon!!!* focuses on continuity (thus its structural emphasis on process), the reciprocity of past, present, and future narrative forms. The thought that new lives, careers, and literary forms will replace those fast fading into history hardly mitigates the novel's sense of loss, however. Barth writes in his cheerful-nihilist mode, his comic mask seldom slipping—but make no mistake, this is an imaginary garden with real pain in it. The third installment (along with the masterful *On with the Story,* the 1996 short story series sandwiched between the novels) in his long farewell to a distinguished career, Barth continues to sing in his chains like the sea. As ever, it's a performance well worth attending. [Charles Harris]

Alfredo Bryce Echenique. *Tarzan's Tonsillitis.* Trans. Alfred MacAdam. Pantheon, 2001. 262 pp. $23.00.

Though a good portion of it is narrated through letters, *Tarzan's Tonsillitis* is much more one man's Bernhardian rambling monologue than epistolary love story. Its narrator would have you believe different, however, and this creates the tension that drives the novel. Juan Manual Carpio, a Peruvian singer-songwriter, narrates the history of his thirty-year love affair with Fernanda María de la Trinidad del Monte Montes, a Salvadoran, whom he meets in 1960s Paris, where they are both a part of the expatriate Boom crowd. Theirs is a star-crossed affair: he, mooning over his absent wife when they first meet, is unable to reciprocate her feelings; she, though still in love with him, marries, has children, and moves back to El Salvador. In his narration Juan Manuel often explains events before presenting Fernanda's letters, which at first bear him out. He also jumps through time and into other characters' heads, speaking at and to himself, often in long, wonderfully convoluted sentences. These twisting digressions (beautifully translated by Alfred MacAdam) are the first clue that there might be an ulterior motive in Juan Manuel's song. As the novel progresses, small discrepancies emerge between the narration and Fernanda's letters. The clarity, emotion, and candor of Fernanda's words puncture the narration's verbal acrobatics. The two voices play off of each other, often contrasting, but also, significantly, harmonizing. For just when the reader begins to wonder if the love affair is mostly a creation of Juan Manuel's mind, a letter from Fernanda will affirm his version of the events. But in the end this is a solo, not a duet—a vain attempt, in reliving the past, to correct past mistakes, to choose what was not and should have been chosen, and ultimately to accept the loss of a lover and the love of a friend. [Gregory Howard]

Mario Vargas Llosa. *The Feast of the Goat.* Trans. Edith Grossman. Farrar, Straus & Giroux, 2001. 404 pp. $25.00.

According to Mario Vargas Llosa, good fiction makes people uneasy. By that standard, his *Feast of the Goat* is a masterpiece, both to the degree it is sure to make readers squirm and for the multitude of reasons it gives them to do so. Set in the Dominican Republic, this triple-plotted novel is at once a fictionalized character study of Rafael "The Goat" Trujillo, the dictator who once ruled that island; of the cell of men who ended his reign by assassination; and of one individual, Urania Cabral, the daughter of a senator who proves his loyalty to the regime by handing over the fourteen-year-old to be deflowered by the seventy-year-old dictator. The novel has already sold 400,000 copies in Spanish, and it's easy to see why: it is a visceral lesson in the complex synergy of political intrigue, sex, machismo, and history, doing a lot to explain the cycle of revolutions and economic dreams unfulfilled that seems to characterize much of Latin America, not just the Dominican Republic. That is—and this is the reason the book deserves an equally wide English readership—without being didactic or absolving Dominicans of responsibility, the novel convincingly demonstrates how all of us in the Americas are Americans, whether or not those readers in the U.S. are aware of the price paid by individuals like Urania for the policies of their own country. Llosa, a former Peruvian presidential candidate, writes as one who knows his political and historical material intimately. The author of novels (e.g., *The Green House*) that explore the nature of narrative, he also writes as one who knows intimately how stories are constructed, be they in the form of literature or the narrative of fear and mythology created by a dictator to stay in power. [Steve Tomasula]

William T. Vollmann. *Argall*. Viking, 2001. 746 pp. $40.00.

Argall, to grossly simplify matters, is the story of two widely known and wildly embellished historical figures, Pocahontas and Captain John Smith, and the less well known Captain Samuel Argall. This main story is one thick thread among many colorful others, including stories about British land ownership, class structure, tribal politics, and the settling of Virginia, all interwoven with purposeful though sometimes meandering digressions and expressed in a dense archaized grammar. The book arrives studded with footnotes, buttressed by a chronology, orthographic notes, six glossaries, and references to source material, and capped off with a formal letter to the "right honourable reader." *Argall* is also the fourth addition to Vollmann's projected Seven Dreams series of ambitious, encyclopedic novels focusing on North America at different historical periods and paying particular attention to the interactions and conflicts between Europeans and native populations. *The Ice-Shirt* imagined tenth-century Nordic invaders. *Fathers and Crows* concerned the Iroquois and French Jesuits of the seventeenth century. *The Rifles* described John Franklin's failed polar expedition. All of the books also tell the parallel story of the books' genesis through Vollmann's personae, who go by various names but usually answer to William the Blind. In these parallel stories, dear readers learn of Vollmann's painstaking but joyful research. In *Argall* William the Blind catalogs the contents of the *Complete Works of John Smith,* a mere six volumes and *Argall*'s primary source. William is a true bibliophile and, for all of the adventure and the placing of himself in harm's way, so is Vollmann. A vast historical imagination is at work here, an imagination that remembers twentieth-century Ithaca, New York, in order to dream convincingly of the seventeenth-century Canadian wilderness. Vollmann's imagination is voracious, intelligent, and by turns critical, scholarly, and playful. It's hard to dream of another to which to compare it. [Paul Maliszewski]

Laird Hunt. *The Impossibly*. Coffee House, 2001. 205 pp. $23.95.

One of the joys of book reviewing is the delight of coming across a brilliant book one might not normally read; one of the difficulties is trying to convey one's enthusiasm without sounding too much the devotee. Put simply, Laird Hunt's *The Impossibly* is one of the most exciting debut novels I have ever read. The prose is a byzantine maze of qualifications, retractions, gaps, and contradictions, detailing the life and loves of some sort of operative (spy or criminal) in some type of organization, in a number of unnamed, presumably European locales. As the character moves from thin to fat to thin again, from young to old(er), from assignment to assignment, from daylight to darkness, the book acquires an absurd but precise energy all its own: like the shelves of the narrator's girlfriend, full of objects that gradually become less knowable, the novel develops with a negative momentum, where the accretion of detail and language detracts from concrete knowledge. As the narrator writes, "To say anything is to complicate it." In *The Impossibly* the ambiguities are meticulously constructed, the ambivalences rigorously maintained. All of this is done with the lightest touch, the surest eye. While most Kafka comparisons are specious and overstated, Hunt's subtle humor, sophisticated intelligence and the graceful timbre of his prose place this novel firmly in the tradition of *The Castle,* as well as Nabokov's *The Eye* and Thomas Bernhard's *The Loser.* This is high praise indeed, but *The Impossibly* is a marvelous, wonderful novel. [Jeffrey DeShell]

Jonathan Franzen. *The Corrections*. Farrar, Straus & Giroux, 2001. 568 pp. $26.00.

For Jonathan Franzen, a writer who has been lambasted by Oprah's minions as too highbrow, too artsy, it must be ironic that the central event of his new novel is a traditional Christmas dinner at home. As *The Corrections* painstakingly unpacks the lives of Alfred and Enid Lambert and their grown children, Franzen introduces an elemental conflict between the authoritarian railroad man, buckling under Parkinson's-induced dementia, and his wife's sentimental "prairie optimism." While the eldest son denies his clinical depression and strives to create a conventional life that will make his overbearing parents proud, his sister, an up-and-coming chef at a trendy Philadelphia restaurant, loses herself in affairs with her boss and his wife. Chip, the favorite son, flees academe after he sleeps with a student, fools around with an absurd screenplay calculated to expose his former lover, and disappears in Lithuania. Franzen brings a postironic sincerity and compassion to his Midwestern *King Lear.* As the Lambert children return to the patriarchal den, Chip wonders, "When had it happened that his parents had become the children who went to bed early and called down for help from the top of the stairs?" The grown children confront the task of charting a life that separates them from their parents' generation at the same time that they must accept the difficult responsibilities of caregivers. Yet as the Lamberts' tale of familial dysfunction turns inward, Franzen's narrative radiates outward, brilliantly weaving a web between the local and the global, the individual and the big picture. An entertaining read that demands our empathy and understanding, *The Corrections* is a great American novel for our time. It is the rare book that engages the heart and the head. [Trey Strecker]

Marcel Bénabou. *Dump This Book While You Still Can!* Trans. Steven Rendall. Intro. Warren Motte. Univ. of Nebraska Press, 2001. 177 pp. Paper: $19.95.

Marcel Bénabou (*Why I Have Not Written Any of My Books*) deserves a prize for creating some of the most intriguing titles of the past fifty years, beyond which lie some of the most playful French writing of recent memory. In contrast to his earlier novels, the focus of *Dump This Book* is on the process of reading instead of writing. The story opens with the narrator discovering a mysterious book amid a pile of volumes given to him by his friend Flauzac. Flipping to its first page, he is assaulted by the author's commands: "Come on, dump this book. Or better yet, throw it as far away as you can." The diatribe goes on for a page, debasing the traditional reasons for reading (such as the desire to find a "bosom buddy" in the author's voice, or "your own image reflected" in the text), giving readers every reason to toss away expectations ("Who cares what you expect, anyway? Whatever it is, you're going to be disappointed") along with the book itself. Although the narrator is put off by these attacks, he believes that there is a secret message hidden in these lines. Determined to uncover this secret, he employs every analytic method he can think of—from Oulipian techniques, to extracting the first letter of each sentence, to reading the pages aloud in the bathtub—yet he is foiled at every turn, a situation that only increases his frustration. In addition, a number of facts about his life come to light and create an equally captivating secondary plot. Slowly, a conspiracy surrounding the volume starts to develop. Reminiscent of *If on a winter's night a traveler,* Bénabou's novel is extremely compelling, even though it constantly forces its readers to question their motives for reading. Steven Rendall's translation is superb, and Warren Motte's introduction is an enlightening look at one of France's top writers. [Chad W. Post]

Nathaniel Mackey. *Atet A.D.* City Lights, 2001. 184 pp. Paper: $13.95.

Do you remember how, back in *those* days, when everyone was partying *real* heavy, there were always a few cats who weren't puttin' the eye on the caboodles, who weren't mainlining the beer from the half-barrel tube, but who were there for the *music?* You could be sitting there talking with one of those cats and he'd be right there until "Unbroken Chain" or "Lester Leaps In" came on, and then he'd be gone—his eyes would roll back in his head, he'd shiver, and then he'd be off—flying a pterodactyl to a beach party hosted by LBJ's daughter. You'd say, "Damn! Let me have what he's had," but you'd already had it. It was just that he could really *hear* the music in a way you couldn't. He could see it, smell it, taste it, touch it. Music was his object. That cat is the narrator of this epistolary novel (third in the series *From a Broken Bottle Traces of Perfume Still Emanate*). He's a tenor sax player in an exploratory jazz quintet called "Molimo M'atet" for whom playing is transcendent, an astral-plane rider whose music leads to grand abstractions, delineating a landscape both hallucinatory and Eastern mystic. This precarious balance between abstract and concrete makes the novel like riding in Atet (the morning boat) through the cloud of unknowing with linguistics as the only paddle and style as the compass. It is some of the most intense, visionary writing about music that I've ever seen. It challenges, it treads, it flies, and it crawls. It's as abstract as the heart of music itself and as concrete as a bicycle crashing to the pavement. [Eckhard Gerdes]

Károly Pap. *Azarel*. Trans. Paul Olchváry. Steerforth, 2001. 219 pp. Paper: $14.00.

Though Károly Pap, laborer, actor and writer, "disappeared" into Bergen-Belsen sometime in 1944, we can count ourselves fortunate that the novel *Azarel* survived. Pap never attempted to conceal his Jewish heritage, as was the fashion of artists during the times of rising anti-Semitism in Europe. Rather, he lumbered on with his writing, revealing both his skepticism and consternation with his Jewish identity, though succumbing to depression when he realized the lack of impact the arts seemed to have on such devastating and tumultuous times. In the novel, Gyuri is the third and youngest son of a modern rabbi and his wife. Gyuri's paternal grandfather, Papa Jeremiah, holds his son and despised daughter-in-law to the promise of giving up one of their sons to him so that he may rear him in the real and true faith of Orthodox Judaism. Papa Jeremiah is fanatically orthodox, contemptuous and hateful of all trends toward progressivism or enlightenment, and considers all seven of his sons to be failures and pagans. Having sacrificed his own desire to immerse himself in the Torah in order to hold a job and support his family, he feels that he is "owed" one of his grandsons. The unfortunate Gyuri is sent to live with Papa Jeremiah in a tent in the yard of the synagogue (thoroughly Old Testament), where he eventually settles into the strange ways of his elder. Eventually, Papa Jeremiah dies and Gyuri is sent back home to live, uneasy in a bourgeois culture he no longer feels at home in. *Azarel* is an unrepentantly semi-autobiographical novel about family, knowledge of self, and the illusory nature of religious devotion. It is one man's account of constant and persistent questioning, though without the pat and standard answers we have all come to expect. [Michelle Reale]

Andreï Makine. *Requiem for a Lost Empire*. Trans. Geoffrey Strachan. Arcade, 2001. 252 pp. $24.95.

Makine's latest novel is a terminal tour of the violent episodes endured by Russia in the twentieth century. A saga that spans three generations of Russian soldiers, *Requiem* maintains an epic feel through its sweeping variation of setting and character. The novel's narrator haunts Third World hotspots around the end of the cold war, reminiscing about his past as he plays at espionage for the homeland. Unable to make sense of the Soviet collapse, he examines his family history for an explanation, beginning with his grandfather, Nikolai. A deserter from the Red Army during the October Revolution, Nikolai sickens of killing and simply returns home, vainly seeking to escape the state-sponsored propaganda that will dog him and his descendents. The most memorable passages of the novel are those dedicated to Nikolai's son, Pavel, who fights as a soldier on the Eastern front in World War II. The cruelty of the Russian officers, who repeatedly send Pavel and his countrymen unarmed to meet the enemy, is equal to that of the German soldiers who wait to kill them. Makine's image of a paralyzed Russian soldier, unable to retreat or advance in battle for fear of being shot by the enemy or his own army, is a fitting metaphor for the inescapable violence of Russia's last century. *Requiem for a Lost Empire* contains a number of episodes in which one of the men seeks to protect a woman from violence. The lives of these degraded women, and the futile attempts to save them, resonate with the vision of Mother Russia, a pure, comforting dream that has been turned nightmarish by repeated violation. Despite the horrific subject matter, this is yet another profoundly humanistic novel from Makine, who continues to earn the sky-high literary comparisons (Proust, Balzac, Tolstoy, Dostoyevsky) thrust upon him. [Jason Picone]

Kate Bernheimer. *The Complete Tales of Ketzia Gold*. FC2, 2001. 192 pp. Paper: $11.95.

The tales in *The Complete Tales of Ketzia Gold*, Kate Bernheimer's intriguing first novel, are the stories Ketzia tells about herself as child and adult and the stories an omniscient narrator tells about her. Much of Bernheimer's book is based on traditional German, Russian, and Yiddish fairy and folk tales. She updates these by changing time, setting and events, and replacing the innocent—or not so—characters of the original tale with Ketzia, Jewish and born in America in the late sixties or early seventies, and with Ketzia's sisters, parents, grandparents and other relatives, and her husband. Thus "Clever Else" in the original Grimms' tale becomes "Clever Ketzia" in the retelling, and poor Else's misfortune as someone with an overabundance of imagination and no common sense at all is mirrored in a broken leg accidentally inflicted by Ketzia on her fiancé and in the unraveling of her marriage. The effect of learning about Ketzia's life in this way is beguiling because although Bernheimer moves the tales out of the once-upon-a-time frame into that of the recent past, she maintains the peculiar quality of the originals, with their mingling of the fantastic and the ordinary. Far from being merely an interesting device, this choice of narrative perfectly reflects the oddity of Ketzia's mind, a mind at times close to psychotic, and battling alienation, depression and despair, yet also capable of astute observations, dry wit and sympathy for others. Dovetailing with the fairy-tale structure and motifs are not only Ketzia's perception of the frequent cruelties and rare delights of life but Bernheimer's knack for capturing the world experienced by a child—how what the child sees and hears is distorted by the inability to distinguish clearly between fiction, dream and reality. A captivating debut novel. [Evelin Sullivan]

Curt Leviant. *Diary of an Adulterous Woman*. Syracuse Univ. Press, 2001. 500 pp. $29.95.

In addition to the main text of the novel, there is an odd "ABC Directory that offers alphabetical tidbits and surprises." (This "Directory" is 111 pages.) Leviant plays with the notion of novels and endings, commentary and criticism. He employs a traditional Judaic format of text (Bible) and commentary (Midrash), but he does more: he shadows the great fiction of Nabokov and Borges. Leviant's novel suggests that love and adultery are, among other things, language games; they are words that have no fixed meaning. It is impossible to omit wordplay from sex or love. Each main character tells a version of the affair(s). Each, in effect, uses language as stimulus or play or secret. Throughout the novel we cannot be sure of meaning. Consider: "Guido is as close as an Italian name can be to *giudeo,* the Italian word for Jew, and still sound like an Italian name. Since the Jews guided the morality of Western civilization, perhaps the word *guido,* or guide, evolved." Guido plays sadistically with Charlie's last name, "Perlmutter," by calling him "Merlputter." "Aviva" is a palindrome—it also means "spying" in Hebrew. And there is further play. Aviva seems to remind both Guido and Charlie of Ava—another palindrome—a woman they both shared in their college years. I could cite many other examples, but they would lead the reader to believe that this novel is simply an erudite puzzle. It is, indeed, a deeply moving demonstration that language has consequences, that it can be destructive. And the novel is a moral work. It ends with brutality, with inexpressible pain. Life "can only be lived, not written about. Some things can never be portrayed in print—or verbalized." [Irving Malin]

Elizabeth Knox. *Black Oxen*. Farrar, Straus & Giroux, 2001. 436 pp. $25.00.

At a moment when we may be tiring of the infinite jestings of postmodern mock-epics, Elizabeth Knox reminds us of their rich satisfactions—call it narrative therapy, a treatment her central character pursues. There is something vivid, even original in the elaborate play of Knox's intrigue: a byzantine plotline that delights in upsetting linearity, that indulges asides with confident, elegant bravura; characters who come and go with astonishing alacrity and who move across a shifting timescape as well as a fluid geography; a delightful confidence in language and a mock-serious indulgence of symbols; a narrative line that accepts the inexplicable; and a determination to skewer an inherited genre—the child-quest for the mysterious parent—by centering the labyrinthine plotline on a disturbed woman who seeks professional help in the California of 2022 to puzzle through whether her father was a human or some alien presence. As with most postmodern gestures at narrative, the tangled lines here do not easily give over to straightening. But *Black Oxen* intrigues rather than tires a reader willing to give into the audacious premise of a novel joyfully able to sustain three narrative worlds: a childhood paradise in late-century Scotland, a fabulous Latin American country undergoing seismic shocks from eccentric revolutionaries, and the California of the narrative present run rampant with ruined celebrities, New Age psychobabblers, and decidedly eccentric millionaires. As crucial (and faux-melodramatic) as the daughter's search for her haunting father proves to be as it unfolds with the full-throttle energy of the nerviest speculative fictions, what enthralls more is the serious game of history: Knox reveals how language assembles, distorts, even invents cultural recollection and, ultimately, the stuff of hope, and how each of us must struggle against the pull of chance to fashion our story. [Joseph Dewey]

Dennis Bock. *The Ash Garden*. Knopf, 2001. 281 pp. $23.00.

The Ash Garden brings together three characters very much products of World War II, its dislocations and violence. Two women, Emiko Amai and Sophie Böll, child survivors of Hiroshima and Linz, live lives of loss despite their "good fortune," which emanates from Sophie's husband, Anton Böll, an atomic scientist who left Germany to work at Los Alamos. Böll discovers Sophie in a refugee camp in Canada in 1943 and plays a critical role in bringing Emiko to the United States for plastic surgery in the mid-1950s. That intertwining of lives forms a central pattern that recurs on several levels of this carefully written and shaped narrative. Emiko's sections of the story appear in the first person, while the Bölls' are told in the third. While the two women lose their families and feel that loss gravely, Böll suffers from an inability to manifest his emotions with any depth. Much like the Edward Teller of the recent *Memoirs* (Perseus, 2001), he too might say, "I deeply regret the deaths and injuries that resulted from the atomic bombings, but my best explanation of why I do not regret working on weapons is a question: what if I hadn't?" Certainly, Böll believes that. Bock, in this first novel, takes us inside the mind of a focused scientist, puts us on the *Enola Gay,* allows us to see the ironies of life and history at work; he succeeds more gracefully than Anton Böll in controlling his creation. While "the ash garden" of Hiroshima nearly finds its balance in Sophie's topiary creations, going to seed because of her illness and consequent inattention, the novel itself, with a touch as delicate and easy as Lily Briscoe's at the end of *To the Lighthouse,* comes satisfyingly together. [Richard J. Murphy]

Iain Sinclair. *Landor's Tower.* Granta, 2001. 345 pp. $24.95.

No one writes like Iain Sinclair. First, there's the idiosyncrasy of his preoc-cupations, among which one might list obscure genre writers, the history and character of London, Jack the Ripper, draw-blood booksellers, leftist politics, the city's—all of society's—disenfranchised. Then there's his style, as gravid and confounding as Europe's ancient encrusted streets. Indeed, his sentences sweat and huff and fart with the meaning packed onto them. In Sinclair's hands, language simultaneously builds the world and con-sumes it. In *Landor's Tower* as in previous novels such as *White Chappell Scarlet Tracings, Downriver,* and *Radon Daughters,* discrete narratives be-gin on parallel tracks and, contrary to all our assumptions, converge. The best way to envision a Sinclair novel may be as a three-dimensional chess set, with Sinclair shuttling vertically, horizontally and obliquely from level to level: historical, socio-literary, personal, political, obsessive. The house game is always fixed. Replacing standard narrative strategies with a series of loose foci, Sinclair allows these to breed among themselves a host of cor-respondences, contradictions, collisions, corrections. It's rather like sitting in the optometrist's chair as he clicks numbered lenses into place, asking Which is clearer, this? this? Here, the story of Walter Savage Landor's re-turn to Wales is interleaved with Sinclair's failure to write a book about Landor and with two booksellers' doomed pursuit of rare editions. One hopes that *Landor's Tower,* along with Granta's reissue of new editions of *White Chappell Scarlet Tracings, Radon Daughters, Lud Heat,* and *Rodinsky's Room,* may bring Sinclair to the attention of U.S. readers. The current state of publishing here certainly does little to encourage that hope. But Iain Sinclair, palpably, is a fine and (I rush to use a word often shied away from) an important writer. [James Sallis]

Jim Crace. *The Devil's Larder.* Farrar, Straus & Giroux, 2001. 165 pp. $20.00.

The Devil's Larder is a collection of sixty-four very short stories—the long-est several pages, the shortest just two words—having to do with cooking and eating all sorts of food, from extravagant dishes to ordinary cans. Crace, the author of six novels, including *Quarantine* and *Being Dead,* sets his stories in an unnamed village. Many of the stories arise from the village's collective identity as a culturally distinct place beset by outsiders. Villagers versus those tourists, those university students, and those rich people just driving through are conflicts that play out in a number of stories told from the villagers' point of view. (When a chef intentionally starts serving plates of bad mussels to visiting troublemakers, the locals come to watch for sport.) Crace's language, always precise and fascinated with naming things, has in this book relaxed somewhat. Crace writes as if he's recording the oral legends of a place we've never been. The narrator in one story says that the devil is seen at night, in the woods, pulling mushrooms from his sack and planting them in the ground. It's an old story, seeming like a lost work of Grimm, something children somewhere are told before bed. At the same time, the details are contemporary—one recent sighting was by people piling out of a bar—and the narrator's voice can be casual, relating his own supernatural encounter as no big deal: "So I was curious when he and I crossed paths." There are many courses here, each prepared superbly, but like any feast, there are a few tastes that repeat from story to story. Crace is interested in our appetites and our ability or inability to restrain them. Feelings of satisfaction here are never far from feelings of discontent, as desire can quickly become disgust. [Paul Maliszewski]

Bruce Olds. *Bucking the Tiger*. Farrar, Straus & Giroux, 2001. 371 pp. $25.00.

Bruce Olds's second novel follows his successful debut several years back, *Raising Holy Hell,* a fictionalized account of the life of John Brown. Olds assembled that first book from scraps of historical documents, newspaper accounts, private correspondence, reminiscences, recollections, and fiction, among other sources. The result was a burning, wavering image of a man: part mad, part angel, part devil. In *Bucking the Tiger* Olds employs the same strategy with the life of Doc Holliday, the consumption-wracked gambler and bogeyman of the Old West. Olds expands his literary range as well, working not only with historical documents but choosing at times to break such documents into verse and reenvisioning Doc's life as poetry. In this he owes something to Paul Metcalf, who transformed nonfictional documents into mixed-genre poetry in works such as "I-57" and "U.S. Dept. of the Interior." He owes something as well to Michael Ondaatje's *The Collected Works of Billy the Kid*—though while Ondaatje's poetry is the strongest portion of his text, Olds's is the weakest. *Bucking the Tiger* explores Holliday's life in incredible and varied detail, leading carefully up to the event that immortalized Holliday—the Shootout at the O.K. Corral—and then moving from there into his slow decline toward death. On either side, Olds presents views of Holliday, his lover, and his gambling and explores the nature of history and myth. Olds never allows us to forget Holliday's illness and is marvelous in his ability to present Holliday as a man in decay. Ultimately, Holliday makes a less intriguing character than Brown did, for Brown was at the heart of an extraordinary conflux of ideas and tensions while Holliday simply is not. There is genuinely brilliant writing throughout, but the cumulative effect is slightly less than that of *Raising Holy Hell*. [Brian Evenson]

Dick Wimmer. *Irish Wine: The Trilogy*. Penguin, 2001. 330 pp. Paper: $13.00.

Irish Wine is an exuberant romp through Ireland, Britain, and the United States. It is part *Candide,* part *Ginger Man,* and part *At Swim-Two-Birds* in its wild pacing, its zany collection of misfits, and its bizarre coincidences and love triangles. There's so much action in these three novellas that it's hard to keep pace; it is as if one were trying to follow a cartoon played at fast-forward. The central figures are Seamus Boyne, a painter living in Ireland, and Gene Hagar, a failed writer who is running his family's pest control business on Long Island. At the outset, both men are down on their luck. At the same time that Boyne is trying to commit suicide, sinister characters are trying to murder him. Hagar hates the family business and his wife has just left him. Wimmer traces the late flowering of Boyne's career as an artist when he is lauded by the art world and raised to the level of celebrity, as well as the rebirth of Hagar as a fiction writer and teacher. He also explores the women, both living and dead, with whom they have shared their lives. Both Ciara, Hagar's lost love and the subject of Boyne's best work, and Tory, Boyne's daughter (who will become Hagar's wife), are delightfully unpredictable. Although Wimmer has a good understanding of the comic possibilities present in the Anglo-Irish world, the best work of the trilogy is to be found in *Hagar's Dream,* the American novella. In particular, the softball games on Long Island involving Hagar, his friends from high school, and Boyne are side-splitting. Among other things, this final novella is as wonderful a send-up of *The Great Gatsby* as one is likely to read. [Eamonn Wall]

Édouard Glissant. *The Fourth Century*. Trans. Betsy Wing. Univ. of Nebraska Press, 2001. 294 pp. Paper: $20.00.

The Fourth Century opens as young Mathieu Béluse, seeking guidance from Papa Longoué, a *quimboiseur,* asks him to "tell [him] about the past. . . . Just what is it?" It is this question that drives the novel, and the past Mathieu desires to know is not only the "unofficial" past of his country, Martinique, but is in fact his own family's past, which spans four centuries. Mathieu and Papa Longoué are the last living members of their respective families, first brought to Martinique as slaves in 1788, and their histories have been intertwined from the start. While the first Longoué escapes from slavery, Béluse remains captive, and in future generations the two lines converge in marriage and in murder. Now the last remaining Béluse has come to the last remaining Longoué to discover the hidden past, the past not in the history textbooks Mathieu has been reading. As the two reconstruct history, we come to see that Papa Longoué is in fact making Mathieu his heir. As much as *The Fourth Century* is a meditation on the complex history of these two families, it is equally (if not more so) a meditation on the very nature of history and of language. I can think of no way to describe the narrative of this novel other than Faulknerian. Glissant's novel seems deeply indebted to Faulkner, as it blurs the lines between past and present, allows for extended stream-of-consciousness narration, and illustrates the ambiguous — and perhaps unknowable — nature of history. (Glissant's *Faulkner, Mississippi* further proves this connection.) The struggle that *The Fourth Century* so beautifully presents in Mathieu and Papa Longoué's search for and reconstruction of the past is in fact a universal struggle that, as Mathieu discovers in the final pages, "has no end and no beginning." [Jason D. Fichtel]

Martin Nakell. *Two Fields That Face and Mirror Each Other*. Green Integer, 2001. 287 pp. Paper: $16.95.

The phrase *novel of ideas* doesn't exactly apply to Martin Nakell's thoughtful *Two Fields That Face and Mirror Each Other* because of the nineteenth-century baggage evoked by the term. And yet some similar description, say conceptual art in the shape of a book, surely applies. Though there is a plot (sort of a family saga in which Grey leaves his lover Gloriana back in New York to visit a family farm in Michigan and attend the funeral of George, a friend's son, who kidnapped and killed his stepbrother before committing suicide), the plot is the least of it. Indeed, the novel is strongest when it functions less like Stendhal's mirror traveling down the road of life and more like textual art on the subject of identity: a weave of meditative sections in which, for example, Grey sitting on a porch in Michigan and watching the repetitive work of a farmer preparing a crop is counterpointed with Gloriana's observation of the emotional cycles that a "tribe" of stock traders goes through trying to predict wheat prices — just one manifestation of the many fields that face and mirror each other. As the characters struggle with a plethora of dichotomies, e.g. how family values in Michigan can translate into the legal defense of a man known guilty of murder in New York, the novel looks deeper into these mirrors facing mirrors until we are considering the nature of narrative itself. And this may be the most convincing aspect of the novel: a demonstration that just when you think it's all been done in the novel, a novel of ideas can still reflect its own rich traditions even as it mirrors them in ways that are meaningful to our contemporary cultural field, where neither people nor institutions can be explained by naive looking. [Steve Tomasula]

Elizabeth McCracken. *Niagara Falls All Over Again*. Dial, 2001. 308 pp. $23.95.

McCracken presents a quirky love story between two physically mismatched misfits: Rocky Carter, fat funny man, and his comedy partner Mike (né Mose) Sharp — Abbott to Mr. Carter's Costello. The tale of their rise to stardom and thirty-year partnership — from the waning days of vaudeville to the golden age of Hollywood — is styled as a memoir told by arch straight man Sharp. Finally, the straight man has the chance to upstage the wag, and this time he gives himself all the best lines. Sharp's reminiscences—from his humble beginnings in Valley Junction, Iowa, as a serious boy with dreams of stardom to the excesses of Hollywood—have all the hallmarks of a celebrity tell-all. Luckily, though, McCracken's narrative gifts lift Sharp's story far above the familiar ghostwritten dross with glossy pictures in the middle. With her ear for snappy dialogue, she re-creates and invents Who's-on-First-type routines for Mose and Rocky, which are a pleasure to read. She breaks all the rules of writing funny: she breaks down the jokes, she explains gags. She even makes pratfalls and mugging *read* funny. Furthermore, she lends lyricism to the schtick: the physical ease between Mose and Rocky is an affecting dramatization of their deepening friendship. Her affectionate treatment of stage business enlivens the world of vaudeville and illuminates a close partnership between two men who depend on each other to deliver the jokes. Unfortunately, success allows Carter and Sharp to get lazy and to make a string of forgettable movies, which recycle the same jokes that made them famous. What was a subtle and sharp story of friendship between two men becomes a series of tragedies and triumphs. In the end, the men's success on the big screen is no match for the offbeat appeal of vaudeville as told in the first half of the book. [Nicole Lamy]

Arnošt Lustig. *The Bitter Smell of Almonds: Selected Fiction*. Trans. Vera Borkovec, et al. Northwestern Univ. Press, 2001. 724 pp. Paper: $25.95.

The fiction of Arnošt Lustig currently in English translation is gathered in two collections of stories, *Street of Lost Brothers* and *Indecent Dreams;* a novel, *Dita Saxova;* and this large, rewarding volume. Each proves to be compelling reading, for Lustig, survivor of three concentration camps, presents the Final Solution as so many variations upon sheer petty cruelty. From the disgruntlement of three Jews huddled together in a camp bunk for warmth as lice and infirmities torment their unspoken recognition of an almost certain fate, to the disappointment of a Prague prostitute who harbors a haughty SS magistrate intent upon eluding his pursuers as capitulation is imminent, Lustig's eerie authority, his feel for this harrowing theme, emerges in the sordid details of what his several characters endure. Whether victims clinging to hope of living another day in the camps or Nazis abusing their prey and themselves to fulfill the Reich's imperious demands, in Lustig's dispassionately lyrical rendition of lives reaching a crossroads, their last, desperate hours stand excruciatingly revealed. Lustig presents his appalling catalog as a series of reversals of expectation. An orphan girl's discovery of responsibility for the murder of her family leads to a passionate expression that catches her ardent lover off guard. Relief among a gathering of civilians in occupied territory at apparently having escaped wartime death subsides as they realize that "safety" remains an absurd concept while armed Nazis prowl the streets. Nineteen-year-old Dita Saxova, who survived the camps when millions died, cannot reconcile herself to any future but frivolity and disappointment in the search for love.

Life is a will-o'-the-wisp, a fortunate escape, grinding hardship for an eva-
nescent reward—what avails, if terror retains the upper hand? Arnošt
Lustig offers no quarter in depicting what happened to so many; he knows
it all too well. [Michael Pinker]

Mónica Lavín, ed. *Points of Departure: New Stories from Mexico*. Trans.
Gustavo V. Segade. City Lights, 2001. 159 pp. Paper: $15.95.

This collection of seventeen short stories brings together Mexican writers
born in the fifties and sixties, many of whom have never been translated
into English. The collection is a testament to the thriving short-story genre
in Mexico, and it provides the reader with a broad selection of literary
strategies and thematic issues. Most important, the collection demonstrates to readers who tend to assume that all Latin American writers practice magical realism that there are a vast array of aesthetic practices
present in contemporary Mexican writing. While the writers included re-
side in different regions of Mexico, the majority are from the capital. Consequently, many of the stories take place in urban settings and show a raw
edge similar to the grittiness found in contemporary Mexican films like
Amores perros. We see the frustration, urgency, and tensions of a woman
who falls in love while in prison in "Queen of Shadow" (Bernardo Ruíz), as
well as the despair and pessimism of an entrepreneur who owns a failing
paint business in "The Big Brush" (David Toscana). These stories show a
Mexican culture hard to romanticize and exoticize. Some of the stories tell
of failed romances, but they display none of the melodramatic tendencies
often associated with Mexican culture. Mónica Lavín's "Why Come Back?"
is a harsh tale of a couple's reconciliation after adultery, and Josefina
Estrada's "June Gave Him the Voice" is a haunting tale of a husband who
finds his wife dead. These two stories dispel many myths of Mexican romance and they provide us with disturbing visions of failed marriages. This
collection of stories makes a valuable contribution to Latin American texts
in translation; it provides readers with a glimpse of the range and intensity
of contemporary Mexican literature. [Sophia A. McClennen]

Erika Krouse. *Come Up and See Me Sometime*. Scribner, 2001. 202 pp. $22.00.

The characters populating Erika Krouse's first book are in many respects
similar to the now-familiar thirtysomething denizens of popular culture:
youngish but consciously aging; cynical but in love; hungry but unsure how,
or if, they might be satisfied. In spite of living in a familiar world, these
characters seem motivated by a far more introspective and personal sense
of exploration than their prototypes. In a brilliant use of structural counter-
point, Krouse punctuates this collection of thirteen stories with the lines of
Mae West. In context, West's words become more than the witty and now-familiar one-liners of the original liberated woman. Ranging in tone from

funny and playful to hard and cynical, these epigraphs provide the book with a sense of cohesiveness and become a unifying concept to a collection whose consistency might otherwise seem incidental. West's humor, insisting upon the limitations and failures of love, effectively reveals the themes of sadness, loss, and loneliness that are the dark center of the book's humor. Krouse's protagonists are marked by a similar darkness, albeit one insisting upon progression and possibility. Other themes, more subtly explored, have to do with a sense of morality and responsibility, as well as a struggle toward self-actualization. Before the penultimate piece in the collection, "Via Texas," one of the few short-short pieces, a lesser-know West line appears: "I'm going to give you a little inside information—I'm going to leave you the first chance I get." In context, it becomes hard to think of West as simply the original liberated woman. The narrator of the story seems as motivated by her fears as by her desires. [Suzanne Scanlon]

Allan Gurganus. *The Practical Heart: Four Novellas*. Knopf, 2001. 322 pp. $25.00.

These novellas remind me of James's ghostly narrative "The Jolly Corner," which explores similar convolutions of art, sexuality, and duplicity. They feature subtle explorations of sexuality and childhood; their titles hint at secretive connections, hermetic yearnings. In "He's One, Too," Dan, the "straight" married man, is caught molesting a teenager. The molestation is really a sting arranged by the adolescent's father, a policeman who arranges and photographs the scene. Gurganus demonstrates that the policeman is a queer double—at least partially—of Dan. The incident—the tabloid scene—becomes a revelation. "Saint Monster," although perhaps forced in its linkage of the Bible and the sexual awakening of the narrator, still manages to discover/recover "seeds." The narrator's portrait of his ugly, weak father is redemptive—and deliberately confusing: Is Clyde really his father? Is Clyde black or white? Gurganus's style rescues the novella from sensationalism and innocence. Consider this one brilliant detail: "And there, conscious in the shallows, one huge black catfish, all mouth and whisker, both knob eyes strenuous, aimed at me . . . It was the mask of Comedy, charcoal-dark, given fins. It appeared aggrieved toward some necessary Wit." The most brilliant achievement of the collection, "Preservation News," is, like the others, a work of preservation—the persistence of memory—and reconstruction. A mansion is linked to the AIDS-wrecked body of Worth, a preservationist. (How often Gurganus stresses structures!) An old woman, now writing the complete account of the building, and Worth are joined by this amazing quotation from Rilke: "It is as if the image of this house had fallen into me from an infinite height and shattered upon my ground." Gurganus, at his best, elevates his material. He, like James, compels us to admire marvelous ruins of body and mansion. They become omens of supernatural intervention. They are masterly renderings. [Irving Malin]

Robert Buckeye. *Pressure Drop*. Amandla Publishing (Box 431, East Middlebury, VT 05740), 2001. 71 pp. Paper: $15.00.

"Buckeye," the constructed persona of the author in this dreamy, philosophical, sexy pressure-dropping novel, finds his way from Vermont to Vieques—less to get away from the pressures at Middlebury College and recover from a virus than to recover from his divorce from Nancy. He follows a friend's advice: "Find someone while you're down there. Spend a few days with her." That someone is the sexy Liz. However, when pressure drops, storms follow, and now that he has left home in order to be himself and find himself, he obsesses about his past lovers, his friends, his place in the world. What he discovers is that he and his fellow travelers are, in truth, all mask-wearers. The reality he had thought he'd find is an artificial construct resulting from a peculiar and precarious balance between ugly Americans (tourists who end up staying, as well as the U.S. Navy personnel stationed on the island), hostile locals, and the disaffected—all of whom don their masks for one another in order to fulfill roles they believe they have to play. Buckeye focuses on this irony beautifully. The escape from reality that is meant to be some sort of rediscovery of a preferred reality is ultimately merely temporary. In a chapter set in a *público* van where the passengers all wear masks—the gringo, the elderly lovers, the angry young *independista,* the nervous nineteen-year-old girl, the lecher, the driver— not only can they not see behind each other's masks, they cannot see out of their own. Masks become blinders. Ironically, when Buckeye returns to Vermont unrefreshed albeit ostensibly sans masks, he remembers his mother's advice: "You do not let them know they've hurt you. You put it behind you." Or, in other words, the masks can't ever come off. [Eckhard Gerdes]

Karen Tei Yamashita. *Circle K Cycles*. Coffee House, 2001. 147 pp. Paper: $16.95.

This collection mixes short story with essay, diary with advertisement, and photograph with recipe, for an intriguing blend that mirrors the lives of its fragmented subjects. Yamashita's visually arresting book concerns the Japanese diaspora in Brazil and their migration back to Japan via a 1990 law allowing descendants of Japanese emigrants to return to their homeland in order to work. Lured back to Japan with promises of wealth and glamorous occupations, these *dekasegi* (migrant laborers in Japan) quickly discover the drudgery of low-paying, dangerous factory work. Estranged from one homeland by distance and the other by language and memory, *dekasegi* turn to one another for community and comfort in their few hours of leisure time. Japanese decorum threatens even this respite, as the cultures collide over issues such as noise level, the proper way to sort trash, and public displays of affection. Yamashita explores this cultural terrain through her journal writing and fiction, alternating the two genres even as she inserts graphics and photographs of each culture throughout her book. The deceivingly light fictions of *Circle K Cycles* gain richness as the short

REVIEW OF CONTEMPORARY FICTION

stories begin to overlap and characters reemerge from different points of view. Supplied both in English and Portuguese, Yamashita's most emblematic story is "Zero Zero One-derful," a prodigious transcript of three phone conversations that one woman holds concurrently. An advisor to other *dekasegi,* Maria Mandalena counsels floundering newcomers while also chatting with a friend on another line. The third line is a phone sex service alluded to in the title and Maria effortlessly negotiates her wildly divergent conversations, switching from one to another in the same manner that Yamashita successfully crosses boundaries of genre. *Circle K Cycles*'s brilliant fusing of forms is perfectly suited to its subject matter, giving insight into the kaleidoscopic lives of *dekasegi.* [Jason Picone]

Mempo Giardinelli. *The Tenth Circle*. Trans. Andrea G. Labinger. Latin American Literary Review Press, 2001. 93 pp. Paper: $13.95.

Mempo Giardinelli's *The Tenth Circle* is a fast-paced survey of an adulterous couple's fall. The quick first chapter comes to a close when Romero, the first-person narrator, "offhandedly" suggests, "We ought to kill your husband." When Griselda responds, "And how would we do it?" their descent into the circles of hell becomes inevitable. Romero, a successful real estate mogul, compares the small Argentinean town of Resistencia to the fictitious Peyton Place—a small New England town where the powerful Martin Peyton rules with ruthless abandon. Like Peyton Place, where "nothing happens until everything happens," the mundane becomes overwhelmed by an ever-widening circle of murders, starting with Antonio, Griselda's husband and Romero's business partner. As they make their dash to Peru, Griselda and Romero find it convenient to continue their murderous spree. In the end, Griselda and Romero pit themselves against each other "because it all came down to the fact that one of us had to kill the other. We had reached a dead-end street, and just as I comprehended it, so did Griselda: either I killed her, or she was going to kill me." *The Tenth Circle,* Mempo Giardinelli's second novel to be translated into English, is similar to his more successful *Sultry Moon,* which topped Argentina's best-sellers list for twenty-seven weeks and won Mexico's National Book Award in 1999. *Sultry Moon* is also a fast-paced thriller in which a successful Argentinean student, a graduate of a prestigious university in France, becomes a violent aggressor on the run over the course of an evening. Even though *The Tenth Circle* repeats a number of the moves made in *Sultry Moon,* the hour spent reading the novel is an hour well spent. [Alan Tinkler]

Manuel Rivas. *The Carpenter's Pencil*. Overlook, 2001. 166 pp. $24.95.

This is the story of Dr. Daniel Da Barca, a Republican doctor in the Civil War, who fought against Franco and survived his prisons. It is begun by a journalist who has been assigned by his paper to write about Da Barca, who has returned from exile in Mexico after Franco's death. It is continued by Herbal, a prison guard during the Civil War assigned to shadow Da Barca while he is in prison. In a bordello he now manages, Herbal tells his memories of Da Barca to Maria da Visitacao, a prostitute from an island off the Atlantic coast of Africa. The journalist's story does not get told, but by framing his story with Herbal's, Rivas underlines how stories should be written and who they are for. For the journalist, the story has nothing to do with himself. For Herbal, it is, in some way, recognition, if not validation, of his own life. One permits poetic license. The other cannot escape what has happened, no matter the poetic license. One is news, information, that one may use, but is not part of one's life. The other is how the tribe makes sense of itself. With Rivas we are in the presence of a storyteller who tells his stories around the fire, rather than that of a novelist, whose books are read in solitude in studies or bedrooms. Call it *testimonio,* oral history, coffee klatch, or the talk of a family reunion or neighborhood bar, but it is the purest form of keeping the past alive and bringing people together. The Carpenter's pencil (which Herbal takes after he shoots him to put him out of his misery) is both a tangible artifact of that past and also a concrete metaphor of how it may be kept alive. [Robert Buckeye]

Ivy Goodman. *A Chapter from Her Upbringing.* Carnegie Mellon Univ. Press, 2001. 223 pp. Paper: $15.95.

In a world in which almost anything can happen, and in which almost anything can be imagined and any imagining publicized as rumor or fact, it is fascinating that human emotions still have the mystique and power to surprise and thrill. This thought came to me after reading several of Ivy Goodman's stories from her collection *A Chapter from Her Upbringing.* Goodman's stories are of atmospheres evoked with precise details and peopled by characters brimming with ambition, confusion, desire, pain, and rage, people aware of their own experience sometimes to the point of paralysis yet able to imagine not merely the social lives but the interior lives of others. It is possible that such stories will never grow old or irrelevant. In one of Susan Sontag's early essays, she says, "*Transparence* is the highest, most liberating value in art—and in criticism—today. Transparence means experiencing the luminousness of the thing in itself, of things being what they are." In Goodman's stories one gets the sense of experiencing people as they (we) are, gifted and flawed. Here are stories of artist colleagues who befriend and exploit each other, a dieting man infatuated with a skeletal (Death-like) woman he sees on the street, an immigrant Jewish woman who begins to feel at home in America when she sees an opportunity to prosper, a fat poor white woman in the midst of a breakup with a handsome but unloving black male, an insensitive doctor, friends whose unlikely friendship ends in betrayal, and a grandmother's indifference proving to be a form of freedom for her grandson; not characters merely, but human beings, every one. [Daniel Garrett]

Suhayl Saadi. *The Burning Mirror*. Polygon, 2001. 240 pp. Paper: £9.99.

Polygon—the paperback imprint of Edinburgh University Press, distributed in the United States by Columbia University Press—publishes an interesting series of Scottish fiction. Many of the books, like those of Kelman and Walsh, are written in dialect—which, although it makes us turn to glossaries at the back of the book, also compels us to read every phrase carefully. *The Burning Mirror* is especially intriguing because the author is a Pakistani living in Scotland. He is "translingual"—at home in at least two languages and traditions. This collection is a wonderful example of the "translingual imagination." One story, entitled "Ninetynine Kiss-o-grams," is a fascinating account of a son who returns to Lahore to claim his inheritance. Although the theme is a traditional one, here it assumes a strange dimension. The narrator seeks an inheritance of land and language. Thus the very style of the writer is cracked or deceptive or duplicitous. The narrator thinks at one point, "I'll choke on ma ane land, he thought and then he almost laughed through the tears, but it was too hot tae laugh. Behind him sat the stupit car he'd used tae get there; it wis meant tae *be only twelve miles, bhai, fifteen at the most,* but it had taken longer than the drive from Glasgee tae Edinburgh on a rainy day, roadworks-an-aw." The fact that we have a sense of displacement, that we are in an odd land of "exile," may trouble us, but we are forced to read closely, to find a home in words. This demanding collection gives us a sense of dizziness, but it is this very vertigo that is one of the beauties of the text. We feel, as did ancient explorers, that we are in a new world. [Irving Malin]

Antony Polonsky and Monika Adamczyk-Garbowska, eds. *Contemporary Jewish Writing in Poland: An Anthology*. Univ. of Nebraska Press, 2001. 349 pp. $60.00.

The third volume in Nebraska's Jewish Writing in the Contemporary World series, *Contemporary Jewish Writing in Poland* gathers stories and novel excerpts along with a few dozen poems by "postwar 'Polish-Jewish' writers." Such writers are defined by the editors as those who work in Polish, treat Jewish material, "define themselves as Jews and stress their ties with Jewish culture." That these writers are "contemporary," however, may be misleading: eight of the collection's twelve authors are dead, and the youngest of the four still alive was born in 1937. Although the collection contains many pages of fiction already available in English (by Adolf Rudnicki, Ida Fink, Stanislaw Benski, and Bogdan Wojdowski), it likewise introduces to American readers several previously untranslated writers: Henryk Grynberg, Julian Stryjkowsi, Stanislaw Wygodzki, Artur Sandauer, Zofia Grzesiak, Leo Lipski, Hanna Krall, and Antoni Slonimski. The selections, perhaps unsurprisingly, focus mostly on prewar Jewish life, the Holocaust, and postwar efforts to come to grips with that catastrophic horror and loss. Cumulatively, these twelve authors create a vivid chronicle of what Rudnicki calls the "Apocalypse . . . people grew used to." And yet, Bogdan

Wojdowski avers, this apocalypse, exposed, must cause the world "to bite down on its fingers to stop itself from crying out in horror." Between these two assessments—between what Stanislaw Wygodzki describes as "the silence and its voice"—can be found the tortured heart of this anthology. A handsomely produced book that includes a glossary and detailed publication histories as well as a substantial introduction and informative headnotes that should help orient readers historically, biographically, and thematically, *Contemporary Jewish Writing in Poland* tells stories both atrociously familiar and startlingly unexpected. [Brooke Horvath]

Frank Lentricchia. *Lucchesi and The Whale*. Duke Univ. Press, 2001. 115 pp. $17.95.

The belly of Frank Lentricchia's *Lucchesi and The Whale* is a thirty-five-page meditation on *Moby-Dick*. Surrounding this are several brief scenarios in the life, career, and fantasies of one Thomas Lucchesi—"relentless reader and rumored writer." While these other chapters (which tend toward the metafictional and the metaphysical) have their moments, they are far less inspired than the central section on Melville. This chapter, "Chasing Melville," takes as its starting point the fact that while the title of Melville's novel is "Moby HYPHEN Dick," the name of the whale in it is actually "Moby UNHYPHEN Dick." From this seemingly minute point, Lucchesi weaves a wonderful reading not only of *Moby-Dick* and Melville, but also of fathers and sons, writers and writing, texts, the universe, death. Occurring in a book that positions itself as fiction takes the pressure off the need for any of these ideas to be "true." But it needn't. As Roland Barthes so aptly showed, criticism may be personal, quirky, creative, and eccentric and feel no less true for all that. What criticism is, at its best, is the joy at the heart of all reading—an agile mind interacting with a text that helps to inspire that agility. Lucchessi's take on *Moby-Dick* may be profound revelation or deconstructionist over-reading, but it is most definitely a pleasure. [T. J. Gerlach]

Micheline Aharonian Marcom. *Three Apples Fell from Heaven*. Riverhead, 2001. 270 pp. $23.95.

In words cheapened by their appearance on the jackets of a thousand and one mediocre books, but necessary here: This is an impressive work dealing with family, memory, and loss. *Three Apples Fell from Heaven* is a first novel inspired by actual events during the years of the Armenian genocide, and as such, it's a catalog of horrors. Among the several narrators who describe their sufferings is an infant left alone to die in a wasteland, the offspring of a tortured father and a mother who perishes of want during a forced march. The tale is terrible, but the brevity of the child's existence spares him many of the brutal details that other chapters do not spare the reader. Scattered accounts of political rape, mutilation, and murder are told in a kind of matter-of-fact poetry and are threaded together by a central figure, Anaguil, an orphaned young woman whose life is saved at the expense of much else. She is taken in by her Islamic neighbors and forcibly assimilated into the culture that seeks to eradicate her own, at once stripped of family, opportunity, and language. The beauty of the novel lies mainly in the questions Anaguil's dislocation raises—how can memory be retained, how can meaning be sought, how can a story be expressed when everything, even one's native vocabulary, is gone? Marcom fluidly weaves English, Armenian, and Turkish as she commemorates public history and private struggle in a work of unrelieved intensity. Marcom doesn't offer much redemption—as one of her anguished narrators puts it, "to die is different from what anyone supposed, in this sacrifice I do not know what is made holy"—but this book is proof that many of the figures on these pages prevail. [James Crossley]

David Albahari. *Bait.* Trans. Peter Agnone. Northwestern Univ. Press, 2001. 117 pp. Paper: $14.95.

In *Bait,* a poet in exile imagines a story he might write, if he were a writer. Recalling his early life in postwar Yugoslavia while sitting in a restaurant on an island in a Canadian city with a writer friend, David Albahari's intent Serbian-Jewish intellectual cannot ignore the appeal of a voice from the past. While atrocities in present-day Bosnia and Croatia slide past him, this poet tries to convince Donald, his Canadian friend, that on some reel-to-reel tapes he has carried around with him for years lies a story beyond his ability to express. Donald's stepfather's rickety old tape recorder has unearthed a voice, a spoken language, once dear but now nearly forgotten, which enthralls the poet. His mother's anecdotal recollection of life during and after the Holocaust, surviving two husbands and untold privations, has to be told. Not even Donald's cajoling skepticism can deflate this conviction. As the disturbing effect of his mother's confessions ensnares him, far removed in time and space from the source, her only surviving son realizes that his Holocaust is not yet over. After his father's death in the fifties, Albahari's unnamed protagonist convinces his mother to record her impressions of her former life, despite her misgivings. Years later, her familiar plain speaking rekindles a sense of his past with unexpected vehemence. Listening to his mother relate her observations, he reels, unnerved by what he believed had been relegated to obscurity. Even hearing his own stumbling efforts to get his mother to say *something* during their recording sessions becomes almost too painful. As his unwound thoughts careen between past and present, the postwar Balkans and nineties Canada, at the prompting of a haunting reminder of a situation he has never put behind him, Albahari's poet submits to his worst fears. [Michael Pinker]

Brady Udall. *The Miracle Life of Edgar Mint*. Norton, 2001. 423 pp. $24.95.

The eponymous protagonist of Brady Udall's first novel possesses the un-canny ability to survive above all else. The very first line of the book, nar-rated by Edgar, sets its morosely droll tone: "If I could tell you only one thing about my life it would be this: when I was seven years old the mail-man ran over my head." Thus begins a whimsical, fresh novel chronicling the misadventures and triumphs of an Apache boy. Udall gleefully peoples this coming-of-age story with eccentrics and outcasts and limns a likeable though flawed hero. Other characters include Edgar's truant mom, whose idea of decorative flair is to string empty Pabst Blue Ribbon cans on the barren trees in their yard; the lamentable, suffering mailman of the open-ing scene; the megalomaniacal doctor who saves Edgar's life and then pro-ceeds to shadow him everywhere like a menacing detective; and Art, an avuncular middle-aged man who rooms with Edgar at St. Divine's hospital and significantly presents to the boy—who, because of his head injury, is unable to handwrite—the Hermes Jubilee 2000 typewriter. Adrift in a wil-derness of people and places, typing (writing) for Edgar becomes a main-stay that provides both solace and sanity. In a prose style that is spare yet exuberant, Udall deftly manages to portray a compellingly human charac-ter awash in a set of sometimes overwhelmingly cruel circumstances with-out resorting to mawkish sentimentality. Edgar's unremitting search for family, friends, and the misinformed mailman betrays a great sadness and longing but also reserves room for wonder, serendipity and, yes, miracles. Though brushes with death figure prominently in this picaresque novel, it teems with a joie de vivre that only the quest for a true "home" can inspire. [Kristin Schar]

Sonia Rivera-Valdés. *The Forbidden Stories of Marta Veneranda*. Trans. Dick Cluster, et al. Seven Stories, 2001. 158 pp. $21.95.

Rivera-Valdés has been praised as one of the most important writers of Cuban descent, and this collection won her the 1997 Casa de las Américas award for short fiction. These nine "true" stories are confessions told to a budding social scientist named Marta Veneranda, whose explanatory note precedes the collection. She collects these stories out of a personal and pro-fessional desire to investigate why "an individual more often hides a chap-ter of his or her past because of the way he or she has perceived and experienced it than because of the greater or lesser weight of criminality or social disapproval of the episode itself." Having discovered that the tools of social science cannot adequately answer this question, she turns to the con-fessional narrative. Rivera-Valdés adds layers of ironic interest to her sto-ries by foregrounding her narrators' emotional ambivalence over their transgressions and by allowing us to speculate about their ulterior motives for revealing them. Most of these stories concern someone who faces a crisis related to sexuality or romantic fidelity. Several of the female informants either experiment with or convert to lesbianism. Other stories involve gay characters confessing the sense of betrayal they feel when they manifest heterosexual tendencies. Another common theme is the difficulty of resisting adulterous temptations, either for altruistic or grossly sensual reasons. Some recurring characters pop in and out of these stories, often in surprising ways. This device gives a complex sense of an interlinked Cuban American immigrant community in New York City that extends across several generations and economic classes. Veneranda hopes that the stories she reproduces will "represent a variety of human conflicts." Each of these vivid, skillfully told tales offers, as Veneranda herself realizes, "not a set of quantifiable data but a new story too fascinating to resist." [Thomas Hove]

A. L. Kennedy. *Everything You Need*. Knopf, 2001. 543 pp. $25.95.

A. L. Kennedy's beguiling tale of love and loss unfolds off the Welsh coast on Foal Island, an isolated writers' colony with a bizarre suicide credo. Nathan Staples, a wildly successful and misanthropic horror novelist trying to write a serious book, extends an anonymous invitation to his long-lost daughter Mary Lamb to join the writers' fellowship. Abandoned by both of her parents, Mary does not know that Nathan is her supposedly dead father, and as she strives to become a professional writer, Nathan struggles to disclose his paternal identity and to restrain his incredible desire for Maura, Mary's absent mother. At times, Kennedy's characters appear to be nothing more than comic stereotypes: the aspiring young novelist, the vitriolic, misunderstood hack, the hedonistic editor. Nathan himself seems to be a classic anti-hero, a man loved only by his dog, yet Kennedy's unwavering exploration of his dark psyche provdes a compassionate glimpse into Nathan's bitter insecurities, his bleak humor, and his humanity. Entwined with the narrative, Nathan's internal monologue and the manuscripts of the stories he invents for Mary enrich Kennedy's generous portrait of a father and daughter finding their way through "the stories we make of ourselves." [Trey Strecker]

Bernhard Schlink. *Flights of Love*. Pantheon, 2001. 308 pp. $23.00.

The author of the best-selling *The Reader* returns with a collection of seven stories vaguely linked by notions of connection and love. The stories themselves, though largely traditional in feel and in their approach to character, show Schlink to be a careful and consummate stylist, someone genuinely aware of the possibilities of working within established form. The characters develop and reach epiphanies, and Schlink generally manages, through slight and subtle means, to convey a genuine sense of what it means to be human. "Girl with Lizard" explores a man's obsession with a painting and the way in which that obsession changes his life. "A Little Fling," more politically charged, is about relationships between individuals in East and West Germany after the collapse of the Berlin Wall. In "The

Other Man," a man discovers after his wife's death that she had had an affair and begins writing to her former lover in the voice of his wife. The main character in "The Circumcision" secretly has himself circumcised out of love for his Jewish girlfriend, but his show of support doesn't quite turn out the way he expects. "Sugar Peas," perhaps the strongest story in the volume, chronicles a man's obsessive voyage among three women over a long period, ending with him paralyzed. In any case, there's more to *Flights of Love* than Schlink's being a former Oprah choice would suggest. Though he doesn't move the literature forward as do German-speaking writers such as Thomas Bernhard, Peter Handke, and Arno Schmidt, he makes a good, quiet showing. [Brian Evenson]

Yehoshua Kenaz. *Returning Lost Loves*. Steerforth, 2001. 263 pp. Paper: $14.00.

Alienation runs like a wild animal through Kenaz's apartment-jungle in Tel Aviv. Each character lives beside rather than with his or her partner, and, just as parallel lines never meet, there is no possibility of a meeting of the minds. Relationships that the reader expects to be based on mutual understanding, such as those of husband and wife, lovers, friends, father and son, or business partners, are totally devoid of intimacy or trust. In sharp contrast, several characters have strong emotional bonds with their dogs: one young woman "can hear the neighbor talking to his dog, she can't hear what he's saying but his voice is the voice of a lover." At first, it seems as if the people in *Returning Lost Loves* are only superficially related to each other, in that they are co-tenants in the same apartment building. About halfway through the book, it becomes clear that a mysterious criminal act is being planned and that a hidden link connects all of the neighbors, who are of diverse ages, social groups, and backgrounds, and who do not particularly like each other. In the end, alienation proves to be the strongest player. It motivates the book's dramatic climax, as it has motivated all of the other actions of the principal characters. In his very thorough exploration of alienation, Kenaz has created many poignant verbal portraits, depicting the subject in evocative language. The translation is good, allowing the reader to comprehend the imprisonment of each of the characters in his or her own private hell. The story turns out to be far more complex and thought-provoking than this reader had anticipated. [Leslie Cohen]

Dagoberto Gilb. *Woodcuts of Women*. Grove, 2001. 167 pp. $23.00.

With *Woodcuts of Women,* Dagoberto Gilb builds on and broadens his storytelling repertoire, which also includes *The Magic of Blood,* stories, and *The Last Known Residence of Mickey Acuña,* a novel. The ten stories in this collection depict men in various relationships with women, from poolside pickup to married with kids. Yet these are not tales of cliché machismo or male posturing. Rather, each narrative explores the often elaborate, sometimes perplexing interactions between men and women. In "Maria de Covina" an eighteen-year-old juggles his fears, flirtations, and affairs with the several women, young and old, who come into his life while he works in a department store. The narrator of "Mayela One Day in 1989" tours El Paso's narrow side streets and queer bars with mysterious Mayela—"red dress and wavy black hair and a blue, cloudless sky, as Mexican as cheap paint, that halos her"—who attracts the keen interest of men and women alike. Sex matters to the men in these stories, though not in a lascivious way. Rather, it's part of the complex company of women. All of the stories, with one exception, depict life along "the Mexican-Chicano border." The characters' code-switching speech is as integral to place as the region's arid heat. "The Pillows" offers a paean to El Paso: "The compact El Paso downtown, and the darkened slot that was the concreted Rio Grande, and Ciudad Juárez beyond that, and then the blackened plain of the desert." Throughout *Woodcuts of Women,* Gilb's prose is sure and unpretentious, the voices real. The stories develop character and reveal situation in a wise, rigorous, questioning, and often good-humored manner indicative of a fiction writer working at the height of his craft. [Peter Donahue]

Richard Klein. *Jewelry Talks*. Pantheon, 2001. 227 pp. $25.00.

The narrator of Richard Klein's *Jewelry Talks* takes both his title and his project from Diderot's *Les bijoux indiscrets*. But whereas that earlier book uses jewelry as a metaphor for sex, Klein's narrator wants "sex to be a metaphor for jewelry." Ostensibly the "anti-autobiography," as he puts it, of Abby Zinzo, detailing to his niece his experiences with both jewelry and transgendering, it is in parts memoir, historical tract, sociological study and lyrical meditation. The "novelistic" element of the book and the more "essayic" concerns never feel quite organic; at times it feels as if one is propping the other up. But then that may be the point. It isn't that connections between the two aren't there. It is that they are so overt, so overly insistent. Gaudy, you might say. *Jewelry Talks* is an excessive book, and one that is in many ways about excess as can be seen in the four women each chapter is alternately organized around—Coco Chanel, the Duchess of Windsor, Elizabeth Taylor, and Katherine Hepburn. The result is a book packed with fascinating tidbits and some quite beautiful philosophical bursts on jewelry and gender and the way the two entwine. [T. J. Gerlach]

Gertrude Stein. *To Do: A Book of Alphabets and Birthdays*. Green Integer, 2001. 144 pp. Paper: $9.95.

Gertrude Stein intended to publish *To Do* as a children's book, but because it seemed to lack narrative interest, it remained unpublished until 1957. I believe children would love the sonically mesmerizing *To Do* were it recited in short doses. The book lends itself to such partitioning. Modeled after the alphabet, it divides into twenty-six sections. That this also signals Stein's modernist concern for the plasticity of language is neither surprising nor paradoxical. F.W. Dupee has called Stein "a Mother Goose with a mind," and her innovation evokes comparison with authors as disparate as James Joyce, e. e. cummings, and Theodor Geisel. Further, *To Do* suggests that Stein's detractors have a misguided view of her methods. Kenneth Burke has called her writing "art by subtraction," and Edmund Wilson has insinuated that her obsession with "purifying" words of their signifying function results in monotonous, meaningless artifacts. But if *To Do* betrays a fascination with reiteration and radical juxtaposition, the book's celebration of the melodic and irrational hardly entails any reduction in its power. Without illusionism, how could the story of Pearl, a girl who eats a certain Mr. Pancake, charm and amuse? And how could the investigation of birthdays, which the characters adjust, borrow, steal, misplace, and simply *lack,* seem absurd yet profound? Stein deconstructs the manifold power of the word even as she remystifies it. Hence *To Do* offers plenty to delight ear and intellect, child and adult. If anything makes the book unsuitable, it is the violence and melancholia that haunt and unify the whole: people are sad and hungry. A brave boy drowns. A vicious cannibal rabbit bursts into flame. A misanthropic youth fantasizes about dogs that depopulate the world at his command. Still, if the young can survive the Brothers Grimm, they will have no trouble surviving Stein. [David Andrews]

Luigi Pirandello. *Her Husband*. Trans. Martha King and Mary Ann Frese Witt. Duke Univ. Press, 2000. 242 pp. $24.95.

Before writing his award-winning plays, Luigi Pirandello began his career writing fiction. His fifth novel, *Her Husband,* written in 1908 and published in 1911, is both a behind-the-scenes satirical scrutiny of Continental theater and a quasi-roman à clef based on the Sardinian writer Grazia Deledda and her husband Palmiro Madesani. As the title suggests, the playwright's husband, Giustino Boggiolo, exists as the satire's focal point. Boggiolo shows no interest in his wife's writing until she receives payment for some. Once Boggiolo realizes that her writing has moneymaking potential, he becomes an ardent supporter and marketer of his wife's works, though he is oblivious to its aesthetic merit. Boggiolo even becomes giddy when he hears from an American critic that American writers are paid by the word. Boggiolo, not surprisingly, longs for Italy to adopt such a sensible system of remuneration. At one point, he even wonders whether some errant scribbling on a torn sheet of paper can be sold. Even though the critics and journalists laugh at Boggiolo for his ardent buffoonery, the satire aligns them with Boggiolo, as the critics are finally less concerned with aesthetic value than with maintaining their respective positions of critical influence, their respective coteries. As the satire exposes the pretentiousness and materialism of the Roman literati, it portrays the effect of the bedlam on the creative prowess of writers exposed to such ineptitude; Silvia becomes unable to write as Boggiolo institutes promotional paraphernalia, including a weekly salon: "Literary Mondays at Villa Silvia." Like many of his other prose pieces, Pirandello's *Her Husband* provides a clear antecedent for his plays, including his enormously influential *Six Characters in Search of an Author*. This successful translation provides English readers access to a compelling work from one of the masters of twentieth-century literature. [Alan Tinkler]

Jeff Noon. *Cobralingus*. Codex, 2001. 120 pp. Paper: $14.95.

Jeff Noon first came to the public's attention as Britain's first cyberpunk with the surrealist science fiction novel *Vurt,* in which desperate urban dwellers enter a virtual world by sucking on feathers. Noon has since shown himself to be a writer of wild imaginative range, one who hopes to shed the science-fiction label so that he may be viewed as an experimental writer. Noon has taken advantage of his interest in music, especially the punk and techno music of Manchester, his birthplace, to showcase one possible route to new literary forms. *Cobralingus,* Noon's eighth work, pushes music as a source of inspiration for literary creation. Noon adapts the techniques of electronic dance music to generate texts, which he calls "metamorphiction" and "dub fiction." In dub, musicians remix recorded material to create new pieces, adding new layers of sound, removing tracks, and changing arrangements. The process is extended in the way a DJ mixes samples. Applying these ideas to language, Noon "samples" literary texts (Dickinson, Shakespeare, Zane Grey) and nonliterary texts (street names, race cards, a shipping forecast), then modifies them through various imaginative "filter gates" (such as "decay," "overload," "randomise," "search & replace," and "find story"). The result is a group of ten experimental pieces with names like "Bridal Suite Production" and "Dubchester Kissing Machine." There are echoes of Burroughs/Gysin's cut-up method, surrealist automatic writing, and, most prominently, the Oulipo's literature of constraint. Many of the pieces take on a visual form reminiscent of concrete poetry, which is enhanced by the inclusion of illustrations by Daniel Allington, adding image to the mix of text and music. Noon has long identified himself as an "avant pulp" writer who aims to fuse avant-garde and popular forms. In *Cobralingus* he's definitely created an experimental work you can dance to. [David Ian Paddy]

Witold Gombrowicz. *Ferdydurke*. Trans. Danuta Borchardt. Foreword Susan Sontag. Yale Univ. Press, 2000. 281 pp. Paper: $14.95.

This new edition of *Ferdydurke* marks the first Polish-to-English translation of Gombrowicz's novel, originally published in 1937, and the important return of a long out-of-print modernist classic. In *Ferdydurke* Joey

Kowalski writes *Memoirs from the Time of Immaturity*. His friends warn him not to publish a book identifying closely with immaturity: who will ever think of him as mature? Joey's aunts—one part family, one part Greek chorus filled with portent, one part cultural nags—beseech him to behave like an adult, with an adult's occupation, or at least an adult's hobby. Joey ignores them. A professor comes to visit him, reads his manuscript, and decides that Joey needs an education. The thirty-year-old writer, much like a Kafka protagonist, is abducted from his adult world. He becomes a school-boy, attending classes, committing turgid Polish verse to memory, conjugat-ing Latin verbs, and battling classmates on the playground. *Ferdydurke* is frequently read as a rousing defense of youthful naïvete and foolishness against the staid values of prewar Polish high culture. High culture does come in for a drubbing, as when a student asks a teacher why he should admire a certain poet and the teacher can manage only circular reasoning: "Great poetry must be admired, because it is great and because it is poetry, and so we admire it." *Ferdydurke* is actually the rare sort of satire in which the ground is always shifting. Gombrowicz identifies with neither high nor low culture. If maturity for him is stapled together with empty homilies, immaturity is a selfish fantasy. Gombrowicz gleefully runs through all the handy props: parochial nationalism, permissive modern parenting, adults' longing after youth, the nobility's romantic view of peasants, the peasants' indulgence of that romanticism, and the belief that what is new must be modern and therefore the best. Nothing was safe from Gombrowicz, and still nothing is safe from him. [Paul Maliszewski]

Steven Kotler. *The Angle Quickest for Flight*. Four Walls Eight Windows, 2001. 443 pp. Paper: $15.95.

After a successful run in hardcover, Steven Kotler's first novel, *The Angle Quickest for Flight*, has been reissued in paperback. Kotler's management of language and structure is commendable—no easy task given that the novel has a cornucopia of characters, including an albino Rastafarian who is an expert spelunker and a woman rumored to be the last descendent of Ghengis Khan. The five primary protagonists join forces to find the Sefer ha-Zaviot, a lost mystical tome of the Kaballah reputed to be a textual shortcut to heaven, while a minor protagonist, the enigmatic Johnii, searches for the sixty-fifth hexagram of the I Ching by attempting to "live out" each of the sixty-four known hexagrams. Johnii accomplishes this through study and travel, which includes time surfing. While researching, Johnii discovers that the Vatican has a concealed library, guarded by a se-cret society, that tolerates no visitors, not even the Pope. The narrative im-plication is obvious—adventure, with the help of an albino spelunker. While at times the novel tends toward established notions of adventure and quest, for the most part the damage is minimal, given Kotler's command of narra-tive form. A slippage occurs for readers familiar with Darren Aronosky's superb and influential movie ; the similarities are at times too thick, par-ticularly during the earlier portions of the novel. In the end, however,

Kotler's authority of subject and character enables readers to overcome the misstep and enjoy this fine first novel. [Alan Tinkler]

Roberto Calasso. *Literature and the Gods*. Trans. Tim Parks. Knopf, 2001. 212pp. $22.00; *The Forty-nine Steps*. Trans. John Shepley. Univ. of Minnesota, 2001. 290pp. $29.95.

Roberto Calasso is one of the most learned and daring voices on the global literary scene. Because of his originality, his work is difficult to classify. Much of his writing looks like scholarly criticism, but his unorthodox style and unbounded imagination make it hard to call his work anything but literature—and that in the unfashionable, purely laudatory sense of the term. On top of this, Calasso's vast erudition is unrivalled, unless one goes back to the days of Erich Auerbach and E. R. Curtius. In *Literature and the Gods* he attempts to revive a sense of the divine in an age when ideals of "society" and "community" threaten to eradicate the kinds of mental experience characteristic of religious awe. Taking the early German Romantics and Baudelaire as his points of departure, Calasso's lectures explore three topics he sees interlinked in postromantic literature: "the reawakening of the gods, parody, and 'absolute literature' . . . literature at its most piercing, its most intolerant of any social trappings." Calasso locates the gods in the private act of reading. Now that "the way of cult and ritual is barred," the only "natural condition" of the gods is "to appear in books—and often in books that few will ever open." Plenty of recent books have predicted the demise of print culture and the ascendancy of the computer. But Calasso sees no cause for dismay in this surface change: "That we may be gazing at a screen rather than a page, that the numbers, formulas, and words appear on liquid crystal rather than paper, changes nothing at all: it is still reading." No matter what the technology, he claims, the mind craves activity, and one of the highest forms of this activity can be inspired only by literature that is "sufficient unto itself." Lest this sound like a mandarin aestheticist pose, Calasso is quick to add that literature isn't "merely self-referential." Quite the contrary, absolute literature is "omnivorous, like the stomachs of those animals that are found to contain nails, pot shards, and handkerchiefs."
   The Forty-nine Steps is itself an omnivorous collection of reviews, prefaces, and essays, mainly on German writers, thinkers, and cultural critics from Marx's generation to Adorno's. Evoking once again Calasso's fascination with the divine, the title refers to Walter Benjamin's method of studying "in the theological sense . . . in accordance with the Talmudic doctrine of the forty-nine steps of meaning in every passage of the Torah." Along with Nietzsche, Benjamin is at center stage in several of these pieces. But the starting point for the tradition these essays focus on is Max Stirner, the most rabid critic of "society's superstitious faith in itself." Some of Calasso's subjects are familiar in English-speaking intellectual circles, particularly Benjamin, Adorno, and Heidegger. Other figures he covers are less familiar, notably Stirner, Robert Walser, and Karl Kraus. As in his earlier book *The Ruin of Kasch,* Calasso manages to rescue Stirner from his subordinate role

in the history of philosophy as nothing more than the target of Marx's and Engels's extensive ridicule in *The German Ideology*. Calasso performs similarly impressive acts of literary retrieval in his remarks on Nietzsche's *Ecce Homo*, Flaubert's *Bouvard et Pécuchet*, and Kraus's *The Last Days of Mankind*.

These two books reveal Calasso doing what he has done so well in his previous work. Combining recent modes of knowledge with an unparalleled ability to generate new meanings from old myths, he provides modern consciousness with a road map through "the treacherous waverings of that uninterrupted experiment-without-experimenter that is the world's recent history." [Thomas Hove]

Paul West. *Master Class: Scenes from a Fiction Workshop*. Harcourt, 2001. 259 pp. $24.00.

In many ways, *Master Class* is an unprecedented book. Indeed, there are Festschrifts and memoirs galore from tyros acknowledging a mentor, but a tribute—and such an affectionate tribute—*from* a mentor is another matter. West painstakingly recalls some of the meetings with his seventeen M.F.A. students, many of whom have developed into promising writers in their own rights. The dominant mood is celebratory, with West extolling virtues, acknowledging success, and encouraging originality in each of his students' works. At the same time, he renders each as a distinct, compelling personality brimming with creative brio. The book re-creates the excitement of spontaneous seminar discussion, as minds come alive and ideas carom from one participant to another. These are the seminars professors yearn for, and West, through his unique, intellectual associativeness, provokes his charges into thrilling insights, while he also frets that he ill prepares them for a publishing market that will want little to do with their brands of originality. All of this perhaps begs the question, why review such a book in a journal dedicated to fiction? *Master Class,* like the work of any artist who pauses to play the role of critic, offers a unique glimpse into West's own aesthetic. He repeatedly encourages his students to create contrasts—"Art goes to sleep without it, and so does the reader"—and to regard the sentence as the origin of creative inventiveness: "The idea is to make the arrangement of the prose unrecognizable ... then restore each [word] to its proper place in the pattern, maybe holding just one or two back. ... " For West, distinctions like fiction and nonfiction are beside the point; instead, the issue becomes the deployment of the intellect and ability to force the reader into a covenant of engagement. [David W. Madden]

Stéphane Mallarmé. *Mallarmé in Prose*. Trans. Jill Anderson, et al. Ed. Mary Ann Caws. New Directions, 2001. 152 pp. Paper: $14.95.

La Dernière Mode (*The Latest Fashion*) was the title of the magazine that Mallarmé edited in which he wrote everything in each issue under different pseudonyms and in different voices. One cannot imagine an enterprise further removed from Mallarmé's own poetic project. His poetry cannot be understood as *dernier mode* unless we read the term as he does (as this book makes us understand). For Mallarmé, *dernier mode* is never anything more than an acknowledgment of failure; we use the latest and most fashionable in language and thought because we cannot make the ineffable speak and we must say something, somehow, to deny what cannot be denied. All of Mallarmé's writing begins and ends with that silence; the *dernier mode* can never be anything more than *premier mode,* endlessly; the blank page stares out from anything written on it. "She dances as if she wore nothing," Mallarmé writes; as if she were, at last, herself, and needed no covering of any kind to explain, justify, place; as if no form can say more than her own. For Mallarmé to write about *dernier mode* is to acknowledge the binary dialectic of the enterprise; if it is not poetry, even if it can never be, it is all, always, *dernier mode.* In these essays and observations about dance, music, art, theater and performance; in his consideration of pipes, furniture, and female bicycling gear; and in his examination of solitude and the bucolic, Mallarmé asks how it is possible to express what cannot be expressed, "the question whether there is any reason to write at all." "One has to locate oneself somewhere," he writes. Mallarmé is like Orpheus, Roland Barthes writes, "who can save what he loves only by renouncing it." We cannot call what he writes literature, even if it might be the only literature possible. [Robert Buckeye]

Czeslaw Milosz. *Milosz's ABC's*. Farrar, Straus & Giroux, 2001. 313 pp. $24.00.

In Polish culture an ABC is a genre of short prose pieces arranged alphabetically, a hybrid form that includes memoir, essay, and anecdote. Often the title only gives a partial hint of the subject: "Adam and Eve," for instance, turns into an epigrammatic reflection on mortality. "Blasphemy" starts with religion and shifts round to considering how the individual relates to communities held together by collective convictions. This marks one of the many points in the collection where the question of allegiance arises. Born in a territory disputed by Lithuania and Poland but then held under the Russian Empire, Milosz has experienced shifts in national and political circumstance that have shaped his writing. Thus he compares the styles of protest in Paris and the U.S. in 1968, discusses dissident Soviet writers like Andrei Amalrik, but reserves his bitterest scorn for the attacks on Camus by Simone de Beauvoir and Sartre for not toeing the pro-Soviet line. In contrast, Milosz's respect goes to independent thinkers like Arthur Koestler, whose *Darkness at Noon* broke the taboo of such allegiance, or Balzac, whose novels, he argues, are constructed on a coherent set of philosophical positions. Given that it became his second country, it is not surprising that America should occupy a large part of Milosz's attention: "What splendor! What poverty! . . . What hypocrisy!" Through its cinema and literature America penetrated his imagination in the thirties—hence his commemoration of neglected writers like Louis Adamic. Milosz reserves special praise for Whitman, Robinson Jeffers, and Robert Frost, and he records what an important part was played by Henry Miller in the sixties. In his envoi Milosz calls the present volume an "instead of" book: instead of a novel, instead of an essay, instead of a memoir. Nevertheless, his *ABC's* manage to combine aspects of all three. [David Seed]

J. M. Coetzee. *Stranger Shores: Literary Essays 1986-1999.* Viking, 2001. 295 pp. $24.95.

Truly skeptical writing—prose that is thoughtful and inquisitive even while it doubts and questions cultural certainties—is rare in our age of critical carping, finger-pointing, and one-upmanship. *Stranger Shores,* by South African writer J. M. Coetzee, the only two-time winner of the Booker Prize, is an immensely pleasurable read because Coetzee submits a global array of authors to the responsible scrutiny of his skeptical gaze. In this collection of twenty-six essays, such seemingly unrelated authors as Daniel Defoe, Harry Mulisch, Joseph Brodsky, and Daphne Rooke become connected by Coetzee's abiding concern with migrants, exiles, and the *heimatlos* (homeless)—those writers who either choose or are forced onto the stranger shores of rootless existence. His critiques explore how these writers migrate among literary techniques as much as they move from place to place. American T. S. Eliot, in Coetzee's view, manipulates the epic form to render himself "English enough" to judge what qualifies as classic European literature. He lauds Caryl Phillips for connecting the persecution of European Jews to the degradations suffered by many Africans, even while he doubts that Phillips's loosely connected stories can rightly be called novels. He questions whether or not Thomas Pringle, a Scottish poet born in 1789, has the right to be called "the founding father of English-language poetry in South Africa." *Stranger Shores* powerfully demonstrates what it means to globalize literary studies, for its juxtaposition of the "classic" (Dostoyevsky, Kafka, Richardson), postmodern (Salman Rushdie, A. S. Byatt, Cees Nooteboom) and postcolonial (Phillips, Amos Oz, Naguib Mafouz) details the differences among these writers even as it elucidates the commonalities of their deracinated experiences. [E. Kim Stone]

Philip Roth. *Shop Talk*. Houghton Mifflin, 2001. 160 pp. $23.00.

In some ways *Shop Talk* is a misleading title, suggesting detailed discussions about the minutiae of fictional composition and inspiration. Instead, Roth discusses Kafka, Bruno Schulz, and Judaism, as well as politics and the media, as banes and inspirations for creativity. All ten profiles are reprinted from earlier sources, of which six are somewhat awkwardly assembled interviews. The first interview, with Primo Levi, is surprising for the contrast between Roth's exaggerations and Levi's rootedness in the commonsensical. After Roth has referred to Levi as a scientist for the third or fourth time, the Italian gently corrects him by calling himself a mere "technician" and concludes the talk by announcing his satisfaction with working in a paint factory because it "kept me in touch with the world of real things." The interview with Milan Kundera is full of sage aperçus. In discussing his adoptive home, Kundera comments that because France is no longer the center of the world, "it revels in radical ideological postures." When pressed to define a novel, Kundera labels it a "long piece of synthetic prose" whose exceptional power "is capable of combining everything into a unified whole like the voices of polyphonic music." The essay about an aging Bernard Malamud is at once lovely and pathetic, as Roth charts an eleven-year separation and a reunion in which the younger writer cannot commend his mentor on work of diminished quality. It is the book's most poignant and unforgettable moment. In spite of its slimness and uneven construction, *Shop Talk* reminds us of Roth's distinct verbal and intellectual capabilities. His questions are often probing mini-essays and his essays delicate forays into the unique gifts of each of his subjects, and the book reminds us that Roth remains a formidable presence in contemporary American fiction. [David W. Madden]

Books Received

Abe, Kobo. *The Ruined Map.* Trans. E. Dale Saunders. Vintage, 2001. Paper: $13.00. (F)

Allen, Jack. *Change of Heart.* Burping Frog, 2001. Paper: $14.00. (F)

Al-Shaykh, Hanan. *Only in London.* Trans. Catherine Cobham. Pantheon, 2001. $23.00. (F)

Alvarez, Aldo. *Interesting Monsters.* Graywolf, 2001. Paper: $14.00. (F)

Arenas, Reinaldo. *Mona and Other Tales.* Trans. Dolores M. Koch. Vintage, 2001. Paper: $12.00. (F, NF)

Arnold, Edwin T., and Dianne C. Luce, eds. *A Cormac McCarthy Companion: The Border Trilogy.* Univ. Press of Mississippi, 2001. Paper: $18.00. (NF)

Auster, Paul. *The Art of Hunger.* Rev. ed. Penguin, 2001. Paper: $14.00. (NF)

Aylett, Steve. *The Crime Studio.* Four Walls Eight Windows, 2001. Paper: $14.95. (F)

Babel, Isaac. *The Complete Works of Isaac Babel.* Trans. Peter Constantine. Ed. Nathalie Babel. Intro. Cynthia Ozick. Norton, 2002. $39.95. (F, NF)

Ballard, J. G. *Super-Cannes.* Picador USA, 2001. $24.00. (F)

Barrett, Andrea. *Servants of the Map: Stories.* Norton, 2002. $24.95. (F)

Baxter, Charles, ed. *Best New American Voices 2001.* Series ed. John Kulka and Natalie Danford. Harcourt, 2001. Paper: $14.00. (F)

Belben, Rosalind. *Hound Music.* Chatto & Windus, 2001. $27.50. (F)

Bell, Madison Smart. *Master of the Crossroads.* Penguin, 2001. Paper: $15.00. (F)

Bellow, Saul. *Collected Stories.* Preface Janis Bellow. Intro. James Wood. Viking, 2001. $30.00. (F)

Berberova, Nina. *Billancourt Tales.* Trans. and intro. Marian Schwartz. New Directions, 2001. $24.95. (F)

Berg, James J., and Chris Freeman. *Conversations with Christopher Isherwood.* Univ. Press of Mississippi, 2001. Paper: $18.00. (NF)

Berger, John. *Selected Essays.* Ed. Geoff Dyer. Pantheon, 2001. $32.50. (NF)

Beti, Mongo. *The Story of the Madman.* Trans. Elizabeth Darnel. Afterword Patricia-Pia Célérier. Univ. Press of Virginia, 2001. $45.00. (F)

Bottoms, Greg. *Sentimental, Heartbroken Rednecks.* Context, 2001. $21.95. (F)

Boyle, T. C. *After the Plague.* Viking, 2001. $25.95. (F)

———. *A Friend of the Earth*. Penguin, 2001. Paper: $13.00. (F)

Brenna, Duff. *The Altar of the Body*. Picador, 2001. $24.00. (F)

Brustein, Robert. *The Siege of the Arts: Collected Writings 1994-2001*. Ivan R. Dee, 2001. $28.50. (NF)

Burgin, Richard. *The Spirit Returns*. Johns Hopkins Univ. Press, 2001. Paper: $13.95. (F)

Cahalan, James M. *Edward Abbey: A Life*. Univ. of Arizona Press, 2001. $27.95. (NF)

Canetti, Veza. *The Tortoises*. Trans. Ian Mitchell. New Directions, 2001. $24.95. (F)

Carey, Peter. *30 Days in Sydney: A Wildly Distorted Account*. Bloomsbury, 2001. $16.95. (NF)

Carson, Ciaran. *Shamrock Tea*. Granta, 2001. $19.95. (F)

Catano, James V. *Ragged Dicks: Masculinity, Steel, and the Rhetoric of the Self-Made Man*. Southern Illinois Univ. Press, 2001. Paper: $25.00. (NF)

Chadwick, Cydney. *Flesh and Bone*. Avec, 2001. Paper: $14.00. (F)

Chessman, Harriet Scott. *Lydia Cassatt Reading the Morning Paper*. Permanent Press/Seven Stories, 2001. $24.00. (F)

Childs, Peter. *Reading Fiction: Opening the Text*. Palgrave, 2001. Paper: $19.95. (NF)

Ciresi, Rita. *Sometimes I Dream in Italian*. Delta, 2001. Paper: $12.95. (F)

Clark, Matt. *Hook Man Speaks*. Berkley Publishing, 2001. Paper: $13.00. (F)

Colombi, The Marchesa. *A Small-Town Marriage*. Trans. and afterword Paula Spurlin Paige. Northwestern Univ. Press, 2001. Paper: $15.95. (F)

Constant, Paule. *Trading Secrets*. Trans. Betsy Wing. Intro. Margot Miller. Bison, 2001. Paper: $20.00. (F)

Cook, Elizabeth. *Achilles*. Picador USA, 2002. $16.00. (F)

Coovadia, Imraan. *The Wedding*. Picador USA, 2001. $23.00. (F)

Couto, Mia. *Under the Frangipani*. Trans. David Brookshaw. Serpent's Tail, 2001. Paper: $15.00. (F)

Craig, William. *Enemy at the Gates: The Battle for Stalingrad*. Penguin, 2001. Paper: $14.00. (NF)

Crews, Frederick. *Postmodern Pooh*. North Point Press, 2001. $22.00. (NF)

Davis, Lydia. *Samuel Johnson Is Indignant: Stories*. McSweeney's, 2001. $16.95. (F)

Delbanco, Nicholas. *The Lost Suitcase: Reflections on the Literary Life*. Columbia Univ. Press, 2001. Paper: $12.00. (NF)

Desplechin, Marie. *Taking It to Heart*. Trans. Will Hobson. Granta, 2002. Paper: $11.95. (F)

Dimond, Arthur. *Blurred Images*. Dry Bones, 2001. Paper: $17.95. (F)

Djebar, Assia. *Algerian White*. Trans. David Kelley and Marjolijn de Jager. Seven Stories, 2001. $24.95. (NF)

Eco, Umberto. *Five Moral Pieces*. Harcourt, 2001. $23.00. (NF)

Egan, Jennifer. *Look at Me*. Nan A. Talese/Doubleday, 2001. $24.95. (F)

Elsschot, Willem. *Cheese*. Trans. Paul Vincent. Granta, 2002. $14.95. (F)

Ernaux, Annie. *Happening*. Trans. Tanya Leslie. Seven Stories, 2001. $18.95. (NF)

Eshleman, Clayton. *Companion Spider: Essays*. Foreword Adrienne Rich. Wesleyan Univ. Press, 2002. $60.00. (NF)

Everett, Percival. *Erasure*. Univ. Press of New England, 2001. $24.95. (F)

Faas, Ekbert, with Maria Trombacco. *Robert Creeley: A Biography*. Univ. Press of New England, 2001. $35.00. (NF)

Faber, Michael. *Some Rain Must Fall*. Harcourt, 2001. Paper: $13.00. (F)

Flisar, Evald. *Tales of Wandering*. Trans. Alan McConnel-Duff and the author. Texture, 2002. Paper: $16.00. (F)

Ford, Charles Henri. *Water from a Bucket: A Diary, 1948-1957*. Intro. Lynne Tillman. Turtle Point Press, 2001. Paper: $16.95. (NF)

Fredman, Stephen. *A Menorah for Athena: Charles Reznikoff and the Jewish Dilemmas of Objectivist Poetry*. Univ. of Chicago Press, 2001. Paper: $16.00. (NF)

Goda, Dee. *Orchid Jetsam*. Tuumba, 2001. Paper: $15.00. (F)

Goerke, Natasza. *Farewells to Plasma*. Trans. W. Martin. Twisted Spoon, 2001. Paper: $14.00. (F)

Gonzalez, Ray. *The Ghost of John Wayne and Other Stories*. Univ. of Arizona Press, 2001. Paper: $16.95. (F)

Gordimer, Nadine. *The Pickup*. Farrar, Straus & Giroux, 2001. $24.00. (F)

Grøndahl, Jens Christian. *Silence in October*. Trans. Anne Born. Harcourt, 2001. $24.00. (F)

Hamilton, Hugo. *Sad Bastard*. Four Walls Eight Windows, 2001. Paper: $13.95. (F)

Hamilton, John Maxwell. *Casanova Was a Book Lover*. Penguin, 2001. Paper: $14.00. (NF)

Harryman, Carla. *Gardener of Stars*. Atelos, 2001. Paper: $12.95. (F)

Hickman, Homer. *Sky of Stone*. Delacorte, 2001. $24.95. (NF)

Hill, Tobias. *The Love of Stones*. Picador USA, 2002. $25.00. (F)

Hogan, Ernest. *Smoking Mirror Blues*. Wordcraft of Oregon, 2001. Paper: $12.00. (F)

Hui, Wei. *Shanghai Baby*. Trans. Bruce Humes. Pocket, 2001. $24.00. (F)

Humphreys, Josephine. *Nowhere Else on Earth*. Penguin, 2001. Paper: $14.00. (F)

Huston, Nancy. *Dolce Agonia*. Steerforth, 2001. $23.00. (F)

Huxley, Aldous. *Complete Essays: Volume III: 1930-1935*. Ed. Robert S. Baker and James Sexton. Ivan R. Dee, 2001. $35.00. (NF)

——. *Complete Essays: Volume IV: 1936-1938*. Ed. Robert S. Baker and James Sexton. Ivan R. Dee, 2001. $35.00. (NF)

Ibrahim, Sun'Allah. *The Committee*. Trans. Mary St. Germain and Charlene Constable. Afterword Roger Allen. Syracuse Univ. Press, 2001. $22.95. (F)

Israel, Alec. *The Kabbalists*. Gefen, 2001. Paper: $16.95. (F)

Jarry, Alfred. *Adventures in 'Pataphysics: Collected Works I*. Trans. Paul Edwards and Antony Melville. Ed. Alastair Brotchie and Paul Edwards. Atlas, 2001. Paper: $14.95. (F, NF, P)

Johnson, Rob, ed. *Fantasmas: Supernatural Stories by Mexican American Writers*. Intro. Kathleen Alcalá. Bilingual Press, 2001. Paper: $14.00. (F)

Joyce, Michael. *Moral Tales and Meditations: Technological Parables and Refractions*. Afterword Hélène Cixous. State Univ. of New York Press, 2001. $18.50. (F)

Karr, Mary. *Cherry*. Penguin, 2001. Paper: $14.00. (NF)

Kelman, James. *Translated Accounts*. Doubleday, 2001. $24.95. (F)

Keret, Etgar. *The Bus Driver Who Wanted to Be God*. Trans. Miriam Shlesinger, et al. Dunne/St. Martin's, 2001. $19.95. (F)

Khai, Nguyen. *Past Continuous*. Trans. Phan Thanh Hao and Wayne Karlin. Afterword Wayne Karlin. Curbstone, 2001. Paper: $15.95. (F)

Kliment, Alexandr. *Living Parallel*. Trans. Robert Wechsler. Foreword Ivan Klíma. Catbird, 2002. $21.00. (F)

Klinkowitz, Jerome. *You've Got to Be Carefully Taught: Learning and Relearning Literature*. Foreword Kurt Vonnegut. Southern Illinois Univ. Press, 2001. $30.00. (NF)

Koestenbaum, Phyllis. *Doris Day and Kitschy Melodies*. La Questra, 2001. Paper: $12.00. (P)

Königseder, Angelika, and Juliane Wetzel. *Waiting for Hope: Jewish Displaced Persons in Post-World War II Germany*. Trans. John A. Broadwin. Northwestern Univ. Press, 2001. $69.95. (NF)

Kostelanetz, Richard. *Metafictions*. Phrygian, 2001. Paper: $5.00. (F)

Kureishi, Hanif. *Gabriel's Gift*. Scribner, 2001. $23.00. (F)

La Farge, Tom. *Zuntig*. Green Integer, 2001. Paper: $13.95. (F)

Lasner, Robert. *For Fucks Sake*. Ig Publishing, 2002. Paper: $14.95. (F)

Leigh, Julia. *The Hunter*. Penguin, 2001. Paper: $12.00. (F)

Levine, Suzanne Jill. *Manuel Puig and the Spider Woman: His Life and Fictions*. Univ. of Wisconsin Press, 2001. Paper: $19.95. (NF)

Link, Kelly. *Stranger Things Happen*. Small Beer, 2001. Paper: $16.00. (F)

Lipsyte, Sam. *The Subject Steve*. Broadway, 2001. $23.95. (F)

Lively, Penelope, and George Szirtes, eds. *New Writing 10*. Picador, 2001. Paper: £8.99. (F, NF, P)

Lucarelli, Carlo. *Almost Blue*. Trans. Oonagh Stransky. City Lights, 2001. Paper: $11.95. (F)

Maalouf, Amin. *In the Name of Identity: Violence and the Need to Belong*. Trans. Barbara Bray. Arcade, 2001. $22.95. (NF)

Makine, Andreï. *Confessions of a Fallen Standard-Bearer*. Trans. Geoffrey Strachan. Penguin, 2001. Paper: $12.00. (F)

Malpus, Simon, ed. *Postmodern Debates*. Palgrave, 2001. Paper: $19.95. (NF)

Mamet, David. *Wilson: A Consideration of the Sources*. Overlook, 2001. $26.95. (F)

Marcus, Ben. *Notable American Women*. Vintage, 2002. Paper: $12.00. (F)

Marías, Javier. *Tomorrow in the Battle Think on Me*. Trans. Margaret Jull Costa. New Directions, 2001. Paper: $15.95. (F)

Martone, Michael. *The Blue Guide to Indiana*. FC2, 2001. Paper: $12.95. (F)

McFarland, Beverly, and Micki Reaman, et al., eds. *Cracking the Earth: A 25th Anniversary Anthology from Calyx*. Calyx, 2001. Paper: $12.95. (F, NF, P)

McKnight, Reginald. *He Sleeps*. Holt, 2001. $23.00. (F)

Meads, Kat. *Not Waving*. Livingston, 2001. Paper: $12.95. (F)

Melville, Herman. *Moby-Dick*. 150th Anniversary Ed. Intro. Nathaniel Philbrick. Penguin, 2001. Paper: $14.00. (F)

——. *Tales, Poems, and Other Writings*. Ed. and intro. John Bryant. Modern Library, 2001. $24.95. (F, NF, P)

Mension, Jean-Michel. *The Tribe*. Trans. Donald Nicholson-Smith. City Lights, 2001. Paper: $14.95. (NF)

Meredith, Christopher. *Sidereal Time*. Seren/Dufour Editions, 2001. Paper: $16.95. (F)

Mezlekia, Nega. *The God Who Begat a Jackal*. Picador USA, 2002. $23.00. (F)

Miller, Arthur. *Echoes Down the Corridor: Collected Essays 1944-2000*. Penguin, 2001. Paper: $15.00. (NF)

Miller, Sue. *The World Below*. Knopf, 2001. $25.00. (F)

Mills, Magnus. *Three to See the King*. Picador USA, 2001. $19.00. (F)

Milosz, Czeslaw. *To Begin Where I Am: Selected Essays*. Ed. and intro. Bogdana Carpenter and Madeline G. Levine. Farrar, Straus & Giroux, 2001. $30.00. (NF)

Mo, Yan. *Shifu, You'll Do Anything for a Laugh*. Trans. Howard Goldblatt. Arcade, 2001. $23.95. (F)

Mogador, Céleste. *Memoirs of a Courtesan in Nineteenth-Century*

Paris. Trans. and intro. Monique Fleury Nagem. Bison, 2001. Paper: $24.95. (NF)

Montale, Eugenio. *Posthumous Diary [Diario Postumo]*. Trans. and annotated Jonathan Galassi. Turtle Point Press, 2001. Paper: $16.95. (P)

Montero, Mayra. *The Red of His Shadow*. Trans. Edith Grossman. Ecco, 2001. $22.00. (F)

Moshiri, Farnoosh. *The Bathhouse*. Black Heron, 2001. $21.95. (F)

Müller, Herta. *The Appointment*. Trans. Michael Hulse and Philip Boehm. Metropolitan, 2001. $23.00. (F)

Munro, Alice. *Hateship, Friendship, Courtship, Loveship, Marriage*. Knopf, 2001. $24.00. (F)

Nahai, Gina B. *Sunday's Silence*. Harcourt, 2001. $24.00. (F)

Naipaul, V. S. *Half a Life*. Knopf, 2001. $24.00. (F)

Nash, Susan Smith. *To the Uzbekistani Soldier Who Would Not Save My Life*. Avec, 2001. Paper: $9.00. (F)

Nicholson, Geoff. *Bedlam Burning*. Overlook, 2002. $26.95. (F)

Nooteboom, Cees. *All Souls Day*. Trans. Susan Massotty. Harcourt, 2001. $25.00. (F)

Nunez, Sigrid. *For Rouenna*. Farrar, Straus & Giroux, 2001. $22.00. (F)

Nye, Robert. *Falstaff*. Arcade, 2001. $25.95. (F)

Oates, Joyce Carol. *Middle Age: A Romance*. Ecco, 2001. $28.00. (F)

Olbracht, Ivan. *Nikola the Outlaw*. Trans. Marie K. Holeček. Northwestern Univ. Press, 2001. Paper: $18.95. (F)

Páral, Vladimír. *Lovers & Murderers*. Trans. Craig Cravens. Catbird, 2002. $27.00. (F)

Paulson, William. *Literary Culture in a World Transformed: A Future for the Humanities*. Cornell Univ. Press, 2001. Paper: $16.95. (NF)

Pavese, Cesare. *The Selected Works of Cesare Pavese*. Trans. and intro. R. W. Flint. New York Review Books, 2001. Paper: $16.95. (F)

Pearson, T. R. *Blue Ridge*. Penguin, 2001. Paper: $13.00. (F)

Pelevin, Victor. *Buddha's Little Finger*. Trans. Andrew Bromfield. Penguin, 2001. Paper: $13.00. (F)

——. *4 by Pelevin*. Trans. Andrew Bromfield. New Directions, 2001. Paper: $9.00. (F)

Perényi, Eleanor. *More Was Lost*. Helen Marx Books, 2001. Paper: $16.95. (NF)

Pérez-Reverte, Arturo. *The Nautical Chart*. Trans. Margaret Sayers Peden. Harcourt, 2001. $26.00. (F)

Perriam, Wendy. *Dreams, Demons and Desire*. Peter Owen/Dufour Editions, 2001. Paper: $19.95. (F)

Perry, A. J. *Twelve Stories of Russia: A Novel, I Guess*. Glas/Ivan R. Dee, 2001. Paper: $14.95. (F)

Pimental, Ricardo. *Voices from the River*. Bilingual Press, 2001. Paper: $12.00. (F)

Pitchford, Nicola. *Tactical Readings: Feminist Postmodernism in the Novels of Kathy Acker and Angela Carter*. Bucknell Univ. Press, 2001. $39.50. (NF)

——. *One Foot off the Gutter*. Seven Stories, 2001. Paper: $13.00. (F)

Plate, Peter. *Snitch Factory*. Seven Stories, 2001. Paper: $13.00. (F)

Powers, Peter Kerry. *Recalling Religions: Resistance, Memory, and Cultural Revision in Ethnic Women's Literature*. Univ. of Tennessee Press, 2001. $27.00. (NF)

Pressfield, Steven. *Tides of War: A Novel of Alcibiades and the Peloponnesian War*. Bantam, 2001. Paper: $13.95. (F)

Quignard, Pascal. *On Wooden Tablets with Apronenia Avitia*. Trans. Bruce X. Burning Deck, 2001. Paper: $10.00. (F)

Reid, Van. *Daniel Plainway*. Penguin, 2001. Paper: $14.00. (F)

Rice, Anne. *Blood and Gold*. Knopf, 2001. $26.95. (F)

Richards, David Adams. *Mercy Among the Children*. Arcade, 2001. $25.95. (F)

Rock, Peter. *The Ambidextrist*. Context, 2002. $21.95. (F)

Rollyson, Carl. *Reading Susan Sontag: A Critical Introduction to Her Work*. Ivan R. Dee, 2001. $27.50. (NF)

Rosenthal, Carole. *It Doesn't Have to Be Me*. Hamilton Stone, 2001. Paper: $14.95. (F)

Rosenthal, Chuck. *Jack Kerouac's Avatar Angel: His Last Novel*. Hollyridge Press, 2001. $23.95. (F)

Ruffin, Paul. *Islands, Women, and God*. Browder Springs Publishing, 2001. $24.95. (F)

Sagastizabál, Patricia. *A Secret for Julia*. Trans. Asa Zatz. Norton, 2001. $23.95. (F)

Schmidt, Arno. *The School for Atheists: A Novella = Comedy in 6 Acts*. Trans. and intro. John E. Woods. Green Integer, 2001. Paper: $16.95. (F)

Schmidt, Heidi Jon. *Darling?* Picador, 2001. $23.00. (F)

Scholz, Carter. *Radiance*. Picador USA, 2002. $24.00. (F)

Scott, Daniel. *Some of Us Have to Get Up in the Morning*. Turtle Point Press, 2001. Paper: $15.95. (F)

Sernovitz, Gary. *Great American Plain*. Holt, 2001. $23.00. (F)

Sheehan, Andrew. *Chasing the Hawk: Looking for My Father, Finding Myself*. Delacorte, 2001. $23.95. (NF)

Shöenfelt, Phil. *Junkie Love*. Illus. Jolana Izbecká. Twisted Spoon, 2001. Paper: $13.50. (F)

Skinner, Jeffrey, and Lee Martin, eds. *Passing the Word: Writers on Their Mentors*. Sarabande, 2001. Paper: $16.95. (NF)

Sontag, Susan. *Where the Stress Falls: Essays*. Farrar, Straus & Giroux, 2001. $27.00. (NF)

Soucy, Gaétan. *The Little Girl Who Was Too Fond of Matches.* Trans. Sheila Fischman. Arcade, 2001. $21.95. (F)

Spark, Muriel. *All the Stories of Muriel Spark.* New Directions, 2001. Paper: $19.95. (F)

Spielberg, Peter. *The Noctambulists & Other Fictions.* FC2, 2001. Paper: $12.95. (F)

Spiotta, Dana. *Lightning Field.* Scribner, 2001. $23.00. (F)

Stasiuk, Andrzej. *White Raven.* Trans. Wiesiek Stasiuk. Serpent's Tail, 2001. Paper: $18.00. (F)

Stavans, Ivan. *On Borrowed Words: A Memoir of Language.* Viking, 2001. $23.95. (NF)

Steimberg, Alicia. *Call Me Magdalena.* Trans. Andrea G. Labinger. Univ. of Nebraska Press, 2001. Paper: $16.95. (F)

Stern, Richard. *Pacific Tremors.* TriQuarterly Books, 2001. $26.95. (F)

Supervert. *Extraterrestrial Sex Fetish.* Supervert 32C, 2001. Paper: $15.00. (F, NF)

Svevo, Italo. *As a Man Grows Older.* Trans. Beryl de Zoete. Intro. James Lasdun. New York Review Books, 2001. Paper: $12.95. (F)

Svevo, Livia Veneziani. *Memoir of Italo Svevo.* Trans. Isabel Quigly. Northwestern Univ. Press, 2001. Paper: $15.95. (NF)

Tharoor, Shashi. *Riot: A Love Story.* Arcade, 2001. $24.95. (F)

Toscana, David. *Our Lady of the Circus.* Trans. Patricia J. Duncan. Thomas Dunne/St. Martin's, 2001. $23.95. (F)

Trevor, William. *The Hill Bachelors.* Penguin, 2001. Paper: $13.00. (F)

Tsypkin, Leonid. *Summer in Baden-Baden.* Trans. Roger and Angela Keys. Intro. Susan Sontag. New Directions, 2001. $23.95. (F)

Ulin, David L., ed. *Another City: Writing from Los Angeles.* City Lights, 2001. Paper: $16.95. (F, NF, P)

Upadhyay, Samrat. *Arresting God in Kathmandu.* Mariner, 2001. Paper: $12.00. (F)

Urrea, Luis Alberto. *Six Kinds of Sky.* Cinco Puntos, 2002. Paper: $12.95. (F)

Vachss, Andrew. *Pain Management.* Knopf, 2001. $24.00. (F)

Vallejo, Fernando. *Our Lady of the Assassins.* Trans. Paul Hammond. Serpent's Tail, 2001. Paper: $13.99. (F)

Verne, Jules. *The Mysterious Island.* Trans. Jordan Stump. Intro. Caleb Carr. Modern Library, 2001. $23.95. (F)

Vukcevich, Ray. *Meet Me in the Moon Room.* Small Beer, 2001. Paper: $16.00. (F)

Wadsworth, Ann. *Light, Coming Back.* Alyson, 2001. $24.95. (F)

Wallace, Daniel. *Ray in Reverse.* Penguin, 2001. Paper: $13.00. (F)

Warner, Sylvia Townsend. *Mr. Fortune's Maggot.* New York Review Books, 2001. Paper: $12.95. (F)

Weiner, Steve. *The Yellow Sailor*. Overlook, 2001. $26.95. (F)

Wilson, Paul. *Someone to Watch Over Me*. Granta, 2001. £12.99. (F)

Wilson, Robert. *The Company of Strangers*. Harcourt, 2001. $25.00. (F)

Winters, Richard. *Ila*. Impatiens, 2001. No price given. (F)

Young, Elizabeth. *Pandora's Handbag*. Intro. Will Self. Serpent's Tail, 2001. Paper: $18.00. (NF)

Zargani, Aldo. *For Solo Violin: A Jewish Childhood in Fascist Italy*. Trans. Marina Harss. Paul Dry Books, 2002. Paper: $15.95. (NF)

Contributors

BRUCE BENDERSON is the author of two books about the Times Square underworld, *Pretending to Say No* (Plume, 1990) and the novel *User* (Dutton, 1994). His book-length essay about the decline of urban bohemia, *Toward the New Degeneracy* (Edgewise, 1997), was also published in French by Payot-Rivages. He is the author of *James Bidgood* (Taschen, 1999), a book about the creator of the film *Pink Narcissus*. He has translated Robbe-Grillet, Sollers, Guyotat, and Virginie Despentes from the French and has written for the *New York Times Magazine,* the *Village Voice, nest,* and other publications. He recently taught creative writing and French literature at Deep Springs College. Benderson is the literary executor of the deceased novelist, Ursule Molinaro.

PHILIP TEW is Course Director for the M.A. Program in Literary Studies at the University of Central England in Birmingham and an Honorary Reader in English & Aesthetics at the University of Debrecen, Hungary. He published the first monograph on B. S. Johnson with Manchester University Press, *B. S. Johnson: A Critical Reading* (published in the U.S. by St. Martin's, 2001). Other publications include essays in the collections *After Postmodernism: An Introduction to Critical Realism* (Athlone Press, 2001) and *Beckett and Philosophy* (St. Martin's, 2001) and the journals *Critical Survey,* the *Anachronist,* and *About Larkin: The Newsletter of the Philip Larkin Society*. A collection on contemporary British fiction, co-edited by Dr. Tew, will be published by Polity Press in 2002. He is joint founder and Director of the London Network for Textual Studies.

ALAN TINKLER is in the final stages of his Ph.D. studies at the University of Denver. His story "Morning Comes by Way of Restless Nights" was published last fall in *Fiction International,* and he is currently at work on a novel that marginally relies on his two-year tour of duty as a Peace Corps volunteer in Papua New Guinea. He is an Associate Editor of *Conjunctions* as well as an Associate Editor for *5-trope,* an on-line journal.

river city

$2000
1st place fiction award

Fiction Entries must
be postmarked by
March 1, 2002

$1000
1st place poetry award

Poetry Entries must
be postmarked by
March 1, 2002

For complete guidelines send SASE to river city
Dept of English, Univ of Memphis, Memphis, TN 38152
email us at **rivercity@memphis.edu** or visit
www.people.memphis.edu/~rivercity/contests.html

European Avant-Garde
New Perspectives

Edited by Dietrich Scheunemann.
Amsterdam/Atlanta, GA 2000. 274 pp. (Avant Garde Critical Studies 15)
ISBN: 90-420-1204-8   Bound EUR 62,-/US-$ 57.-
ISBN: 90-420-1593-4   Paper EUR 27,-/US-$ 26.-

This collection of critical essays is designed to lay the foundations for a new theory of the European avant-garde. It starts from the assumption that not one all-embracing intention of all avant-garde movements - i.e. the intention of "reintegrating art into the practice of life" (Peter Bürger) - but the challenge of new cultural technologies, in particular photography and cinema, constitutes the main driving force of the formation and further development of the avant-garde. This approach permits to establish a theoretical framework that takes into account the diversity of artistic aims and directions of the various art movements and encourages a wide and open exploration of the multifaceted and often contradictory nature of the great variety of avant-gardist innovations.

Following the theoretical foundation of the new approach, individual contributions concentrate on a diverse range of avant-gardist concepts, trends and manifestations from cubist painting and the literary work of Apollinaire and Gertrude Stein to the screeching voices of futurism, dadaist photomontage and film, surrealist photographs and sculptures and neo-avant-gardist theories as developed by the French group OuLiPo. The volume closes with new insights gained from placing the avant-garde in the contexts of literary institutions and psychoanalytical and sociological concepts.

The main body of the volume is based on presentations and discussions of a three-day research seminar held at Yale University, New Haven, in February 2000. The research group formed on this occasion will continue with its efforts to elaborate a new theory of the avant-garde in the coming years.

Editions Rodopi B.V.

USA/Canada: One Rockefeller Plaza, Ste. 1420, New York, NY 10020, Tel. (212) 265-6360, Call toll-free (U.S. only) 1-800-225-3998, Fax (212) 265-6402

All other countries: Tijnmuiden 7, 1046 AK Amsterdam, The Netherlands. Tel. ++ 31 (0)20 611 48 21, Fax ++ 31 (0)20 447 29 79

Orders-queries@rodopi.nl   **www.rodopi.nl**

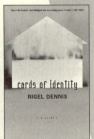